Fundamentals in the
Philosophy of God

57618

ARNOLD J. BENEDETTO, S.J.
Professor of Natural Theology at
Jesuit House of Studies and Spring Hill College,
Mobile, Alabama

*Qui ne prendrait la cause . . . de
Dieu en main, mon cher Théotime?*
(St. François de Sales)

The Macmillan Company, New York
Collier-Macmillan Ltd., London

NIHIL OBSTAT: Rt. Rev. Msgr. William J. Cusick, D.D., P.A.
                 Censor Deputatus,
                 January 30, 1961

IMPRIMI POTEST: Andrew C. Smith, S.J.
                 Vice-Provincial of the New Orleans Province,
                 December 13, 1960

IMPRIMATUR: ✠ Thomas J. Toolen,
                 Archbishop-Bishop of Mobile-Birmingham,
                 January 30, 1961

BL 182
B 46 f

© Arnold J. Benedetto, S.J. 1963

First Printing

Library of Congress catalog card number: 63–7394

The Macmillan Company, New York
Collier-Macmillan Canada, Ltd., Galt, Ontario
DIVISIONS OF THE CROWELL-COLLIER PUBLISHING COMPANY

Printed in the United States of America

Preface

This book is written as a textbook in the philosophy of God, intended primarily for undergraduate students. We have aimed throughout at clarity of exposition and solidity of doctrine, judging it better that students should have a thorough grasp of the more important points in the philosophy of God rather than a superficial acquaintance with a greater number of details. We mean the text to require labor on the part of the students, but we trust their labor will prove to be pleasant, labor that the students will consider amply rewarding as they come to see ever more clearly the deep reasonableness of the basic positions of Scholastic theism.

The book does not intend to make textual exegetes out of students, nor to produce historians of philosophy. It is written for undergraduates anxious to acquire the mature intellectual appreciation of God befitting their age and corresponding to their education in other fields.

The book is not meant to be particularly original. To aim at novelty in writing about God does not recommend itself; the theme is too sacred. What elements of originality there may be in the actual text concern largely the distribution of the subject matter, the manner of treating the various topics, and the omission of certain traditional problems. We have, for example, put the discussion of God's creation and conservation early in the book, emphasizing the pertinence of these topics to the immediately preceding chapters that prove the necessary existence of God as the uncaused Cause and the intelligent and free Designer of the universe. We also depart from the practice of some recent textbooks in the space we give to the treatment of the "negative attributes" of God. Five chapters out of the twelve are devoted to these attributes, with the hope that the sacred terms reserved exclusively for the transcendent Being will become meaningful to the student.

We do not discuss the various interpretations of St. Thomas's famous *Quinque Viae* for proving God's existence; we do not go into such questions as whether or not creation in the creature is a predicamental relation; we refrain from debating the recondite problems involved in varying theories about God's concursus and foreknowledge. Such questions may very well find place in textbooks for graduate students, but they do not seem to us to call for discussion in a text for undergraduates.

In the doctrines we propose, we have certainly not tried to be independent just to be independent; we do not care to be a maverick expositor. On the other hand, we are not preoccupied with presenting and defending the thought of this or that specific school of philosophy and with making our students its ardent partisans. We are confident, however, that we keep within the broad area of traditional Scholasticism. In fact, our aim has been, as far as possible, to find some ground of common agreement among Scholastics. The importance of this subject—the rational science of God—seems to call for this. Indeed, we would be most happy if this work were found serviceable by teachers of differing views; it would thus in itself constitute an argument for the thesis that defends the existence of a *Philosophia Perennis*.

We would like to be profuse in our expression of thanks to those who have helped in preparing this book for publication; they have preferred that we not be so. We must be content, then, with a brief but heartfelt word of appreciation to those students who volunteered their help in preparing the typescript for publication and to our confrere, the Rev. S.Y. Watson, S.J., who generously agreed to read the manuscript and who has made many valuable suggestions.

Contents

THE EXISTENCE OF GOD

CHAPTER

1

OUTLINE

Introduction

I. THE "CASE FOR GOD"

Leibniz's classic treatise. In the year 1710 Gottfried Wilhelm von Leibniz published a book entitled *Theodicy, Essays on the Goodness of God, the Freedom of Man, and the Origin of Evil*. The word which Leibniz coined, "Theodicy," is derived from the Greek (*Theou dikaia*) and means "the cause of God." In the preface to his work, after telling us of his aims, Leibniz goes on to state, "My hope for success therein is all the greater because it is the cause of God I plead." And at the end of his book Leibniz gives several appendices, one of which is a Latin summary of the whole work put into Scholastic form. The title given by Leibniz to this summary is "*Causa Dei*," that is, "The Cause of God."

In Leibniz's context, the word "cause" is not taken in the philosophical sense of an agent that produces something, but in the legal sense of a "case," that is to say, in the sense of an argument or plea on behalf of someone, as, for example, a defense attorney's plea for his client. The attorney undertakes the client's "cause" or case.

When one realizes this, Leibniz's title no longer appears as an innovation, for it has always been a fairly common enterprise of serious and devout thinkers to try to justify the ways of God to man. We find this, for example, as far back as the Old Testament book of *Job*, where the stranger, Elihu, introduces his discourse thus: "Attend to me yet a little and I will teach thee, for I still have words to say on God's behalf; I will take my reasons from afar and will show forth the justice of my Creator." [1] And the pagan philosopher, Seneca,

---

[1] *Job* 36: 2–3 (translation by G.O. Neill in *The World's Classic: Job*, Milwaukee, Bruce, 1938, p. 139).

in introducing his essay on Providence, says: "I shall be pleading the cause of the gods." [2]

Limitations. Although Leibniz was a philosopher, his *Theodicy* did not discuss the "case for God" solely from a philosophical viewpoint; the argument also involved the doctrines of revealed religion. Moreover, as its sub-title indicated, the book did not deal with all the aspects under which God can be considered by a philosopher. Despite these limitations, however, the practice became popular, soon after Leibniz, of giving the title *Theodicy* to purely philosophical treatises that deal, at least in general fashion, with all the problems concerning God, His existence, and His attributes.

Traditional usage, then, despite Leibniz and despite etymology, justifies the practice of entitling a philosophical treatise on God, "Theodicy." The term is still in current use: for example, in his famous encyclical letter, *Humani Generis,* when Pope Pius XII referred to the philosophical discipline that treats of God, he called it simply "Theodicy." [3] The term, however, does not seem currently to be the most popular. To many, the word is associated with the rationalism of the eighteenth century, when the heirs of Descartes tried to deduce all philosophical knowledge independently of experience of the sensible world.

II. "NATURAL THEOLOGY"

"**Theology.**" On etymological grounds a good case could be made for naming the philosophical treatise on God simply "Theology," for this word means "the study of God." Such a word would have the further advantage of being parallel with the names commonly given, at least in by-gone days, to the other sections of philosophy. Thus, as the study of *being,* as such, is sometimes called "ontology," the philosophical study of *animate* nature is sometimes

---

[2] *Causam deorum agam* (*De Providentia* I.1). See the title of Thomas Bradwardine's most famous work: "The Cause of God, against Pelagius" (*De Causa Dei contra Pelagium*). Bradwardine died in 1349. See, too, the motto on our title-page, borrowed from St. François de Sales (died 1622), *Treatise on the Love of God,* Book 4, Chapter 5.

[3] *Acta Apostolicae Sedis,* Vol. 42, 1950, pp. 574–575.

called "psychology," and the philosophical study of the *material universe* is sometimes called "cosmology," so the philosophical study of God would conveniently be named "theology."

Two kinds of theology. The historical situation, however, prevents such simplicity. Jews and Christians insist that God has made a special revelation of Himself; He has not merely manifested Himself in a general and indirect way in His effects. He has also directly revealed certain truths about Himself and has told us about Himself and about His plans in a way that we could never have discovered by ourselves without this special revelation. He has revealed strict "mysteries." What He has told us is of such paramount truth and importance that if any science deserves the title "Theology," then certainly it is the science that studies the data furnished by God Himself in this special revelation. And so, indeed, the word "Theology," without qualification, has come to mean the study of God based on what God has chosen to reveal directly about Himself (even though not all His revelation is of strict mysteries).

The merely philosophical study of God, that is, the study based on what God has only indirectly revealed about Himself (namely, in His effects—the world, or creation), is indeed sometimes called "theology," but with a qualification, for example, "Rational Theology" or "Natural Theology." This latter phrase is perhaps the one most commonly given to our science. It seems to have been given as a title of a treatise first by Raymond de Sabunde in the fifteenth century,[4] but probably the most famous of the books bearing the title "Natural Theology" are the ones written by Christian Wolff in 1736–1737 and William Paley in 1802.

To differentiate between the two theological sciences, the one ("theology") based on the special data of revelation and the other ("theodicy") based on the ordinary data of experience, the terms "Dogmatic" (or "Supernatural") Theology and "Natural" Theology are commonly employed. The two sciences have the same basic subject matter—God. They both reason about this subject matter, but philosophy reasons on it without the special light of faith, while dogmatic theology reasons on the data concerning God furnished by revelation and is constantly guided in its speculations by the light of

---

[4] See Baldwin's *Dictionary of Philosophy and Psychology*, Vol. II, 1911, under the entry "Natural Theology."

faith. Dogmatic theology is not a branch of philosophy, whereas natural theology emphatically is. Philosophy aims to know the ultimate cause(s) of things; it should push its investigations until it reaches the absolutely ultimate cause of all things, and this is God.

III. THEODICY: AN APPRECIATION OF DATA PRECISELY AS DATA, OF CREATURES PRECISELY AS CREATURES

Starting point of theodicy. To have a comprehensive understanding of God, to appreciate God completely and directly "from within," one would have to have an infinitely perfect intellect—one would have to be God Himself. What we humans learn about God in theodicy will not be derived directly from contact with God; rather, it will be deduced from what we know about non-divine realities.

We do not start in a vacuum; we do not argue *a priori* from mere concepts. The data of experience will be our starting point. The objects around us with which we constantly come into contact—the earth, the air, minerals, plants, animals, other men; events that ceaselessly occur; the objects, likewise, and occurrences that are within us (our feelings, our perceptions, our thoughts, our volitions, our choices)—all of these form the starting point of our philosophical discussions about God. God will be known through the relations that these data must have with Him. We reflect on the data, and they prompt us to ask questions whose answers demand that we concede that there actually exists some being who has divine perfections, that there is, in the real order, a divine existent.

God known indirectly. We do not grasp this divine existent (God) directly; we know of His existence and properties from the clues left in the data of experience, which we do know directly. The data could not be what they actually are, indeed, they could not even be at all, unless—so we shall argue—there exists some being who is essentially different from these data, and who is the ultimate and adequate cause of the data. He must have an existence that is self-explanatory, that in itself calls for no further questions; He must have whatever perfections and modes of being are requisite for Him to be the ultimate and adequate explanation of the data of experience. He must also have whatever other perfections necessarily follow from these requisite perfections and modes of being.

Theodicy explains what it really means to be a creature. In a way, we could say that theodicy does not, and cannot, explain God; it does, however, explain non-divine things. It shows us that they are not fully explicable so long as we admit the existence only of beings such as we immediately experience; it shows that reality cannot be confined to the types characterized by the "data"; it shows that there must be some "transcendent" being, some being that "goes beyond" the data in His mode of being and in the perfections with which He is endowed.

We might say, therefore, that the process of arriving at God by starting with the so-called "data of experience" is simply the process of coming to appreciate the fact that the data of experience are truly *data* (a Latin word originally signifying "things that are given"). These "data" are truly *given*—by a beneficent Giver! We come to appreciate that what is "out there" might *have not existed* at all, that it cannot be "taken for granted." We start out with what are actually called *data*, but which are known at first as something simply existing as this or that thing; then we find out that they really are, in the most literal sense of the word, *data*, that is, things given, gifts (and, therefore, requiring a Donor). We call them creatures, using the word unreflectingly, but, philosophically, we come finally to realize that they are rightly called creatures, we realize what it truly means to be a creature. Knowing what it means to be a creature, we know, indirectly but quite scientifically, that a Creator exists and what qualities He must have, since His creation is such and such. The quest for God turns out to be an investigation of what it truly means to be a creature.

IV. POPULAR KNOWLEDGE ABOUT GOD— SCIENTIFIC KNOWLEDGE ABOUT GOD

Pre-scientific knowledge about God. In our present civilization it would be difficult to find anyone growing into adulthood who has not heard something about God or who has no ideas on the subject of God. Even the atheist (one who denies that there is a God) associates some meaning with the term "God." There is a definite object of his denial. It is not that he has never heard of the idea of God; he has heard of it but has concluded that the idea is of nothing objectively real.

Thousands of years of history and tradition have handed down from generation to generation some knowledge (at least, what purports to be knowledge) about God, a personal, supreme Being on Whom the universe depends, an uncaused, eternal, all-perfect Being. It would be ridiculous to ignore the fact that ideas of God have had a tremendous influence on the history of man, his life, his manners, his morals, his literature, his art, his every occupation. There exists, then, a sort of ready-made knowledge of God, a popular, non-critical, pre-scientific variety, based partly on human faith and human traditions, and partly on a spontaneous and elementary reasoning about the origin and destiny of the universe.[5]

A striking example of such reasoning is furnished by the case of Helen Keller. Despite the extremely fragmentary contact she had with the outside world, despite the fact that her teachers studiously avoided all references to God and religion in Miss Keller's early training, still, at the age of nine, she spontaneously argued that the origin of the world and the origin of life required some supreme being.[6]

The popular knowledge of God, the spontaneous reasoning to Him, is certainly not false knowledge, at least not necessarily false. But again, certainly, it is not the knowledge which theodicy, as a science, aims to furnish. Still, we may grant that one of the ways of elaborating theodicy would be to take the popular brand of knowledge about God, purify it of its misconceptions, and give the residue a solid basis in metaphysics, the science of being as being.

Perfection of scientific theodicy. It is the aim of scientific knowledge to bring one to an understanding of the truth; science appeals not to popular beliefs and traditional statements but to the intrinsic evidence of the object to be understood or of objects related to this. When we see that a matter is such and so, when we know that we know its truth, when we know why we know it, when we know why

[5] See Jacques Maritain, *Approaches to God*, translated from the French by Peter O'Reilly, New York, Harper and Brothers, 1954, pp. 1–15.

[6] Helen Keller, *The Story of My Life*, New York, Grosset and Dunlap, 1904, pp. 368–370.

the matter cannot but be as we know it, then we have the best kind of knowledge obtainable. Our knowledge is, then, in the classical meaning, scientific knowledge.

The popular mind—the mind of the average educated man—has some hazy knowledge about many scientific matters, for example, about the law of gravitation. Again, it knows, from magazine articles, newspapers, television, and movies, something about the hydrogen bomb, rocket missiles, and artificial satellites. But the popular mind does not *understand* such matters, it does not truly grasp the laws that enable the scientists to make their machines work, to plot orbits, or to invent new devices.

The scientist (and this word, again in the classical meaning, includes the philosopher), however, has a reflective and critical knowledge; he knows what is true in his particular science, why it is true, and why it cannot but be true. This ability and prudence to distinguish what is certain from what is merely probable in their knowledge, what is ascertained from what is only hypothetical, is a characteristic scientific quality, befitting not merely physical scientists but also, and especially, philosophers.

Now, theodicy wants to be scientific knowledge about God. We study theodicy in order to see whether the traditional doctrine about God's existence and nature is really true; we want to know that we know it, we want to realize how and why we know it and why it cannot be otherwise than as we know it. Or, from a different point of view, we study theodicy in order to come to understand our universe according to its most ultimate cause.

It may very well be the case that theodicy will not teach us much beyond what the popular mind already knows about God; still, the popular mind does not understand why the doctrines it holds about God are true, and necessarily so. Nor has the popular mind ordinarily examined its beliefs enough to stand its ground when these beliefs are subjected to scientific scrutiny. The popular mind, driven into a corner, admits that it says "yes" to the truths about God because it "feels" or suspects them to be true, because it has a natural and unshakable conviction about them based on a spontaneous, noncritical inference, or because it takes them on faith—but not because it grasps the necessity of their being true.

V. THE ASSENT OF REASON—
THE ASSENT OF FAITH

Occasionally a book of natural theology may be found bearing the title, "Philosophy of Religion." Because a real and very important relationship exists between theodicy and natural religion, and, again, between natural religion and revealed (or supernatural) religion, we believe it opportune to discuss here, in two further sections of this *Introduction*, first, the differences between the assent of reason and the assent of faith, and, secondly, the question of the relation between the "God of philosophy" and the "God of religion."

Truths that can be accepted both by faith and by reason.   Almost all the truths that we shall learn in theodicy may be found in the Judaeo-Christian revelation; they are truths that have been "revealed." One may, therefore, accept them *on divine faith*. Likewise, if one hears these propositions from the lips of some human teacher whose intelligence he respects and whose word he believes, then he may accept them *on human faith*. On the other hand, if he reasons them out for himself, he is not making an assent of faith but is engaging in philosophizing. The fact that the truths are knowable from revelation, that is, to use the specialized language of Scholastic theologians, acceptable from a "motive" of respect for divine authority, does not prevent a philosopher from thinking them out for himself (except in the case of a strict mystery). This does not mean, for example, that a Christian who is a philosopher is not sincere, that he is a sham philosopher, that he does not seriously employ his reason.

Man is a very complex animal; we do not live our daily lives aseptically safeguarded from the influence of tradition, history, and culture. Still, when we reason to a truth, we are philosophizing. The mere fact that, if we do not advert to the intrinsic evidence, we can still accept this truth with an act of faith, does not mean that we cannot be philosophical if we so choose. A teacher may tell his class the answer to a difficult mathematical problem without showing the class the steps leading up to the answer. The teacher may then assign the working out of the problem to the pupils for their home-work, and the mere fact that they already know what the answer is, and that they assent to it by an act of human faith in the authority of their teacher, does not prevent them from sincere and honest work on the problem. If and when they work out the answer to the problem for themselves, then they know that the answer is true, and they know it this time not from faith in any authority, but from an understanding of the intrinsic evidence, from the very nature of the case. They have come to see why the answer given is correct and inevitable. Their working on the problem has led them to conclude that the answer is necessarily true. Their assent now is the assent of reason.

Motive of assent. What determines whether a man's act of assenting to a proposition is an act of faith and not an act of reason? It is the motive of the assent. What is it that moves the man to say "yes" to the various propositions presented to him? If the motive of assent is the objective evidence seen by him as necessarily true, he is making an assent of reason, or an act of "science." If the motive of assent is the authority of someone's word, he is making an act of faith in the proposition. When the authoritative voice he is reverencing is that of God, then the act of faith is an act of *divine* faith; when the authority he is heeding is that of some fellowman (his parents, his teachers, his minister or pastor, etc.), he is making an act of *human* faith.

With regard to strict mysteries, only an act of faith can be made. With regard to truths that are objectively accessible to human minds, these, if revealed by God or related by humans, may be accepted by an assent of faith. One *can* make an act of faith in these truths, and if one is actually motivated to say "yes" by reason merely of the authority of a speaker, then he really *is* making an act or assent of faith. However, where a true proposition is not a strict mystery, if the man clearly sees the intrinsic evidence for its truth, then his intellect cannot but yield to that evidence. The man cannot but say "yes." In fact, if he adverts to and grasps the internal evidence, he must give an assent, an assent of science; this is the only assent possible; he cannot at the moment make an act of faith.

Examples. Let us take some concrete cases and investigate the assents that are, or can be, given to the following three propositions:

Proposition A: "There exist three Persons but only one Nature in God."

Proposition B: "The human soul is immortal."

Proposition C: "The world was created by God out of nothing."

PROPOSITION A	can be assented to by faith—and *only* by faith
PROPOSITION B	can be assented to by faith is demonstrable by reason unaided by revelation historically, was demonstrated by reason unaided by revelation
PROPOSITION C	can be assented to by faith is demonstrable by reason unaided by revelation historically, was not demonstrated by reason unaided by revelation

Comments on the chart. Proposition A (concerning the Trinity) was revealed; *de facto* (as a matter of fact, historically), it was not known independently of revelation; and *de jure* (by right, by reason of its very nature), it is not even knowable independently of revelation. Proposition B (concerning immortality) was revealed; *de jure*, it is knowable independently of revelation; and *de facto*, it was known independently of revelation (e.g., by Plato). Proposition C (concerning the fact of creation) was revealed; *de jure*, it is knowable independently of revelation; but *de facto*, it was not known independently of revelation.

Proposition A can be accepted only with an assent of faith; propositions B and C can be accepted also with an assent of reason; indeed, they can be accepted through reason by one who has never heard of revelation and thus has no motive to make an assent of faith. And even if one, having accepted revelation, has made an assent of faith in the fact of immortality and of creation, he is not prevented from making, at another time, an assent of reason motivated by the mere force of the intrinsic evidence of the truth in question and not, as in the assent of faith, by the authority of the revealer.

VI. THE "GOD OF PHILOSOPHY"— THE "GOD OF RELIGION"

Attitude of "all or nothing." Unfortunately for dispassionate and intelligent discussion, theodicy has fallen upon somewhat evil days in this present blasé, yet sensitive, post-war generation (though the complaints about the science of theodicy are almost as old as the science itself). If one presents a theodicy without linking it to a positive religion, his work is said to be sterile, unreal, and a bloodless abstraction; he is reminded that, nowadays at any rate, there are no "theists" or no *mere* theists"; that is, people who admit God are either Catholics, Moslems, Jews, Protestants, and so forth, but are never "merely theists." From the logical point of view, however, such an observation is no more pertinent than would be the statement: "Red things don't exist; what exist are dark red things, and light red things, and medium red things and so forth." Things that are dark red are still red. Catholic theists, Presbyterian theists, Moslem theists, and Jewish theists are still theists. Theodicy merely furnishes theism, nothing more; but anything "more" presupposes the theism. If, on the other hand, in his theodicy one mentions religion and/or faith, his work is denounced as an unscholarly descent into apologetics, indoctrination, or pseudo-philosophy.

Theodicy's only answer is to ask that it be given a fair hearing. More should not be expected of it than its nature is capable of giving or is meant to give. Theodicy is not the only theological science; much less is it the only science. Not to say everything, however, is not the same as saying nothing. To say little is not necessarily to say nothing important. A full, integral education requires contributions from history, literature, the physical sciences, theology, and so forth. Philosophy is not the totality of knowledge, and theodicy is not the totality of knowledge about God. *Non omnia possumus omnes!* The demand for "all or nothing" from any one human science will inevitably be answered by nothing. Theodicy, however, with all its limitations, does have contributions to make.

The revolt against theodicy. The failure to abide by the pedestrian, but eminently sane, rule of not asking more of philosophy than it is philosophy's task to give, has at times provoked useless polemic, expressed by the statement of the antithesis: the "God of philosophy" and the "God of religion." Usually the aim of such rhetoric is to state, cleverly and emphatically, that the two "gods" are opposed, that the "God of religion" differs from the "God of philosophy" as the real from the unreal, as the true from the false. Even talented thinkers and writers who have achieved, deservedly, a great reputation will sometimes lightly dismiss the "God of philosophy." The classic case is that of Blaise Pascal, in the *Memoriale* which he wore over his heart and in which is found the famous phrase, "God of Abraham, God of Isaac, God of Jacob, not the God of the philosophers and scholars." Immanuel Kant felt it "necessary to deny *knowledge* in order to make room for *faith*." [7] In our own day the following statement is attributed to the famous theologian Karl Barth: "Faith takes reason by the throat and strangles the brute." [8] The contemporary Existentialist Karl Jaspers tells us that "a proved God is no God." [9]

There is, then, a certain temperament that seems to resent, as an intrusion, the entry of reasoning or even of any intellectuality into the realm of religion. Proponents of this position feel religion is the realm of faith and love and grace, not of knowledge; faith is to be sought for by the heart and will, not by the mind and intellect.

Difference, but not contrariety. Certainly, if all that is being thus defended is the doctrine that to *know* God is better than merely to *know about* God, or that *sanctity* is a nobler perfection than *knowledge*, one should readily concede the correctness of the position, however carelessly it is worded. A devout Christian will rightly insist, for example, that "*to know* Jesus Christ"—on the level of personal commitment, by putting on His mind and heart, to know Jesus "by connaturality"—is indeed to have achieved a much higher and much more important knowledge than "*to know about* Jesus Christ" on a merely academic level, as an historian or a bibli-

[7] I. Kant, *Critique of Pure Reason*, 2nd ed., 1787, p. XXX.

[8] Quoted in *Newsweek*, May 2, 1955, p. 90. See Barth's Gifford Lectures: *The Knowledge of God and the Service of God*, London, Hodder and Stoughton, 1938, Lecture 1.

[9] K. Jaspers, *The Perennial Scope of Philosophy*, New York, Philosophical Library, 1949, p. 32.

cal archeologist or even as an exegete of the New Testament might know Him.

That the "God of philosophy" and the "God of religion" do not altogether coincide must immediately be granted. But the difference is not between opposites, nor between incompatibles, nor between adequately distinct ideas and realities. Rather, the difference is like that which exists between a less perfect and a more perfect approximation, or between a part and a whole, or between the natural and the supernatural.

A "religion" that excludes the intellect is not a religion but a superstition and a degradation. For some, indeed for many, the intellectual factor may simply be a reasonable conviction based on human faith or on elementary pre-philosophical reasoning. One certainly does not have to be a philosopher in order to have a religion. But neither does philosophy as such make one irreligious. Real religion is not cheapened, nor made less concrete nor less appealing, simply because its adherents can find some rational grounds for holding its presuppositions. The "God of religion" is not honored by a flight from reason on the part of His worshippers. As Father Sertillanges says, "There is a kind of worship that makes us want to blaspheme." [10]

Revealed truths cover a wider area than philosophical truths. No philosopher who does not simply equate human mind with infinite mind will deny that God can reveal about Himself what the most brilliant philosopher could never have suspected. And if God has made such a revelation, then assuredly the God of (revealed) religion is one about whom we know more than we do about the "God of philosophy." God alone comprehends God. Although we can learn something about God from philosophy, there is a far greater amount that only He can tell us. And He has told us some of these truths— so believers in divine revelation and positive religion insist. God has told us a tremendous number of things about Himself, important things, beautiful things, inspiring and enrapturing things—all of which, or much of which, man could never know apart from revelation.

[10] A.D. Sertillanges, O.P., St. *Thomas Aquinas and His Work*. London, Blackfriars Publications, 1957, p. 139.

Philosophy is not history. The most deeply penetrating philosophy will never discover the particular, contingent events of history; it cannot inform us, at the end of a syllogism, what a free agent will do. Much of what is known of the "God of religion" is known precisely through history, particularly through Sacred History (often defined as "God's acts in history"), in short, through the Jewish and Christian scriptures. But that there is a "double truth" about God —one for the philosopher and another for the believer—is simply nonsense, whether this is affirmed by the philosopher or by the believer.

Philosophy and the "personal" God. Philosophy does not tell us about God's personal and intimate dealings with individuals and nations, but the possibilities of such dealings are not excluded by philosophy. Indeed, philosophy even shows us that God is personal— in the sense that He is an independent, complete, individual nature, endowed with intellect and will. Also, the general fact of Providence —meaning that if there is a history of the universe, then it is a divinely planned one—is something derivable, in a *general* manner, from philosophical speculation and analysis. As for *individual* applications, these are set forth, not by philosophy, but by Scripture, theology, history, literature, and mystical writings. Interior prayer life and personal appreciation of the wisdom and love of God in dealing with His creatures are not forbidden a man who is a philosopher; nor is it necessarily a philosopher's temptation to shy away from such appreciation and prayer. Is a medical doctor forced by his professional activities to lose reverence for the human body, or must an art critic lose any taste he may have for artistic achievement?

When something affects us directly—when we know of its influence on us or on persons, places, and times that are near and dear to ourselves—then we tend to consider that thing as "more real" and, if it is a person, as "more personal" than we consider other things and persons. The norm for what is "personal" and "more personal" in this sense thus involves more than intellectual factors. Even so, a man who is a professional philosopher is not precluded from putting his relations with God on a personal basis.

In short, the "God of philosophy" is included in, but does not extend as far as, the "God of religion" (at least, not as far as the God of *revealed* religion). Philosophy (the same may be said of theology) is not the totality of knowledge—nor does it purport to be.

VII. OUTLINE OF *FUNDAMENTALS IN THE PHILOSOPHY OF GOD*

This book will be divided into two parts, the first of which will deal with the existence of God, and the second with the essence (or nature) and attributes of God. It is impossible, of course, even to deal with the problem of the existence of God without simultaneously, at least implicitly, dealing with the problem of the nature of God. The second part of the book is, therefore, implicitly contained in the first part.

Part one. Our treatment of the proofs for the existence of God will be set out in three chapters. *Chapter 2* takes the data of experience, discovers at least some that are truly produced, argues that it is impossible for all existents to be products, and so concludes that there must be an uncaused cause in existence. *Chapter 3* will present the proof that the order within the universe has been caused by a supremely intelligent cause and that the determination and specification of those possibilities to be actualized presupposes dominion, choice, or will in the ultimate cause of the universe. *Chapter 4* will attempt to say something about the mode of production of the universe, that unique action known by the term "creation."

Part two. The second part of the book will deal with God's nature and attributes. There will be a special introductory chapter (*Chapter 5*) on how we come to know something about the divine nature. This chapter is a very important one, establishing as it does the validity of the concepts that we apply to God and setting up the norm for distinguishing literal and symbolical predications of God. Then comes discussion of the various transcendent modes of God's being. *Chapter 6* will discuss God's transcendent perfection, that is, His infinity. *Chapter 7* will discuss God's transcendent unity, that is, His absolute simplicity or freedom from all composition, and also the uniqueness or numerical oneness of His nature. *Chapter 8* is concerned with God's transcendence over change. *Chapter 9* will discuss the divine transcendence over time, that is, God's eternity. *Chapter 10* will discuss the divine transcendence over space, that is, God's immensity and omnipresence. These chapters on God's transcendent modes of being will be followed by a chapter (*Chapter 11*) on the divine intellect and will. A final chapter, *Chapter 12*, will speak of Providence and the problem of evil in the universe.

Some thinkers and writers occasionally imply that God's existence is not proven until His transcendent attributes are *explicitly* established. In truth, God's existence, essence, and attributes are all really identical. Still, no one can prove everything at one time. All of natural theology is but one extended proof of God.

LEADING IDEAS of Chapter 1

1. "Theodicy" or "Natural Theology" is the study of God by the light of natural reason (that is, reason unaided by supernatural revelation).

2. The philosophical search for God turns out to be an attempt to appreciate creatures precisely as creatures, that is, as something totally "given," and therefore presupposing an adequate "giver."

3. Theodicy clarifies and makes systematic much of the "every-day knowledge" that most people have about God.

4. To accept a statement on the authority of another is to make an act of "faith" (and if the authority is that of God, the "faith" is "divine faith"); to accept a statement because one grasps its truth from within (sees the internal evidence) is to make an act of "understanding."

5. Some propositions about God are *de jure* knowable (and, of course, *de facto* known) only through supernatural revelation; other propositions about God are *de jure* knowable, but historically—*de facto*—were not first known independently of revelation; still other propositions about God are both *de jure* knowable and also were historically—*de facto*—known independently of revelation.

6. The difference between the "God of philosophy" and the "God of religion" is like the difference between a part and a whole, or between the less complete and the more complete.

7. Personal religious faith and commitment have nothing to lose by serious philosophical consideration of God.

SUGGESTED READINGS for Chapter 1

N.B.1. Other lists of suggested readings may be found at the end of each of the appropriate chapters in the following works:

C. Bittle, O.F.M. Cap. *God and His Creatures, Theodicy*. Milwaukee: Bruce, 1953.

A.R. Dulles, S.J., J.M. Demske, S.J., and R.J. O'Connell, S.J. *Introductory Metaphysics*. New York: Sheed and Ward, 1955.

M.R. Holloway, S.J. *An Introduction to Natural Theology*. New York: Appleton-Century-Crofts, 1959.

N.B.2. In the readings we suggest at the end of our own chapters, we shall use the titles, *Basic Writings, Truth of the Catholic Faith*, and *Power of God*, respectively, for the following English translations of works of St. Thomas Aquinas:

Basic Writings of Saint Thomas Aquinas, edited and annotated by A.C. Pegis. Two volumes, New York: Random House, 1945.

On the Truth of the Catholic Faith (Summa Contra Gentiles), translated by A.C. Pegis, J.F. Anderson, V.J. Bourke, and C.J. O'Neil. Four volumes in five, Garden City, N.Y.: Hanover House, 1955–1957.

On the Power of God (Quaestiones Disputatae de Potentia Dei) literally translated by the English Dominican Fathers. Three volumes in one, Westminster, Md.: Newman, 1952.

On the Historical Circumstances of Leibniz's Theodicy:

G.W. Leibniz. *Theodicy, Essays on the Goodness of God, the Freedom of Man, and the Origin of Evil*, translated by E.M. Huggard, edited with an introduction by Austin Farrer. London: Routledge and Kegan Paul, 1951, "Introduction," pp. 34–47, and 63f.

On the Nature of the Philosophy of God:

M.D. Chenu, O.P. *Is Theology a Science?* New York: Hawthorn, 1959, pp. 25–28.

F.C. Copleston, S.J. *Aquinas*. Baltimore, Penguin Books, 1955, pp. 42–44.

On Faith and Reason:

St. Thomas. S.T. II-II.1.4 and 5 (*Basic Writings*, Vol. 2, pp. 1059–1062); C.G. I.7 and 8 (*Truth of the Catholic Faith*, Vol. 1, pp. 74–76).

Brother Benignus, F.S.C. *Nature, Knowledge and God.* Milwaukee: Bruce, 1947, pp. 435–460.

G.C. Colombo, S.J. "The Analysis of Belief," *The Downside Review,* no. 247, Winter 1958–59, pp. 18–37.

E. Gilson. *The Spirit of Medieval Philosophy.* New York: Charles Scribner's Sons, 1940, chapters 1 and 2.

On the Purpose of Revelation:

St. Thomas. S.T. II-II.2.4 (*Basic Writings,* Vol. 2, pp. 1079–1080); C.G. I.4 (*Truth of the Catholic Faith,* Vol. 1, pp. 66–68).

On Pascal's "reasons of the heart" and the "God of philosophy":

F.C. Copleston, S.J. *History of Philosophy, Vol. IV: Descartes to Leibniz.* Westminster, Md.: Newman Press, 1959, pp. 160–167.

CHAPTER

2

OUTLINE

22

The Existence of God as Uncaused Cause

I. INTRODUCTION: GENERAL PRESENTATION OF THE ARGUMENT

The purpose of the present chapter is to show that from the existence of experiential realities that undergo change we can prove the existence of God as of an uncaused cause, a self-existent or self-sufficient being, a necessary and immutable being, and the ultimate source of contingent and changeable beings.

The argument, briefly, is this: In the data of experience we find beings that are contingent in their existence, that is to say, beings whose intrinsic constitution, whose make-up, whose essence or nature, does not necessitate their existence. Since such beings do not exist necessarily but are indifferent with respect to existence, then the fact that they actually do exist must be attributed to some other, really distinct, being, which we call their cause. Contingent beings, thus, are caused beings. Now, not all beings can be caused beings; hence there must exist some being—at least one—that is uncaused and non-contingent.

The whole of theodicy is but the amplification of this basic argument, the unfolding of what is implicitly contained in it. The uncaused cause is thereby explicitly shown to be God.

This basic argument is quite simple. However, to understand and not merely to memorize the ideas and principles that underlie it and to answer the difficulties that are raised against it, a good deal of time and space is required. The main ideas calling for development are these:

"Contingent beings need a cause";
"It is not necessary for every cause to be a caused cause";
"It is impossible for every cause to be a caused cause."

23

II. CONTINGENT BEINGS NEED A CAUSE

A. Change Is Not Self-explanatory.

The argument, strictly speaking, is from the contingency of the data of experience. But since this contingency is not immediately manifest as such, it is something that itself has to be reasoned to. Perhaps the greatest difficulty in coming to know that God exists does not lie in passing from the idea of contingent being to that of necessary being, but in recognizing some data of experience precisely as contingent. Once we acknowledge this contingency, we can go on and argue to an absolutely necessary being—God.

Very telling evidence for the contingency of a being is its changeability. This changeability we know from witnessing the changes or modifications that the being actually undergoes. Hence we start our argument by appealing to the fact of change. If a being changes, we have a changeable being.

Change presents a problem. We constantly experience change: we grow fat or thin, we become tired, we get sick, we feel glad or sorrowful, we increase our knowledge, we forget, we change our minds. Likewise, the things around us manifest change: they change in shape, speed, and direction; they change in temperature; they change in color. Some changes are relatively superficial (a man gets sick), while others are quite radical (a man drops dead). But any real change, superficial or radical, presents a real problem: it requires an explanation, and this explanation will have to include more than the change itself and more than the being in which the change occurs.

If change were adequately explained in complete independence of any reality other than the changeable being, hence uniquely by the intrinsic constituents of the thing which undergoes change, then what the thing *becomes* would already have its full, adequate, and completely actual explanation in that which the thing *already is*, namely this specific existent; the thing and its future newness would be unrelated to any other reality in the universe, would be independent of any outside, or really distinct, object, and would be free of external influence; there would be no such thing as one being affecting another being.

If change were intelligible independently of a cause external to the change, if change could be self-explanatory or adequately accounted for by the being of the changeable being, then nothing would need an explanation, there would be no problems; "explanations," "questions," and "reason" would be meaningless expressions. The "contingent" would be "explained" by itself, that is, by the contingent, that is, by the "unnecessary," hence, not really explained at all.

Illustration. Let us represent to ourselves something which is found successively in two distinct states: first, as a large cube of marble (A), and then, as a statue of a man (B). Since state B contains a configuration that is not actually that of state A, then surely we cannot say that state A, simply of itself, explains state B. That which previously was cubical is not, of itself alone, the adequate determinate reason for subsequently having the shape of a man. The transit that is effected from state A to state B, the actual variation and the new configuration, depend on something more than the cubical marble. Leave the marble alone in the quarry, and it will never take on the configuration of a man. Only a sculptor can cause the marble to have the new shape. Even if you object that the physical and chemical elements (wind and rain, lightning, and other natural forces) can make the marble lose its cubical shape and take on some other one (perhaps even making an impressionistic statue of a man) you will not be refuting, but confirming, the point we are trying to make. You are admitting that when change occurs, then forces are at work distinct from the being in which the change occurs. You are admitting a really distinct cause.

Even in the case of changeable living beings, which are in some sense the partial cause of their new "perfections," that is, of their new qualities or attributes, external agents are needed when and in so far as these living beings undergo real change. Put a fertile egg on a glacier in the Arctic Circle, and you will get no chick. Put it in an incubator, and in about three weeks the transit from potential chick to actual chick is effected. Something more than the egg is required for the coming into existence of the chick. Something more than an old thing is required when the old becomes new.

Often this "something more," this cause, is a plurality of distinct beings; often the active power needed for the production of a single

new effect is the combined active power of many beings, each of
which is thus only partially responsible for the effect. The point is
that the change itself is not self-explanatory and that the changeable
being, however much it determines some aspects of the change, is not
the adequate explanation of the change.

Metaphysical proof that change needs a cause. Let us now
present the metaphysics of the proof that change is due to something
other than the being that undergoes the change.

Presupposing the truism that what does not yet exist is not active,
and that a being is not yet, actually, what it will be after some change
has occurred in it and it has acquired some new perfection, we must
admit that for a thing

to undergo a change,

to receive a perfection or some new quality,

to be the subject (the "patient") in which some action is occurring,

to be "reduced from the state of passive potency into act"

IS to pass—at least under some aspect—from non-existence into existence,

IS to COME INTO EXISTENCE (at least relatively, that is, according to some new quality or some new configuration of attributes),

IS to exist as BEING ACTED UPON.

On the other hand, presupposing the truism that you can't give
what you haven't got, or its more technical equivalent, that "the
greater does not come from the lesser," we must also admit that for a
thing

to cause something to change,

to be the donor of a perfection or of some new quality,

to be the "agent" from which an action proceeds,

to "reduce into act" something which was in the state of passive
potency

IS to ACT, that is, IS TO EXIST AS ACTING.

So, to be coming into existence (at least relatively, that is, in the
sense of getting some *new* perfection or coming to exist *differently*)
is to be in the "state" of *becoming*; whereas to act, to be producing
a certain perfection, is to be already in the "state" of *existing* and

to be already perfect. Now, "becoming" and "existing" are two different states, as opposed as motion and rest, as "being in motion" and "being at rest," or as "being passive" and "being active."

Nothing, therefore, can be at one and the same time, with reference to one and the same perfection (determination), both cause and effect, both the new being and the producer of the new being.

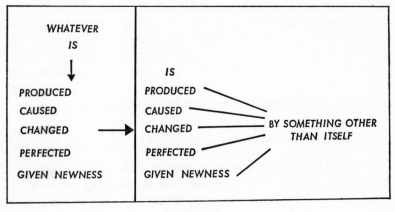

Figure 1.

You can't be both the pitcher and the catcher at once in the same ball-game!

B. Changeable Beings Are Contingent Beings.

Contingence more radical than change.   It is not enough to say that change needs an outside explanation; even more radically, the total being that is subject to the change cannot be a self-existent being but must be totally caused. It *is* contingently *this* being (since change can make it *that* being), but it is also, more profoundly, a *contingent being.*

A changeable being cannot but be radically contingent, not only contingently *this,* but contingently a *being.* It cannot have as an ingredient any self-existent part. If a being is partially contingent—and its dependence on an outside cause for the fact of its change shows that it is at least partially contingent—then it is totally contingent. A thing cannot be half-necessary in the existential order. Not only is the new (and the old) determination something dependent on, contingent upon, an outside cause, but the very substrate or common element that was determined by the old perfection and is now determined by the new is something that cannot possibly be self-existent but is *absolutely* contingent.

Contingency of the substrate of change. A substrate that can receive a plurality of different and successive determinations is indifferent intrinsically to sustaining this or that determination. Incapable of existing without a determination and of itself determining what determination it shall have, it is totally dependent on outside causes for its determination and is, therefore, totally dependent or contingent in its very reality as an underlying substrate of change. This point will be further developed in *Chapter 4*.

C. Contingent Beings Are Caused Beings.

Change is possible only in a contingent being. A contingent being is an existent that does not have within itself an absolute, unconditioned necessity for existing. *What* a contingent being is—a man, a mouse, a house, a tree, a rock—does not account for the fact that *it exists*. A man is a man; an existing man is a human existent. But men do not have an absolute, inner necessity of existing at all. Otherwise there would be no dead men. Nor would any men have been born, i.e., have come into existence; they would all have always existed, and existed without changing. Whatever is absolutely necessary is not contingent; what is not contingent is not capable of beginning to exist, nor of passing out of existence, nor, consequently, of undergoing change.

To come to exist by reason of a change occurring in some already existing reality is to come into existence under some new aspect after having been existent according to some other aspect. But if a being begins to exist, or ceases to exist, even in the merely relative sense of undergoing change from being *this* to being *that*, then it is a being that is not self-existent but existent through some outside influence. When change is occurring in an existent, the existent in question is ceasing to be this thing and is becoming that thing, it is passing from (relative) non-existence into existence. A being that changes is a

being to which something is happening; it itself is constituted of
contingent ingredients. It would not change if its intrinsic constitution existed of absolute necessity.

Contradiction between "changeable" and "absolutely necessary."
If we were to say that by its own very nature a being necessarily exists
—and is, therefore, self-explanatory and self-sufficient—and yet necessarily becomes "other," we would be saying at the same time that this
being is not necessarily what it is (since it changes). We would be
saying that the constituents which intrinsically make it what it is are
(while remaining unchanged themselves and without the intervention of any outside influence) the reason why this "necessary" being
passes through really distinct stages. But this is to contradict one of
the most fundamental intuitions of our intelligence, namely, the principle that "That which is, is."

That which exists is, in a formal sense, intrinsically explained by
that which intrinsically constitutes it; these intrinsic constituents cannot, merely by themselves and without outside aid, make the reality
become really "other." It is impossible that the supposedly necessarily existing constituents of a being—making it to be what it is—
nevertheless precisely oblige it, in independence of all outside influence, to become different from what it is. We do not explain why
A becomes B merely by affirming that A is A. Identity suffices for
identity, for sameness; it does not account for difference, diversity,
"otherness."

Necessity and immutability. What necessarily exists is necessarily immutable. A necessarily existing reality, one that exists of
unqualified, unconditioned, absolute necessity, is necessarily whatever it is; it is necessarily unchangeable, it has no passivity or determinability, it is purely act, sheer positive perfection. It is unintelligible that a self-existent, necessarily existent being should have any
passive potentialities and thus be related to, dependent upon, ori-
entated towards, something distinct from its own all self-sufficient
self. It is unintelligible that passive potentialities receive their complement totally from the being that has the passive potentialities.

A word on the pantheists. Certain philosophers, called "pantheists," hold that there is only one being in existence and that this one
being necessarily modifies itself. The self-consciousness which each
of us has suffices to give a practical refutation of pantheism, while

a demonstration of the contradictoriness of the qualities possessed by the pantheists' one being would constitute its metaphysical refutation.

Summary of Section II. Thus far we have come to realize that besides the existence of beings that undergo change, or that come to be, or that contingently exist, we must also admit the existence of beings that cause the change, that account for what comes to be, that explain the beings that contingently exist. We have learned, briefly, that: change exists, therefore causes of change exist. More universally: products exist, things come into existence; therefore at least one producer exists. Contingent realities exist; therefore at least one cause upon which contingent realities depend likewise exists.

Digression on a point of vocabulary. Before going on with the main topic of this chapter we would like to introduce a few paragraphs on a point of vocabulary. This digression, we trust, will help prevent confusion from arising when other textbooks or St. Thomas himself and his modern commentators are consulted.

The general argument that we are giving in *Chapter 2* may be called, indifferently, "the argument from contingency," "the argument from causality," "the First-Cause argument," "the argument from effects," or "the argument from change." But we would readily admit that these titles could be misleading, since they might induce the reader to equate the argument with more specialized arguments.

In writers, for example, whose philosophical use of the words "necessary" and "contingent" consciously depends upon that of St. Thomas, any being that does not have as a constituent part a "prime matter" or substantial potential principle, capable of being subjected to some substantial form other than its present one, is considered to be an "absolutely necessary being." [1] Such a being (for example, an angel or a human soul) might be totally dependent upon some really distinct cause (a creator) for its existence; but it cannot have come into existence by way of strict generation (the production of a new substance out of a previously existing one); neither has such a being an intrinsic principle of "corruption" (whereby it could cease to be what it is by becoming substantially different). Such a being

---

[1] See Thomas B. Wright, "Necessary and Contingent Being in St. Thomas," *The New Scholasticism*, Vol. 25, 1951, pp. 439–466.

might even be made up of matter and form in the order of substance, but because the form in question completely actualizes the potency of the matter (as St. Thomas believed to be the case in the planets and other celestial bodies), the being is not capable of "corruption." In this use of language, an "absolutely necessary being" could still be a product, not something generated, however, but something created. It would be "absolutely necessary *per aliud*" or have its "absolutely necessary existence" caused, in contrast with God, Who alone is "*per se* absolutely necessary" or Whose existence is uncaused and self-sufficient.

Similarly, with these writers "contingent" is not co-extensive with "caused" or "created"; it is used only of terrestrial bodies, capable of undergoing substantial change. Every "contingent" being in this sense of the word is a caused being, but not every caused being is contingent.

However, we ourselves, throughout this book, use the phrase "absolutely necessary being" in reference only to a being which not only cannot cease to exist by "corruption" but which is altogether self-sufficient, totally uncaused, unconditioned, and independent, existing of itself and having no need of something distinct from itself to account for its existence. Similarly, we use the adjective "contingent" to describe any caused being, any being whose existence is "*per aliud*" and not absolutely, unqualifiedly self-sufficient. So long as it does not exist by its very nature, so long as its existence is not self-explanatory and self-sufficient, such a being is "contingent," even if such a being did not "come into being by *generation*" and even if it has no positive *intrinsic* principle of "corruption."

Hence our argument—"the general argument from contingency" —is not simply to be equated with St. Thomas's more specialized "Third Way," which is sometimes spoken of as his "argument from contingency."

Our general argument also employs the words "change" and "effect" and "dependent cause." But this should not be taken to mean that we are attempting to give the more specialized Thomist "First Way" (from motion or change) or the "Second Way" (from dependent causes). These latter two Thomist arguments are sometimes interpreted as proving God's existence on the score that a mover or a cause which is (proximately) *capable of* acting becomes a cause that is *actually* acting only by the intervention of some superior mover or cause. The inferior agent (capable of causing) is thus *intrinsically* modified into an actually acting agent, the modification being due to a created additional entity that only an uncaused, eternally acting, immobile mover bestows and can bestow. Our argument does not proceed along such paths.

We wish to retain somewhat popular modes of speaking, and so we call a thing a cause even if it is not here and now found with an effect, just as people call a doctor a doctor even when he is not actually treating a patient, or just as they call an Olympic runner a runner even when he has paused for breath (or, for that matter, even when he is asleep in bed). Of course, it is certainly true that if something is here and now being actually effected, then there is in existence here and now a being that is actually (and not merely potentially) causing what is being effected: there is here and now an actual cause in existence. This point will be stressed in *Chapter 4*. Only, our present argument does not rest upon a claim that there is an evident necessity of admitting that the difference between a "potential cause or potential mover" and an "actual cause or actual mover" is an *intrinsic* difference which is and can be accounted for immediately by God and only by God. Change or newness is in the recipient or even is simply the effect itself—it is not in the agent. Fulfilling the conditions prerequisite for the exercise of A's causality is not necessarily to be intrinsically modifying A. Our argument should not be confused, therefore, with an attempt to give the mind of St. Thomas in the "First" and "Second" Ways.

We believe, along with many others, for example the distinguished Thomist, Father Garrigou-Lagrange, O.P.,[2] that there is a "general proof" of God's existence that underlies all more specialized proofs. It is to this general proof that we give the name "the argument from contingency."

Let us now return to the exposition of this general argument. So far we have argued that changeable being is contingently existent being and that contingently existent being is caused being and therefore needs a cause.

[2] R. Garrigou-Lagrange, O.P., *The One God*, translated by Dom Bede Rose, O.S.B., St. Louis, Herder, 1946, pp. 138–139; and *God, His Existence and His Nature*, translated by Dom Bede Rose, O.S.B., St. Louis, Herder, 1946, Vol. I, pp. 251–261.

III. IT IS NOT NECESSARY THAT EVERY CAUSE BE A CAUSED CAUSE

A need for caution. The doctrine that *contingent* beings are caused beings is a very far cry from any claim that "*every* being has a cause." However, because of the possibility that some might not appreciate sufficiently this distinction, and in order to forestall difficulties against our description of God as an uncaused and immutable being, we shall proceed to further analyses.

If every being were necessarily a caused being, then, since every cause is a being, every cause would be something caused, and an "uncaused cause" would be a contradiction in terms. And thus, were we to try to prove the existence of God as of an uncaused cause, we would be doomed to failure from the very outset. On the other hand, if we were to start out by saying that "Not every being is a caused being" or "Not every cause is a caused cause," would we not already be affirming—without any warrant—the existence of at least one uncaused being, at least one uncaused cause? Would we not be begging the question of God's existence?

A. "Essential" Propositions.

To appreciate the distinctions that are called for, let us consider the proposition "It is not necessary that every cause be a caused cause." This proposition is not needed *logically* for the demonstrative value of our proof for God's existence, for it does not play the role of a logical premise in that argument; the argument proves, even if we do not refer to this proposition. However, it is a proposition which is very helpful *psychologically* for understanding the argument, it is one which enriches our appreciation of the conclusion of the argument, and it forestalls many difficulties.

Difference between statements about essences and statements that affirm "extramental" existence or reality outside the mind. When we say "It is not necessary that every cause be a caused cause," we mean to make a statement about the "essential" order, that is, we are talking about the necessary connections, or lack of these, between the intelligible notes or aspects of the nature of a cause and of its properties. We are not, in such a case, explicitly affirming the existence of anything, whether of a cause or of something caused. Rather we are trying to come to an understanding of what is relevant and what is irrelevant if we are ever to be justified in affirming that there exist beings which are truly causes, beings which are truly effects, and beings which (if at all) are both causes and effects. We are not trying to show that an uncaused cause is positively possible, nor are we arguing that we can see how it is possible for a being not to be caused; we are very interested, however, in emphasizing that it is unwarranted to state that an uncaused being or an uncaused cause is impossible.

The notion "cause" is not the same as the notion "caused cause." The notion "cause" prescinds from (neither affirms nor denies) the notion "caused." There is no logical justification for concluding, "X is a cause (or simply: X is a being); *therefore* X is something which is caused." Whether a being is caused or uncaused cannot be settled by us on the evidence furnished by it when considered simply *as a being*, or even *as a cause*. If we are to know it as something caused, this will have to be manifested by some show of contingency on its part, some deficiency, some lack of self-sufficiency. On the other hand, if we are to know it as a cause, it will have to manifest itself as such by the exercise of transitive activity, that is, by influencing or producing something distinct from itself. A being may well be both a cause (a productive being) and an effect (a produced being), but, as we saw in the previous section, it cannot be both cause and effect simultaneously according to the same aspect. Hence, if we know that a being is an effect, we know that it is not the only being in existence—its cause also exists. If, however, we know that a being is a cause, we know that it has (or at least can have) an effect, but we do not know whether or not it itself has a cause; hence we are not justified in straightway affirming that this cause is itself an effect.

The role of "essential" propositions. The present proposition, "It is not necessary that every cause be a caused cause," is, then, an "essential" proposition. It simply makes a statement about the nature or essence of a cause. It tells us that the essence, "cause," does not as such include the characteristic, "something caused," that such a characteristic is irrelevant to a cause as a cause.

What we human beings know of the nature of *cause, as such*, will certainly be dependent in some way upon our experience of some concretely existing cause or causes; these *concretely existing* causes, if we duly examine them and reason about their actual, concrete, integral being, will become known to us not merely as "something productive" but also as "something caused." Still, our knowledge is not a merely passive registering by our senses of concrete sense-phenomena; neither is all our knowledge mere experience. We also have the ability of abstracting, of reasoning, and of "understanding"—abilities with which to come to grips with the intelligible aspects that underpin the sense-world.

The understanding abstracts the absolute nature of "cause" from the concrete determinants (and even from the actual exercise of existence) that are concomitants of this or that particular concrete cause existing in the world of sense-phenomena. "*Abstract* natures" or "*absolute* natures" do not prescind from existence altogether; rather, they imply it hypothetically (otherwise they would simply be inconceivable and therefore never abstracted); but when *considered* in themselves absolutely, abstractly, as hypothetically existent, they are *not affirmed* as actually exercising existence, they are simply apprehended as forms determining reality (if and when reality is given); they are natures considered "essentially" or "formally." These "absolute" or "abstract" natures, these "metaphysical quiddities," are not "unreal" in the sense that they *exclude* existence; they are not "real" in that they do not *affirm* the actual exercise of existence (no *concept* does that!—this is reserved to intuitive knowledge or else to the judgment or second operation of the mind), but they are "real" in that what they signify are the conditions, determinants, constituents, or properties and laws of what is real, when, and if, there is anything in the real, concrete order.

Need of reflection and clarification of concepts. The *imagination* glides swiftly:

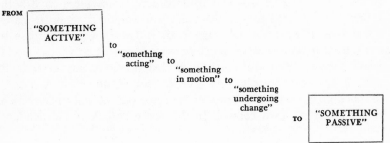

But we must be on guard and not let the *intellect* be led astray; we must forestall an erroneous judgment that would amount to saying "Whatever is active is passive."

Most of our intellectual mistakes are caused by insufficient reflection. We often surreptitiously put into our ideas a content that is unjustifiable, or we confuse our sensory imaginations with our intellectual operations (our concepts and our judgments); we are sidetracked by the irrelevant. A red (and impermeable) hat kept Joe's head from getting wet in yesterday's rain. Joe's advice thereafter is: "Always carry something red along with you when it's cloudy!"

We should by now have come to realize that it is always some reason, other than the fact that a thing is a cause, to which we must appeal if we are to explain why the thing in question is also a mutable thing or why it is a caused being. For it does not change simply on the score of being a cause; it is not a product simply because it can produce. An agent does not, itself, necessarily change when it acts.

Appearances to the contrary.   When there is question, in the concrete, of a material substance (A) causing some effect in another material substance (B)—and this is always the case when there is question of the data of *sensible* experience—physical contact is necessary between the two bodies. Now, while this contact enables A to act on B, it also enables B to act on A. In the physical realm of bodies, to every action there is an equal and opposite reaction; physical action comes in *two's*. Our private interests may inspire us to call A the agent and B the recipient or patient, or if the only action whose cause we are investigating is the one taking place in B, then we say that A is the cause. Still, both A and B are agents, and both A and B are patients, though neither is both agent and patient under the same aspect nor through numerically the same action. Not being interested in the reaction that B produces in A, we tend to think of B solely as a passive recipient. But corporeal substances have both active potencies and passive potencies, and corporeal action is really interaction. Hence, not only does body A (which we presuppose is not self-existent) receive its active power and in that sense is a caused cause, likewise A's condition is such that it cannot act on body B until it has been brought into contact with it, and thus A is conditioned in its exercise of causality by some outside influence, which is not under A's own control. In this sense also, A is a dependent cause. Finally, the reaction of B upon A produces an effect in A; something in A is caused by B. Thus, A is far from being immobile, though *considered precisely in its aspect as a cause*, A still is immutable. What may appear to us as a cause undergoing change in the very act of causing, is a composite being that has, in differing respects, both activity and passivity.

As for spiritual activity, this is not interaction. A teacher does not give up the knowledge that he gives out, even if he becomes physically worn out by the reactions that affect his physical nature when he translates his thoughts into messages communicated through the corporeal media of sound and gesture.

B. Cause—Caused Cause—Uncaused Cause.

"CAUSE"	includes: "having active power" neither includes nor excludes: "having active power from another being"
"CAUSED CAUSE"	includes: "having active power" also includes: "having active power from another being"
"UNCAUSED CAUSE"	includes: "having active power" excludes: "having active power from another being"

Explanation of the above table. To state that a concrete thing is a *book* is not to state that it is a *theodicy* book. To state that a thing is a cause is to state that it is known to us as active, as having certain perfections *in act* and as capable of communicating these perfections and of making new beings exist; but it is not to deny that this cause might itself have certain other perfections only in potency and, therefore, cannot give (whether to itself or to another) that which it does not actually have. A being which is in one way active may in another way be passive. Still, "to be active" is not "to be passive," and "to be a cause," while implying "to have active power," does not imply "to have received active power." A self-existent, and consequently auto-dynamic being, unlike an "automobile" or a "self-made" man, cannot be shown, merely from its concept, to be an impossibility.

To demonstrate that such a being is not only *not impossible*, but actually necessary, if things come into existence, if things undergo change, or if there are things that exist contingently, is to prove the existence of God.

Again, when we merely state of a being that it is a cause, we as yet say nothing about the origin of its active power—not even that this has an origin. We may argue, of course, that existing active power, that any existing cause, must be either self-sufficient in being or owe its origin to some other being; we may acknowledge that in the concrete order every cause must be either a caused cause or an uncaused cause (though a true *realization* or appreciation of the implications of such disjunctive propositions is not something naively come by and is indeed almost the whole burden of theodicy). Still, if all we know about a being is that it is a cause (and therefore active), we are not justified in saying that it is something produced. On the other hand, we cannot affirm, *a priori*, that such a cause is an uncaused cause. It is not of the essence (the quiddity, the formal content, the objective concept, the absolute or metaphysical nature) of a "cause" to be a "caused cause."

Although it is essential to a "producer" that it have active power, or that it be able to produce, still it is not of the essence of a producer that it itself be "something produced." A thing is meaningful to us to the extent that it presents its intelligible structure to us. Objects of experience present themselves to us as active, and they also present themselves to us as passive. But none of them force us to say that "what is active" is also, necessarily, "what is passive."

Where an active being also has some passivity and changeability, this being is not adequately self-explanatory, it is not fully intelligible merely by reason of its intrinsic constitution. The intellect is not justified in seeking an extrinsic explanation for a thing which is adequately explicable by its own intrinsic constituent nature. But when a being manifests itself as contingent (for example, by revealing changeability, perfectibility, passivity, finitude, or composition of activity and passivity), when a cause manifests that it itself is caused, that its being or that its act of causing is itself dependent or affected or conditioned by something other than the cause itself, then we reasonably judge that some further being, ultimately an uncaused cause, is needed to furnish an adequate explanation of that being's existence.

Possibility of an uncaused cause. Can there really be such a thing as an uncaused cause? Certainly its existence will not be known merely through a definition or description. Its very possibility will be *positively* known only after we know that it is actual, that is, only if and when we prove that God does exist. The objective validity of this notion, "uncaused cause," is certified only by proving that some cause exists which cannot possibly be a caused cause. Our notion of an "uncaused cause" and our knowledge that such a thing is possible is thus derived only indirectly from experience; it presupposes discursive reasoning and judgments; it is an analogical notion, not derived from, nor perfectly proportioned to, the object of which it is predicated. Still, we can already say—from what we know about any cause, about caused causes, and about the mind's ability to reason and judge (by affirmation and negation)—that we do not see any impossibility in an "uncaused cause," and that it is therefore not meaningless to raise the question: "Does any cause really exist that is an uncaused cause?"

IV. IT IS IMPOSSIBLE FOR EVERY CAUSE TO BE A CAUSED CAUSE

A. Preliminary Remarks.

In an earlier section we argued that since in the universe of our experience there exist contingent beings (known as contingent, or as not intrinsically necessary, by the fact that they undergo change), then there must also exist some being as the cause or source of these contingent beings. Most simply, we argued that since certain things exist as products, then some other being(s) must exist as their producer(s) or cause(s).

The proposition that we have just finished discussing, "It is not necessary that every cause be a caused cause," did not prove the *existence* of anything; but it did show us what is demanded and what is not demanded by a being by the fact simply that it has the nature of a cause. If such a being is to exist, it must have *active power*, but it is not necessary for it, precisely as a cause, to *have received* active power. It is *not necessary* for every agent to be a product.

Section IV goes a step further and argues that it is *not possible* for every agent to be a product, for every cause to be a caused cause. Applying such a principle to the existential order where changes and new beings are obvious data of experience, we must conclude that unless some existing cause is an uncaused cause, there would be no causes, and therefore no change, nothing new, no products, at all in existence. Briefly, the argument is this:

Change exists and is not self-explanatory, hence some cause of change exists;

But no cause at all exists unless an uncaused and unchangeable cause exists;

Therefore an uncaused and unchangeable cause exists.

Or, even more fundamentally:

No products without a producer;

But no producer without an unproduced producer;

Therefore, since products exist, there must also exist an unproduced producer.

B. Development of the Proposition, "It Is Impossible for Every Cause to Be a Caused Cause."

A caused cause not an ultimate explanation. A cause can account for an effect insofar as it has, *within itself,* active power or energy. But if the energy which it has is *received* energy, if the cause merely has energy *within* itself but not *of* itself, if the energy it has is *caused* in it and is *derived* from some other being, then it cannot account *adequately* or ultimately for another being or any new aspect in a being. Precisely of itself, no cause that is *caused,* that is, no caused cause as a recipient, contributes in the slightest degree towards the explanation of a new reality. To the extent that a being which is a cause is caused, it is passive; it is on the receiving end and not on the contributing end. Insofar as a being which is a cause happens to be passive, it is energy-less, its energy is equivalent to zero.

Even though a caused cause—since it is a cause and has in itself active power—does give some explanation (an immediate and proximate explanation) of change or of a being that comes to be, still, a caused cause, because it is not the source of its own active power but has this power "derivedly," leaves us in suspense. It cannot be the *ultimate* or *adequate* explanation of change or of new being.

Qualitative inadequacy. The inadequacy of a caused cause, or of a whole series of caused causes, is not precisely a *quantitative* inadequacy. It is a *qualitative* one; hence it cannot be removed by appealing to *other caused* causes. There must exist some cause *essentially* different from a caused cause, some producer essentially different from a produced producer.

Univocal causality. An adequate explanation of an effect cannot be found in a univocal cause, that is, in a cause which is essentially similar to its effect. The being which is an effect is a being that does not have in its essence the adequate explanation of its existence; that is why we say that, if it is to exist at all, it requires an extrinsic cause. But since a univocal cause has the same kind of essence as its effect, therefore every univocal cause is a caused being, and so an inadequate cause. Since the inadequacy of a new being for explaining itself is manifested in the thing's very mode of existence (in our present case, the fact that this being exists changeably, or the fact that it is new), then not only must the adequate cause of this being be essentially different from its effect (in the sense that it cannot belong to the same species as the effect), this cause must also transcend its effect in its very mode of existing. No *derived* being, no matter what its species or essence, can be the *ultimate* explanation of another being.

Example. A new-born bear cub is a contingent being and needs an outside explanation. It needs such an explanation most fundamentally because of its contingency. That this contingent thing is *a bear* is, in the immediate circumstances, due to its parents or generators (univocal causes, these); but that the bear, as *a contingent being,* should be actually existent at all requires something that is not of the bear species at all, it requires something that is not of the class of existents that *exist contingently.* Changeable beings, new beings, and produced beings require something real—therefore, something that is a *being,* something *existent*—for their explanation; but for that being to be the adequate explanation of the changeable, new, and produced beings, it cannot itself be changeable or produced or new. In the lapidary formula of the subtle Franciscan Doctor, Duns Scotus (died 1308): "The whole collectivity of dependent beings is dependent, and it is dependent upon nothing within that collectivity." [3]

Numerical multiplication not an explanation. To invoke a cause or producer which itself is subject to change or is itself produced is only to multiply the number of things that need an outside explanation; this will but complicate the problem quantitatively, while leaving it qualitatively and metaphysically untouched. The popular imagination inclines people to think that to repeat a phenomenon is to explain it. A bit of intellectual insight, however, should make us realize that a problem is not truly solved merely because it has been multiplied.

If it is change which, in a being, indicates that this being is not necessarily existent but contingent, therefore not self-sufficient, and consequently in need of an outside explanation, then the only kind of outside explanation which can render change and changeable being adequately intelligible must be a being which does not have in itself any change to be accounted for. Only an unproduced producer, an uncaused cause, would be the *ultimate* intelligible explanation of any new being, any product, anything dependent. The first cause must be uncaused; the first source, or "prime mover," of changeable being must be unchanged and unchangeable.

Metaphysical import of "first." Note that the word "first," or "prime," that we have just used is to be taken in a *metaphysical* sense that describes the ontological nature of the being to which the words are applied. The idea corresponding to these words prescinds from the idea of a *temporal sequence* or *temporal priority.* Of course, nothing can be conceived as prior, in time, to an unproduced, necessarily self-existent cause or to an immutable, self-explanatory active power; indeed, what is "immutable" is simply not "in time" at all.

[3] Scotus, *Ordinatio,* in I, d. 2, Pars Prima, q. 2, n. 53 (Vatican edition, *Opera Omnia,* Vol. 2, 1950, p. 157).

The "first" cause, therefore, is not "first" in the sense of being the remotest ancestor in a species. It transcends the species and does not belong to the species at all (otherwise, it would be essentially and existentially of the same nature as the species, and hence a *derived* individual). It has an ontological, or natural, priority over all other causes and over all its effects. It is "first" in the sense of "ultimate," "underived," "unqualified," "unconditioned," "absolute," "supreme," or "presupposing nothing else in its own order" (which in the present case is the "order of being and of activity").

Perhaps the word "first" or "prime" spontaneously evokes the idea of succession in time; still, even independently of theodicy problems, there are many everyday usages in which the word "first" or "prime" does not have a temporal or quantitative, but a qualitative, sense. George Washington was a "first" in certain orders in American history: he was, chronologically, the "first" president; but he was also "first in war, first in peace, first in the hearts of his countrymen." The United States has a "first lady"—has, indeed, had a succession of "first" ladies. The "first" in theodicy class may mean the earliest arrival, the brightest student, the most successful examinee, or the one whose desk is closest to the teacher. Certain countries have their "prime" ministers. A butcher can furnish you with "prime" ribs.

Who made God? Since, if any products are to exist at all, there must exist a first (that is, an uncaused) cause, it is not a meaningful question to ask: "Who made the first cause?" Our knowledge that God exists comes to us only when we realize that it is not possible for all that exists to be produced or to be changeable. Our argument has never invoked, even implicitly, the proposition: "Every being has a cause," or "Existence as such needs an outside explanation." Only contingent being needs a cause or outside explanation. The cause of contingent being cannot have any potentiality or contingency. It is totally in act.

That is why one who appreciates the argument from contingency will not be unduly swayed by such statements as the following autobiographical remark of Bertrand Russell: "I believed in God until I was eighteen, when I found in Mill's *Autobiography* the sentence: 'My father taught me that the question, "Who made me?" cannot be answered, since it immediately suggests the further question,

"Who made God?" ' In that moment I decided that the First-Cause argument is fallacious." [4]

Two implications. By now it should be evident that our thesis has been established, namely: the existence of God as a necessarily existing being, a self-sufficient being, an unproduced producer of being, and an immutable and uncaused cause of contingent being can be proved from the existence of experiential realities that undergo change. But there are two implications of our argument that deserve to be developed before we close this chapter. These are: the purity of God's dynamism, and the irrelevance of an infinite series of causes in proving God's existence.

C. An Uncaused Cause Is Pure Act.

Primacy of dynamism. In recent generations, especially, there have risen up those who say that what the world needs is a new conception of God, that it needs a dynamic, changing, evolving, developing God. They misunderstand the nature of dynamism and of change; worse, they misunderstand the nature of the true God. An immutable being who is purely act is not lacking in dynamism; indeed, only Pure Act can be perfectly dynamic, it alone cannot be in any respect passive when it acts. To insist on the necessity of the immutability of God is not to accord a primacy to the lifeless and the static over the living and the dynamic; it is rather to accord a primacy to activity over passivity, to perfection over determinability, and to possession and ownership over reception and acquisition.

Self-existent active power is simply self-existing being, an uncaused cause of being, a being that in no respect depends on something outside itself for its being and for its acting. What is self-existent owes its existence to nothing but its own very being, its own absolute nature; if it exists at all, it exists of absolute, inner, independent necessity. That which exists necessarily and, therefore, is necessarily whatever it is, is necessarily immutable. Since its being exists of necessity and is due to itself alone, such a being is not in potency to its dynamism nor to any of its perfections; it is Pure Act.

---

[4] *The Philosophy of Bertrand Russell* (The Library of Living Philosophers, Volume 5), edited by P.A. Schilpp, Evanston, Ill., Northwestern University, 1944, p. 8.

A thing's activity is affected or determined by whatever affects or determines a thing's nature or being. A thing *acts as it does* because it *is what it is.* A thing that has its active power from itself (and only such a being, with *underived active power*, can give an *ultimate* explanation of anything contingent) must also have its very nature, its being, from itself, i.e., it must be self-existent as well as autodynamic. A being which is active of itself (i.e., which possesses unproduced, uncaused, active power) is simply identified with its existence; it is subsistent activity, utter dynamism, pure activity, Pure Act.

Immutability not the same as inertia. Here we must not yield to the human tendency of thinking that if God is immutable, then He must be inert and stagnant. "Unwashable Jones," if he is a human, is in a very bad way; he is very imperfect, no doubt about that! But if Jones is an angel, a spiritual substance, then his "unwashability" is rather a property of his pure excellence, his spiritual perfection. A thing is not perfectible if, of its own intrinsic nature, it is already all-perfect; a thing cannot receive what it already actually has. You can't teach calculus to an Einstein; the infinitely perfect being receives nothing.

This immutability of the Pure Act, the uncaused cause, is not inertia; much less is it inability to act. To be immutable does not necessarily mean to be unable to produce anything. It simply means not having the passive potency that is required in order to undergo change or to be perfected. A thing is changeable or perfectible only insofar as it is in some way potential, or passive. If a thing is entirely in act—and an uncaused being, a being which is totally self-existent, has to be entirely in act, with no potentiality whatsoever—it can act and it can produce new reality, but it cannot be affected by others and it cannot be reacted upon. Just because Tom, Dick, and Harry can do nothing to Raphael does not mean that Raphael can do nothing. An "uncaused being" is not synonymous with an "unproductive being." Pure Act is identified with its activity. The unmoved and immutable cause is utter dynamism.

Intimations of Pure Act. If ever there is something that is truly active, it is the immutable Creator. Such immutable dynamism we do not immediately experience in the data around us; indeed, it transcends our human comprehension. We do not have an adequate understanding of it even when we realize that it must exist. Yet, even we, who busy ourselves about many things, can appreciate the fact that a motionless gazer, lost in ecstatic contemplation of the sublimity of a sunrise seen from atop Mt. Everest, is still thoroughly active. To be enjoying infinite delight or to be appreciating infinite beauty, even if it is not to be undergoing change, is not simply to be limp and inert. The infinite perfection of Pure Act will be explicitly treated in *Chapter 6*.

D. Post-script on an Irrelevance.

Arguments relying on, or concluding to, the impossibility of an infinite series.   Besides presenting arguments for God's existence like the one given above, some philosophers pursue another line of argument, in which a *quantitative* factor plays (or seems to play) an essential role. The *qualitative* factor, of course, cannot be dispensed with, but the emphasis in this other type of argument is largely on number and time. These authors argue that *SINCE it is impossible* (so they claim) *to have an infinite regress* in produced beings or in caused causes, *THEREFORE, there has to be a temporally first* caused cause, one that was produced a finite "number of years" ago, and that since this "first" caused cause cannot be explained by total nothingness, it must have been caused by an eternally existing un-caused cause, an *absolutely first* cause. In such an argument, the "impossibility of an infinite series" is taken as a *premise leading to* the conclusion that God exists.

Other philosophers seem to argue that since there has to be an uncaused and independent being to account for any products at all, then such a "first" or uncaused being exists, and further, that *since THERE IS A FIRST being, therefore there is NO INFINITE SERIES* of beings at all. Here the "impossibility of an infinite series" is not a *premise leading to*, but a *corollary flowing from*, the conclusion that God exists.

Irrelevance.   For our own part, we would like simply to empha-size the *irrelevance* of the possibility or the impossibility of an infinite series to the argument based on the qualitative inadequacy of change-able or produced beings. Contingent beings exist; they could not exist unless an uncaused cause existed. That the multitude of contingent beings is large or small, finite or infinite, is irrelevant. Nothing contingent would be at all, unless some uncaused cause existed. It was the impermeability of his hat—remember?—and not its redness, that kept Joe's head dry.

How old is the universe? How many caused causes are there? How many generations of men have existed? Can the elephant species have always had some individual(s) realizing it, even though no individual elephant has always existed? Can every monkey have had a grandfather? Our argument did not enter into such problems; nor is their solution pertinent to the problem of proving God's existence. We were giving not the history of the chicken but the metaphysics of the egg. Genealogy is not an explanation of generation.

We concentrated on the metaphysical aspects of mutable beings and argued simply that without the influence of an uncaused cause there would be no beings in existence; that without an immutable being there would be no mutable beings existent; that without an unproduced being there would be no products; that a universe of contingent reality (no matter how old it is) is dependent upon God whenever and so long as it exists; that such a universe is dependent for its every moment and not merely for its (debatable) "first" moment; and that certainly not all beings can be elephants or monkeys.

A classic phrase. The phrase "It is impossible to proceed indefinitely, or to infinity, in a series of caused causes" is a fairly traditional phrase. In fact, it goes back, in substance, at least to the time of Aristotle. Not all who quote the phrase mean that every multitude has to be finite. What some of the great thinkers of the past meant when they stated that "an infinite regress is impossible" can be stated in the following fashions: "An infinitely prolonged explanation is no explanation"; "You will not find in an indefinite backward (or upward) prolongation of caused causes an adequate explanation of any effect"; "Any series of causes that eliminates an uncaused and independent cause could never exist"; or, "One must get outside the set of caused causes—even if the set contains an infinite multitude of individuals—if he is to render the universe intelligible." The upshot of the debate about whether an infinite regress is possible is that "it makes no difference whether there is one intermediate or more, nor whether they are infinite or finite in number"[5] for the important fact is that not all movers can be intermediary movers, not all causes can be caused causes.

As Father D'Arcy says of St. Thomas' arguments: "It should be noted that he is not arguing from the impossibility of an infinite series. He means that the addition of dependent things *ad infinitum* will do nothing to get rid of the dependence."[6] And E.L. Mascall writes in similar fashion:

> The real point of the argument is, I am convinced, not that we *cannot* proceed to infinity, but that it does not get us any nearer the solution of our problem if we do. . . . "*Non est procedere in infinitum,*" not in the sense that the infinite regress is impossible but that it leads us no nearer to the solution of our problem. . . . The explanation of motion therefore cannot be found in the realm of mobile beings; it must be sought in a different direction altogether.[7]

Illustrations of the irrelevance. An appeal to an infinite multitude of caused causes will not eliminate the necessity of some cause existing which is not a caused cause. For, a series of caused causes, even though infinite in multitude, cannot constitute an ultimate and therefore an absolutely adequate principle or source of new being nor an explanation of contingent being. Continuous addition of things which do not have their active power *of* themselves will never give you a collection of things which does have *of* itself active power.

One blind man cannot see the moon; neither can two, a hundred and two, a million and two, nor an infinite multitude of them! An infinitely long pipe or channel will not account for a city's water-supply; you still need a fountain-head, a source. You can imagine one planet reflecting light upon another planet, and this second one reflecting it upon a third, and so on, perhaps indefinitely. Still, every single planet would be in darkness were it not for a sun, a *source* of light.

[5] Aristotle, *Metaphysics*, Book 2 ("little alpha"), c. 2. Actually, Book 2 is by a pupil of Aristotle, not by Aristotle himself.

[6] M.C. D'Arcy, S.J., *St. Thomas Aquinas*, London, Benn, 1930, p. 161.

[7] E.L. Mascall, *Existence and Analogy*, New York, Longmans, Green & Co., 1949, pp. 73–74. Compare F. Copleston, S.J., *Aquinas*, Baltimore, Penguin, 1955, p. 118 f.

Similarly, it is vain to appeal to "circular causality," as though the universe were a "mutual aid society." Two sailors ship-wrecked on a desert island cannot support themselves by taking in each other's wash. No man can be his own grandfather.

The insufficiency of a caused cause, as meant in our argument, lies precisely in the fact that such a cause would not exist if it itself were not caused by some other cause. No matter how much you multiply caused causes, you will never achieve a cause, or a complexus of causes, which would possess active power *of itself*; thus you will never have a cause truly sufficient for the production of the perfection in question.

If the ultimate reason why the cause of a given effect has energy is to be sought for outside that cause, then an infinite series of causes all of that same type will not adequately explain the effect. If no cause in a series is sufficient, then to account for the effect you must admit that outside the series there exists a different type of cause, one, namely, which does have, *of itself*, the capacity to give new perfection.

There are some fairly persuasive arguments (as well as a number of clearly specious ones) to prove the impossibility of any infinite series (a multitude without a temporally first term) *in the concrete existential order*. But even if one claims that an infinite series of caused causes is possible, such a series will not adequately explain a product or a change; one must admit that besides that infinite series there exists an uncaused cause.

Warning given by St. Thomas. St. Thomas Aquinas did not find suasive the arguments given by his contemporaries to prove that the world is not eternal. And he warns apologetes against trying to argue to the impossibility of an eternal world with arguments based on the impossibility of an infinite succession. As early as his *Commentary on the Sentences* he says that the "demonstrations" given to prove that the world is not eternal would "turn to the derision of the faith rather than to its confirmation, should anyone relying on such reasons strive to prove against the philosophers that the world had a first moment." [8] The same warning recurs in later works.[9]

[8] In II, d. 1, q. 1, a. 5, sol.
[9] S.T. I.46.2,c. (*Basic Writings*, Vol. I, p. 453); C.G. II.38 (*Truth of the Catholic Faith*, Vol. II, p. 113).

LEADING IDEAS of Chapter 2

1. Contingently existing beings, known as such from the changes they undergo, are caused beings.

2. Not all beings can be caused; some being must exist of absolute, intrinsic necessity.

3. If a being is partially contingent, it is totally contingent; nothing can be half-necessary in its existence.

4. What is absolutely necessary cannot undergo any change; hence change in a being is a manifestation of that being's contingency.

5. If a cause exists which is itself caused, the fact that it is caused is something accruing to it from outside its essence and properties; for it is not necessary that a cause be a caused cause.

6. A cause that has received its existence, and, consequently, has its active power as something derived, cannot be the ultimate explanation of any product.

7. In the phrase, "First Cause," the word "First" signifies: ultimate, underived, absolute, unconditioned; it does not have any temporal significance.

8. An uncaused cause, being totally self-sufficient, is not in potency to any perfection but is purely act.

9. The inadequacy of a series of caused causes for explaining an effect is a qualitative inadequacy that cannot be remedied merely by multiplying, even to infinity, the caused causes.

SUGGESTED READINGS for Chapter 2

On the General Argument:

D.J.B. Hawkins. *The Essentials of Theism.* New York: Sheed and Ward, 1950, pp. 15–63.

R. Kane, S.J. *God or Chaos.* New York: P.J. Kenedy and Sons, 1912, pp. 50–57 and 95–102.

On the Use of the Terms "Necessary" and "Contingent":

M.J. Charlesworth. "Linguistic Analysis and Language about God," *International Philosophical Quarterly,* Vol. I, 1961, pp. 148–152.

P. Corcoran. "St. Thomas Aquinas and Sir Edmund Whittaker; the

Third Way of St. Thomas," *The Irish Theological Quarterly*, Vol. 19, 1952, pp. 175–184.

J. Hick. "God as Necessary Being," *The Journal of Philosophy*, Vol. 57, 1960, pp. 725–734.

Joseph DeFinance, S.J. In a book review, *Gregorianum*, Vol. 43, 1962, p. 174.

On the First Three "Ways" of St. Thomas:

St. Thomas. S.T. I.2.3 (*Basic Writings*, Vol. I, pp. 22–23).

R. Garrigou-Lagrange, O.P. *God, His Existence and His Nature*, translated by Dom Bede Rose, O.S.B. St. Louis: Herder, 1946, Vol I, pp. 261–302.

M.R. Holloway, S.J. *An Introduction to Natural Theology*. New York: Appleton-Century-Crofts, 1959, pp. 80–118.

Jacques Maritain. *Approaches to God*, translated by Peter O'Reilly. New York: Harper, 1954, pp. 16–49.

On the Infinite Regress in Causes:

Brother Benignus, F.S.C. *Nature, Knowledge and God*. Milwaukee: Bruce, 1947, pp. 486–489.

G.K. Chesterton. *The Everlasting Man*. New York: Dodd, Mead and Co., 1949, pp. 1–6.

For Some Misconceptions of the Theistic Arguments:

C.J. Ducasse. *A Philosophical Scrutiny of Religion*. New York: Ronald, 1953, pp. 334–335.

Bertrand Russell. *A History of Western Philosophy*. New York: Simon and Schuster, 1945, p. 462.

Elmer Sprague. *What Is Philosophy?* New York: Oxford, 1961, pp. 56–66.

CHAPTER

3

OUTLINE

The World, a Product of Intellect and Free Will

I. INTRODUCTION

The satellite and the atheist. Back in 1957 when the Russians put Sputnik I, the first artificial satellite, into orbit, certain Communist writers in Europe hailed this pioneering achievement as somehow showing that God is superfluous. Referring to this conclusion, Archbishop (later Cardinal) A.J. Muench made the following comments:

If these boasting atheists, who shout that they have dethroned God, would think but a little, they would see in their scientific achievement of sputniks a clinching proof of a Supreme Intelligence. For, if a great deal of intelligence is required to launch a globe no bigger than a medicine ball with a weight of about 184 pounds, certainly an intelligence infinitely greater than that of the wisest man was needed to devise and make the billions of huge stars and planets in the universe, and then have them adhere for countless ages to fixed positions and orbits in the firmament so that astronomers are able to make most precise calculations regarding them.[1]

This incident serves as a fitting introduction to the present chapter, whose purpose is to show that the uncaused cause which is needed to effect the universe must be an intelligent and free agent, indeed supremely intelligent and supremely free, hence supremely personal. The existence of contingent beings calls for an uncaused cause; the existence of order in contingent beings calls for intelligence and freedom in the uncaused cause.

[1] Quoted in *The Catholic Week*, organ of the Mobile-Birmingham diocese, October 30, 1959, p. 6.

Appeal of the argument from order. The argument from order to a divine intelligence is probably the most popular, the most readily understood, and the most widely accepted argument for the existence of God. Even the agnostic Immanuel Kant, prior to criticizing the argument, pays tribute to it: "This proof always deserves to be mentioned with respect. It is the oldest, the clearest, and the most accordant with the common reason of mankind. . . . It would therefore not only be uncomforting but utterly vain to attempt to diminish in any way the authority of this argument." [2]

To many persons the admission of a supreme intelligence as the origin of the obvious order in the visible universe is so spontaneous as to be almost instinctive. They make this admission even though they have had no formal training in philosophy. It is this admission (usually coupled with the recognition of a moral order imposed upon, not created by, man) that makes them religious-minded and that gives them a sense of the divine.[3]

Summary of the argument. To furnish the student with a prospect of what we shall say in this chapter, we shall summarize it now as follows. In the beings that we come across in our experience, we find evidences of order. These beings—many of them at any rate—obviously have a plurality of parts that are so related as to constitute not an aggregate but a unified whole. This is particularly evident in living things, some of which are extremely complicated in the arrangement and constitution of their parts.

Now, where there is a real unity constituted of a plurality of parts, where there are related beings—or functionally related elements or parts—that together constitute a whole (and do not form just an aggregate of juxtaposed, independent entities), where there are beings dependent upon others and making mutually advantageous unions with these others, where there is relationship of appetite and good, where there is relationship of tendency and goal—there we have order. And where we have order, we have what in the ultimate analysis is explicable only by an intellect. The thing ordered, if it is less perfect than a human being, does not itself possess an intellect;

[2] *Critique of Pure Reason,* A 623–624, B 651–652, Norman Kemp Smith translation.
[3] See, for example, Whittaker Chambers, *Witness,* New York, Random House, 1952, pp. 15 f.; also, Avery Dulles, A *Testimonial to Grace,* New York, Sheed and Ward, 1946, pp. 50–57.

but there would be no ordered things at all if intellect were not present in their originating cause.

Hence outside (distinct from) the ordered universe—and this means outside (distinct from) man himself, to the extent that man is not self-ordered—there must be an intellect that effects, controls, and directs the universe.

Because, too, the order in question is explicable only if there is a choice, the intelligent being who organizes and directs the universe is also endowed with free will.

II. THE FACT OF ORDER IN THE UNIVERSE

A. General Survey.

The world, our universe, is not an aggregate of independent beings that have no influence on one another; it is rather a vast concatenated system, with its members constituting a hierarchy of goods or values, the inanimate world inferior to the animate, the nonsentient world inferior to the sentient, and the whole irrational world inferior to man.

Order is proclaimed by every diurnal revolution of the earth— the revolution of the earth about its axis that causes the phenomena of day and night. Order is manifested by the earth's travels in its annual circuit around the sun; this journey, since the earth's axis maintains a constant inclination, causes the panorama of the seasons: summer, autumn, winter, spring, with the accompanying phenomena of growth, decline, decay, and regeneration. There is order in the adaptation of soil, atmosphere, and light to the growth of plants, thus to the growth and good of animals, and thus ultimately to the wellbeing of the human race. We are not here claiming that absolutely everything in the universe can be seen to benefit man. We do insist that much of the universe can be seen to benefit man, and we consider it evident that there are various levels of reality, of which man is the highest of those we experience. In this sense we claim that there exists a hierarchy as well as an order.

Science and order. Countless books and articles have been written proclaiming the reign of order throughout the universe: books of physics and chemistry, of geology and zoology, of astronomy and cytology, of biology and psychology—books on every conceivable facet of every suspected constituent member of the universe. Not all of the writers of these works, we must admit, are conscious that they are proclaiming a reign of order, for some of them do seem to believe that to have stated *what* happens, or at most, to have established what it is out of which visible things are made, is to have furnished the full intelligible structure and meaning of the universe. They confuse statistics and descriptions with understanding; they identify observation and the forming of statistical averages with the entire scope of human knowledge. Yet, their books and articles often furnish excellent "material" for a starting point of a teleological argument for God's existence—the argument that the world's order was *intended*.

Such books and articles describe, for example, the awe-inspiring order of the world of the astronomer. Or they set forth the tremendous physical laws of gravitation, electricity, heat, and light. Or they describe the natures and qualities of the various species of material beings as governed by the marvelous laws of chemistry. Biology tells us of the intrinsic order and adaptation reigning in every leaf of every tree, in every blade of grass, and, indeed, in every cell of every living creature. Physiology sets forth the order implicit in the functioning of the vital parts of animals and men: the order implied in every breath taken by every being that breathes, the order that is proclaimed in every flicker of every eye-lid and in every beat of every pulsating heart. Every one of the sciences, willy-nilly, is a declaration of the order in the universe; for each one is a detection of at least some of the laws that account for the universe's unity in variety.

Thousands upon thousands of cases of order could be cited. One could go into detail about the planetary system, the structure of our earth, the tides, the oxygen cycle, the fixation of nitrogen, the complex patterns in a butterfly's coloring, the survival devices of the thousands of species of insects, the structure of birds' wings, the instincts of animals (e.g., the nest-building and migratory instincts of birds or the communal life of a bee-hive), the adaptation of living things to environment, the powers of self-healing, including even the power possessed by certain animals of the regeneration of limbs, the fantastic fact of light, the structure of the eye and its relation to light, the structure of the ear and its relation to sound-waves, the relations of lungs and gills to oxygen and vital energy, the nature of homeostasis, the facts of embryology (e.g., the development, from yellow yolk and egg white, of the thousands of species of birds varying enormously in color, shape, flight, and song), the stomach that secretes gastric juices that digest all flesh save the stomach's own—the list could go on endlessly.

B. Specific Detail.

After these brief indications, it will be helpful to give, by means of quotations, a few detailed descriptions of order in the universe, especially of teleological order (unification of a plurality of elements for an end). We have chosen to furnish the student a sort of cross-section of the cosmos, giving him examples derived in turn from the inanimate world, the plant world, the animal world, and the world of man.

The inanimate world. Let us take, for instance, the gravitational attraction that bodies exercise upon one another. The discovery of its law, as described in vivid fashion by Anthony Standen, will bring out the order in the astronomical world:

It would be hard to find, in the whole history of human thought, a grander conception than Newton's laws of motion and the theory of gravitation. This is an amazingly bold assumption, or rather pair of assumptions, that are now so much a part of all our thinking that it is difficult to realize their astonishing and striking character. It is first assumed that a moving body does not, as everyone would at first suppose, require a force to keep pushing it along, but on the contrary would go on moving for ever if it were not for some force *stopping* it.

The second assumption is, on the face of it, even more preposterous: it is that any two objects, anywhere, are all the time "attracting" one another. Not the faintest suggestion is put forward as to how this mysterious "attraction" takes place, although it works at a distance, even a very great distance, with no sign of anything to account for it in the space between the two objects.

Making these two wild and improbable-sounding assumptions, and a few sub-assumptions concerning the magnitude of the attractive force and of the effects of "force" on objects, the most amazing results come out. All the phenomena of astronomy, which had baffled the acutest minds since the dawn of history, the movement of the heavens, of the sun and the moon, the very complex movements of the planets, suddenly tumble together and become intelligible in terms of one staggering assumption, this mysterious "attractive force." And not only the movements of the heavenly bodies, far more than that, the movements of earthly bodies too are seen to be subject to the same mathematically definable law, instead of being, as they were for all previous philosophers, mere unpredictable happen-so's.[4]

Why should not all bodies repel, rather than attract one another? Our universe, certainly, under such an hypothesis could not subsist. It is also marvelous how things are adapted to gravitational attraction on earth. Our very bones would snap under stresses far less powerful than those at the surface of the sun; our muscles, just right for walking on the earth, would cause us to jump up and down like a kangaroo on the moon. In our ears, too, are marvelously sensitive receptors, geared to gravitational pull, enabling us to keep our balance and sense of direction.[5]

The miracle of photosynthesis. Let us turn to some examples of order in the realm of living beings. Every seed is a marvel of finality. For instance, an acorn, although it contains only a fertile germ cell and a supply of food, and looks nothing like leaves, bark, limbs, or wood, changes in time into all these by growth, until it ends up with the beautiful form and size of a mighty oak, producing more acorns.

But many other marvels are possessed by so commonplace a thing as a tree:

Leaves are . . . the lungs of a tree, though their manner of breathing is peculiar to the plant world. The underside of each leaf is pitted with thousands of porelike stomata, or infinitesimal openings. Through these stomata leaves inhale and exhale oxygen and carbon dioxide. But leaves emit generous amounts of water vapor and vastly more oxygen than carbon dioxide, which, in fact, is released only as a waste product. Thus the breathing of trees purifies and tempers, even renews, the air around us. . . .

[4] J. Anthony Standen, *Science Is a Sacred Cow*, New York, E.P. Dutton, 1950, pp. 62–64.
[5] See *Catholic Digest*, May 1955, pp. 78–81. On the "equilibratory mechanism" of the ear, see F. Kahn, *Man in Structure and Function*, translated by G. Rosen, New York, Alfred A. Knopf, 1953, Vol. II, pp. 614–623.

Leaves soak up energy directly from the sun and convert water and air, plus chemicals and minerals from the soil, into a great body that may weigh 1,000 tons and tower 300 feet into the sky. The tree accomplishes this feat by the remarkable process of photosynthesis. . . . Bundles of specially organized leaf cells called chloroplasts produce chlorophyll, the familiar green substance of all growing plants. Chlorophyll, in turn, picks out just the rays of sunlight it needs to transform water and air into the substance of branches, trunks, and roots. Specifically, the leaf rearranges carbon, oxygen, and hydrogen into a variety of carbohydrates, usually sucrose, one of the basic foods of all living things. The leaf then converts the sugar into starch, which is stored in leaves, seeds and roots. Since the tree cannot digest starch, the leaf with incredible virtuosity changes the starch back into sugar as the tree demands food. . . .

Photosynthesis creates the world's food supply. All plants and animals feed upon the organic substances which leaves and grasses convert from unassimilable elements into digestible material. Falling to the ground leaves and twigs decay and combine with the soil's nitrogen to create the humus which fertilizes the forest floor. . . .[6]

The insect world. We now go from the plant world to the animal world. Instead of the countless items of wonder and amazement which we could list, let us rather record a brief, general description of insects:

If a wizard could construct a tiny machine designed to walk and fly, with automatic appliances for finding and consuming fuel, for building itself a suitable garage or shed, for repairing breaks in its parts, and finally, for reproducing other machines like itself, his name would be world famous overnight. . . . Persons would flock from near and far and empty their purses to view the mystery and magic and wonder of his creation. An insignificant insect . . . is just such a magic automation.[7]

Animal instincts are a most fascinating subject. How is it that mere animals recognize the proper food and distinguish it from what is poisonous? How is it that the wax-worker bee unwittingly uses

[6] Wm. A. Dayton, "Wealth and Wonder of Northern State Trees," *The National Geographic Magazine*, Vol. CVIII, pp. 672–673, copyright 1955 by National Geographic Society. Used by permission of the National Geographic Society. See also John B. Sheerin, C.S.P., "Only God Can Make a Tree," *The Homiletic and Pastoral Review*, Vol. LIV, July 1954, pp. 861–864.

[7] Robert Southard, *Almighty Magic*, a pamphlet, St. Paul, Catechetical Guild, 1943, pp. 21f.

the appropriate principles of mechanical engineering in building her cell in such a way as to give it a maximum of strength and capacity, using a minimum of material? [8]

Development of an embryo. Consider the marvels that operate in the formation of man's body. In the development of the embryo:

(A single fecundated cell proceeds) to play the roles of physicist, chemist, sculptor and architect. . . . Out of the blood in the mother's womb it proceeds to fashion such divergent structures, of different physical and chemical elements, as bones, muscle, sinews, nerves, cartilage, skin, blood, hairs and teeth. . . .

Let us concentrate, however, on one of its achievements—that of building nerve cells. There in the darkness of the mother's womb, whither neither light nor color has ever penetrated, the fecundated ovum, developing into the embryo, takes the common material and transforms it into nerve cells which will respond later on only to light and color. How does it do this? How does it know that there exist light and color? It has had no experience of either.

Then, out of that same material, it fabricates there in the silence of the womb other nerve cells which will respond later on only to stimuli of sound. Others it builds into nerve cells which are adapted only to stimuli of temperature. These respective types of nerve cells it places in their appropriate places in the developing embryo—in the end organs with corresponding centers in the brain.

How does the fecundated ovum, without hands or tools of any kind, build finely spun nerve cells with different kinds of antennae, the details of whose architecture even the trained eye of the neurologist, armed with a high-powered microscope, is unable to trace? How does that speck of protoplasm build a heart and gear it into an elaborate musculature that will keep it pumping blood through the body all the days of a life stretching close onto a century? How does it fabricate eyes, which make the finest camera seem rudimentary and awkward in comparison? How does it fashion ears which make our dictaphones seem like crude and unwieldy contraptions? How does it achieve that miracle of miracles, that mystery of mysteries, the crowning achievement in the biological world—the brain of man? [9]

[8] See J.A. O'Brien, *Truths Men Live By*, New York, Macmillan, 1948, pp. 46–48.
[9] *Ibid.*, pp. 50–52.

Organs of reproduction. The adaptation of the reproductory organs, male and female, is another marvel of nature. Paul Janet writes of this:

Of all the facts of coordination, none is more remarkable or more complex . . . than the existence of sex, that is, of the means used by nature for the perpetuity of the species. There is not merely question . . . of the appropriateness of an organ for a function, but . . . the appropriateness of one organ to another organ. . . . It is a completely mechanical adaptation of two apparatus distinct but so related to each other that the form of the one is determined by the form of the other, a reciprocal determination that obviously presupposes a relation to the future, in a direction inverse to that of the ordinary relation of cause to effect. These two organic apparatus . . . are both, and reciprocally, related as means to ends. . . .

Here one can no longer say that we are mistaking a simple effect for an end, a result for an intention. The organs of the sexes are not the effects of each other; the male organ is not the cause of the female organ, nor vice versa; these two organs are two distinct and independent effects—and yet they cannot be explained except by each other. This is precisely the relation of finality. . . . In the case of the two organs of sex . . . cooperation . . . supposes the application of one to the other and a momentary conjunction that makes of them one—a phenomenon that could not occur without perfect coincidence of form and structure. . . . Here practice and conjunction, far from explaining the formation of the organs, precisely presuppose it; if there is to be any conjunction it is necessary that adaptation and reciprocal suitability already exist. One cannot say that this adaptation is brought about through time, for without it the species cannot subsist; before this adaptation could have been effected the species would have perished. . . .

In addition to the appropriateness of organ to organ, there is also that of organ to function: and it is the combination of these two kinds of appropriateness that makes the finality of this case impose itself on the mind in a most imperious and overpowering fashion.

Finally, this one function, accomplished by two organs, is precisely that by which the individual assures the perpetuity of the species, doing so, at least in the case of the lower species, without its knowing or willing it. Thus, on all the levels of this phenomenon, we see the determination of the present by the future: the structure of the two organs is explained only by the conjunction that is to occur; this conjunction only by the function that results from it, this function, finally, only by its effect, the production of a new being, itself called in turn to perpetuate and to immortalize the species.[10]

The human body. Let our final details illustrating the fact of order in the universe be taken from the general structure of the human being. Man has always been a source of wonder to himself: the wonderful constitution of his body, with its various organs and appetites, and of his soul, with its mind and will. All these are matters of perpetual amazement to man in his reflective moods. We shall be content here to give a paraphrase of a description of the marvels of the human body by Dr. L. Murat.

Dr. Murat likens the human body to a vast agglomeration of factories of which the individual cells, about fifty million million in number, are the workmen. These individual cells, like the organs and tissues and other larger structures within the body, cooperate in perfect harmony for the well-being of the individual and for his preservation.

Among the various but coordinated factories in this vast organization we can single out several very interesting ones. There is the factory of oxygenation, namely the lungs that take in the air and put its energy-giving oxygen into the blood. The lungs are like a fueling station. Then there is the refinery that makes food products assimilable into the organization; this refinery is the stomach and the intestines. The liver is, as it were, a factory for generating heat and motor force—it is a dynamo and also a pharmaceutical laboratory. The spleen is a factory for making red corpuscles and a warehouse for storing up iron. The kidneys are a filtering and purifying system. The heart is a wonder-world all in itself. It is a huge pump acting both as a suction pump and as a pressure pump. Connected with this pump are arteries and veins that constitute a system of pipelines going to and from all parts of the body. There is a factory for electricity, the brain, from which radiates and to which converges the complicated network of innumerable conductive wires, the nervous system with its manifold electrolytic currents.

Distributed through the entire system there is the highly interest-

---

[10] Paul Janet, *Les Causes Finales*, 2nd ed., Paris, Félix Alcan, 1894, pp. 70–74. The teleological complementarity of the sexes in the case of human beings—persons, therefore, not mere animals—is of an even more profound nature. See L.F. Cervantes, S.J., *And God Made Man and Woman*, Chicago, Regnery, 1959.

ing mechanical apparatus for movement: levers, springs, gears, mortises, pulleys with oil-cans, and protective sheaths; in other words: bones, muscles, aponeuroses, tendons, ligaments, articulations, and synovial membranes.

The eyes are marvelous optical instruments, with lenses, reflectors, shutters, diaphragms, and photographic plates. There is an apparatus for defense and for labor: the arms, the fist, and the fingers. There are, in the ears, marvelous instruments for the recording of sound: an acoustical horn, a violin, a resonator or microphone, and a music-box. There is a veritable electric telephone in the auditory nerve. The larynx is a gramophone and a musical oboe. The taste buds constitute an apparatus for testing and controlling alimentary products. Finally, there is the over-all enclosure, insulatory and elastic, protecting the entire apparatus: the skin. In all this, despite the architectural complexity of the ensemble, there are harmony, rhythm, aesthetic coordination, facility of functioning, and silence.[11]

III. ORDER IS DETECTED ONLY BY AN INTELLECT

Domination by man through intellect. The order in the data of experience, such as we have been describing it, is not the object of pure sensation. Certainly the things which are ordered are seen and felt and heard and tasted, but the order *as such* is not detected except by the understanding. Man's intellect, that is, his power of understanding, gives him a unique position in the universe; it makes him —or allows him to become—the master of the visible world. Because he can perceive the coherence and systematic character of phenomena, he can dominate them; their qualities somehow become his own, and he can utilize them, making their powers his powers and directing their forces to his own purposes and advantage.

Man's intellect makes him "the tool-using animal." Tools, it was said long ago, are the extension of man's hands. Man's intellect en-

11 The paraphrase that we have given of Dr. Murat's description, is based on a quotation given by Father Pedro Descoqs in *Praelectiones Theologiae Naturalis*, Paris, Beauchesne, 1932, Vol. I, p. 355, note 1.

ables him to make tools. Thereby all the universe is at man's disposal. He tames the waterfalls; he utilizes electricity, radio waves, heat, and light; he studies the natures of things and gains control and direction over them. Even the higher forms of animal life he "domesticates" for his own ends. Knowledge—not sense perception, but intellectual knowledge; not the knowledge that registers appearances, but the knowledge that understands relations—is, indeed, power.

Indeed, a most fitting occupation of man as man is this understanding of the specific determinations or *natures* of things, that is, the apprehension of the *patterns* imbedded in things and of the consequent *laws* that direct in determinate ways and in accordance with definite relationships the forces within things. Natures, or patterns, and their consequent laws—these are the intelligible aspects of things; these are what constitute or bring about order in the universe; but only an intellect can detect them, and only an intellectual being can originate them. An intellectual being is both practical and contemplative.

The appreciation of order.   What a painting—what its beauty, its harmony, its purpose, its meaning—really is, is not discoverable by chemical or physical analyses. The most important thing about a picture, as a picture, even a skilled scientist, merely as a scientist, will not apprehend. One who stands too close to a mosaic will fail to understand it; all he sees is little square stones of varying hues, juxtaposed to one another. Because he is not in the appropriate condition or situation he does not detect the order, the pattern, the design, and the beauty of the mosaic. From the merely material point of view, a page of Shakespeare is but black liquid that has dried out in various scratchy patches on some flat pieces of calendered cellulose. The grasp of order, beauty, and meaning calls for more than chemical and physical analyses, and it calls for using more than the senses.

Order, not sensible but intelligible.   The microscope reveals the microscopic aspects of things; the telescope reveals the telescopic aspects of things; the spectroscope reveals the spectroscopic aspects of things; and the senses reveal the sensible aspects of things. But it is the intellect that reveals the intelligible aspects of things. The intelligible aspects of things constitute their order; order is something more than the plural individuals that enter into the order, but not a "more" in the sense of being an "extra" *chemical* element or a "further" *physical* property. The whole thing which is an order **is**

something more than just the sum total of individual, juxtaposed parts.

A microscope does not detect order, a telescope does not, and a spectroscope does not. These instruments make evident to human eyes the operation of some of nature's otherwise invisible parts and thus make it possible for the human intellect to find the order, or some of the order, in the complexities of certain things in the universe. They bring about favorable conditions for the discerning of certain aspects of order by the intellect—although the intellect has to have already discerned some order if it is to invent and utilize these helpful instruments at all.

Order, in a word, is the *intelligible* aspects in things. It is the relation that gives unity to plurality, that connects things or parts in such a way as to make a whole. Now only intellect understands wholes as such, the influence and causality of the parts. The eye and some of the other senses register in succession what happens in succession, but the mind reads, in what succeeds, the various relations of dynamic order that are therein involved; it understands the order, it does not merely see succession. The mind realizes connections of causality, dependence, means and end, and natures and properties; it *appreciates the irreversibility* of existential happenings, it *does not merely not see reversion occurring.*

The positivist's analysis. A "positivist" believes that the whole scope of knowledge consists in registering the succession of sense phenomena in the material universe and in tabulating the statistical averages of recurrences of events in these or those conditions. He is interested only in *what results* from *what,* that is, what *succeeds* what; he does not admit that other questions are meaningful. He will observe, for example, a certain living object. He will find that its constituent elements are carbon (C), hydrogen (H), oxygen (O), nitrogen (N), and potassium (K) in various proportions. He sizes up the living thing as an agglomeration, symbolized by CHONK. He does not detect order, for order is not a sixth element (Q) detectible and measurable like the five elements we have listed. What the positivist does not detect, he denies. Denying, or at least not admitting, order, he naturally finds meaningless everything due to order, such as beauty, harmony, purpose, adaptability, utility, intelligibility, or meaning itself.

But for the teleologist, order pervades CHONK and each element in CHONK—it is not something superadded. It does not convert CHONK into CHONKQ. The teleological argument is not based on a reasoning that would say that "Mother Nature" or "Chance" or "Unknown X" makes CHONK, whereas God makes Q; neither does it say that God makes what would otherwise just be CHONK be actually CHONKQ. No; order is immanent in CHONK. It is the nature, the patterns, and the laws of CHONK; it pervades the basic natures of the elements themselves, it is in the properties that flow from those natures, and it is in the unifying relations that are established as a result of those properties and natures. God creates everything that enters into CHONK and into all the rest of the ordered universe; but the order is not distinct from the ordered universe, no more than truth or intelligibility is distinct from being. In making our universe be, God makes its order.

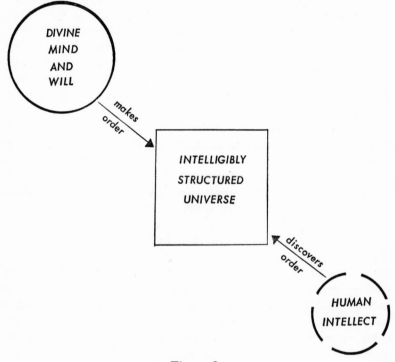

Figure 2.

IV. ORDER IS EFFECTED ONLY BY AN INTELLIGENT AGENT

Intelligibility proceeds from an intellect. Order discovered is not merely a sign that there is an intellect in the one who has made the discovery, it is a sign that there is an intellect in the one who has made the ordered being. The uniting, the correlating, and the directing of different elements, pieces, or parts, or the coordinating of various forces to produce a joint effect that is a good or value, e.g., an object of beauty, cannot be satisfactorily explained unless one admits an intelligent being as the ultimate producer of the whole (the components and the composition).

For, the part-whole relationship, the means-end relationship, the appetite-good relationship, the tendency-goal relationship, the instinct-survival relationship, and the environment-adaptation relationship are relationships of a finalistic system. They are the effects not merely of an *efficient cause* but of a cause that *intended* something; they are the effects not merely of a cause that has power but of a cause that has intelligence; they are the effects not of a cause that acted through mere blind necessity, but of a cause that acted insofar as it was directed, ultimately at least, by an intellect. The argument is not that every intelligible object is endowed with intellect, but that intelligible aspects of an object exist in an object only if an intellect in some way has been the ultimate source of the object.

The "related to" has "proceeded from." Good, beauty, utility, adaptation, purpose—all these are extremely real, but they are metaphysical, not physical, aspects of reality. When analyzed by the understanding that apprehends them in the data of experience, they are seen to be not simple, self-explanatory substances but the result of certain relationships that physical substances or parts have to other substances or parts. To effect such results, the parts or components of these good, beautiful, or useful things must be made for one another, that is, adapted or correlated to one another in their very natures.

We argue that these parts are, therefore, not self-sufficient nor independent in their reality. They and the beings that they compose and the resultant aspects of good, beauty, utility, etc., must be something caused, for what is *related to* something else *proceeds from* something else (not, usually, the same something else); what is *ad aliud* is *ab alio*. The something else from which they ultimately proceed must be, not a blindly operating efficient cause, but a being that has an *understanding* of parts as parts, a power of *adapting means* to ends, and an appreciation of good or value or end as such. Just as a user of a utensil must have intelligence, so must its maker. Since nature can be understood, its maker must itself have an understanding to have put intelligibility into nature.

Relatively simple beings, like the atoms and molecules of chemical elements, have their own characteristics and so enjoy a sort of independent existence; yet they are constantly found united and constituting new and more complex wholes. Instead of going a separate, independent way, with their activities unrelated to other beings, they rather join forces, they fuse their differences, and they combine into new beings, sometimes highly organized and complicated compounds. Where entities are thus related, where there is interdependence and activity, we have a sign that the beings are caused. When the effect is not an isolated case but is repeated generation after generation, especially as in the case of living things, we are driven to conclude that the effects in question are certainly not "chance" effects, nor even "mechanical" effects; they include aspects which are mechanical, yes, but more than mechanism is involved— mind is radically required, not in the effect, but in its ultimate and adequate cause.

Unreasonable to deny intellect as source of order. The things existing around us, independently of us, at least *seem* to have order. Is it reasonable to claim that the manifestations of intelligent activity, and the manifestations of sheer unintelligence, on the part of others than ourselves would be perfectly alike, utterly equal, and completely indistinguishable; that brute power and intelligent power cannot be distinguished except in our own personal self-consciousness? When a being that lacks intelligence produces effects that constitute an ordered whole, surely it is reasonable to say that some intellect, distinct from that being, is at the origin of that being or at the very least is in control of the forces of that being, directing and co-ordinating its elements and forces with the rest of the universe.

The universe seems to act according to laws that direct things to their own good or to the good of more perfect things, especially to the good and utility of man, the "lord of the visible universe." These laws seem to "conspire" in the making, not of a chaos, but of a cosmos, a "universe," a whole in which parts mutually complement one another. We have an effect, or at least a phenomenon, that is just the sort of phenomenon that would be had if an intellect were in the background originating and directing things. Are we to say that unless we ourselves are conscious of having imposed order on things, we have to conclude that these things have no detectible order? As though the only way to be certain that intelligence is at the origin of something is to be ourselves the conscious cause of that something; as though we cannot recognize as an effect of an intelligent agent anything that exists independently of our own personal activity; as though we cannot know that something *was intended* unless we ourselves *intended* it!

Paul Janet says very well:

How is it conceivable that so many diverse causes, acting without an end, should coincide so well in their common action with that end? Remember, we have the right to say here, as men of science do in similar circumstances, that all takes place as if the causes of these phenomena had foreseen the effect which they behoved to produce; would it not be strange if a blind cause should act precisely in the manner in which one not blind would do? Consequently, unless it be proved that such facts have not been foreseen, the presumption is that they have been. It lies with those that deny it to furnish the contrary proof.[12]

Intended effects.   A typewriter does not intend to write; but it *is intended* to write. Even if I myself did not make the typewriter, its order, its complexity, and its usability bear all the earmarks of an intention. It would not exist if there were no intelligent agents who could write; it would not exist if there were no intelligent agents who knew that others could write. We all admit that this or that human

12 Quoted by G.H. Joyce, S.J., *Principles of Natural Theology*, 3rd ed., New York, Longmans, Green and Co., 1934, p. 126.

artifact (for example, a typewriter) has purpose implicit in it, that it is designed, and that some cause has effected it with an end in view, has given specific direction to the generic forces of its parts, and has intended it to be utilizable for this or that desired effect. Are we to rule out, *a priori*, the possibility of the universe being a *divine artifact*? That it is a divine *fact*, produced by an uncaused cause, we learned from the previous chapter. The order, the utility, and the beauty in the fact prove that it is a divine *arti*fact. Where the myriad parts of the universe could, absolutely speaking, be a confused jumble, a total hodge-podge, and an agglomeration of relatively useless and ugly things, nevertheless we have an harmonious *universe*—an interrelated complexity and a serviceable and an extremely beautiful and fascinating abode for intelligent man.

Sole reasonable explanation: an originative intellect. What could possibly prove that an ultimate cause is intelligent, if order in its effects does not? It would be incredible that the achievements of blind unintelligent power would present themselves to man's intellect as full of intelligibility, or that originated beings would have order and value, but their origin have neither intellect nor goodness.

Moreover, man's intellect itself is one of those contingent, non-self-explanatory beings; it is an ordered reality that is produced. Will the ultimate cause of intelligence in man be less perfect than man—will it lack intellect—yet nevertheless produce intellect in man (not just in one man, but in the whole race of men); will it be mindless, yet account for intelligibility in man himself as well as in the beings that are less perfect than man?

Approaching the question from a somewhat different point of view, John L. Stoddard writes:

In the consideration of this subject one thing impressed itself upon my mind with constantly increasing emphasis. It was the absolute impossibility of believing that in this limitless expanse of flaming suns and countless constellations, *no one understands its origin and mysteries more than we do*, and that our feeble, finite intellects form the highest limit of intelligence existing in this wondrous scheme of things! That thought is blasphemous in its conceit, and paralysing in its influence. We may talk academically of a "godless world" but when we really face its possibility, we find that there is nothing more appalling in its horror, than the conception of a boundless universe, eternally evolving in perfect order and in full activity . . . without a Mind to comprehend, or Will to guide it! [13]

If a being is to be the ultimate cause of why such and such a thing exists, operating in a definite fashion and producing a definite good, then that being must itself be endowed not only with power but with intellect, must understand the relationships of means to end, must understand the natures of the things that it causes, and must exercise control over them. The subhuman things that operate in nature for a good end are not themselves endowed with intellect, yet they act as though directed by intellect. The cells of an embryo, for example, cannot know the body into which they are being formed; yet they proceed to multiply in orderly fashion and to arrange themselves, some to form bone and others to form tissue, eyes, the various vital organs, skin, teeth, or hair. They act as though they were obeying some directing force, some law governing both their ensemble as a complex unified whole and themselves as individual cells that nevertheless are related parts. The thing happens not just once—a casual incident—but millions of times. As Chesterton would say, it begins to look like a plot. Over and over again, for example, humans are reproduced, and the species continues. Adaptations and changes occur, yes; more or less perfect specimens are produced; but still there is the constant tendency to reproduce one basic pattern: the masterpiece which is man.

The ultimate maker, then, must be endowed with mind, with an appreciation of the natures of things and of the forces or properties belonging to these natures; it must comprehend the laws inherent in these things, and it must have some controlling influence over these natures and their forces. The maker of such things must have, or be, an intellect, working in, controlling, and directing these beings; it must be a being that intends the good that is effected by the combinations.

[13] John L. Stoddard, *Rebuilding a Lost Faith*, New York, P.J. Kenedy and Sons, 1923, p. 42. Italics in the original.

V. THE ORDER IN OUR UNIVERSE CALLS FOR AN AGENT WHO IS NOT ONLY INTELLIGENT BUT ALSO FREE

The universe an effect of a choice. The data of experience demand that we admit free will, not only our own (testified to by our immediate experience), but also some free will distinct from ours and from the universe itself: a will that has decided that there shall be a universe rather than none at all, a will that has selected this particular universe rather than some other one, and a will that has chosen the ultimate elements that are this universe's ingredients or, what amounts to the same thing, has determined, from the myriad possibilities of being, what particular basic natures shall exist, and consequently, what patterns and laws shall reign in the actual universe.

The possibilities of existence are limitless. No finite number would answer the question: how many beings are existible, or even, how many varieties of being are existible? The actualities, however, that do exist in the concrete are quite definitely circumscribed in time, place, number, and variety of nature. But the sum total of these physical actualities is not coextensive with the sum total of metaphysical possibilities. What but a choice of a free will can account ultimately for the discrepancy between the possibilities and the actualities? There is a certain arbitrariness about the whole universe. There is definite order, yes; there are definite physical necessities or laws, yes; but there were thousands of other orders possible. For the particular particles that enter into the present composition of this universe there were thousands of other combinations possible.

Constitution of our universe reveals choice. The metaphysician will ask, "Why is the number of particles just the precise number that it is, no more and no less? Why are the laws what they are?" It is no final answer to say, "Because the particles are what they are." For the particles do not have to be at all; there could have been other particles with other natures. Why does a falling body fall with a rate of acceleration of thirty-two feet per second per second? Why not thirty-three or why not only thirty-one? Of course, the reason for this is the nature of the matter out of which the falling body is composed and the nature of the matter of the body towards which it is falling; the mutual gravitational attraction of these two natures accounts for the rate of the falling body. But why must matter have precisely that kind of nature? Nature, with all its seeming necessities, is shot through with contingency. We certainly do not mean to imply that there are no strict physical necessities in nature, but physical laws are, from the metaphysical point of view, only proximate, not ultimate, explanations.[14]

Why do not pine trees just keep on growing taller and taller and taller? Why do not humans just grow fatter and fatter and fatter? Why are there, relatively speaking, limits at all? Why are there species? Why do species repeat themselves throughout the centuries? Why are there two sexes and not sixty-nine? Why their complementarity? Sheer chance? Adaptation? Wring "adaptation" all you will, still you will never eliminate teleology out of the *ad* and the *apt* in what is *adapted*. Why do things, singly and in species, work for their own good and for the good of the species? It is true to say that *that is their nature*; only, why do *these* natures exist? Are they the only possibilities? The adequate cause of the universe is infinitely imitable; the imitability is not due to free will, but the actual imitations are; the concrete number of species and individuals is ultimately traceable—through as long an evolution as you please—to a will that made a choice among the multitudes that were possible. Free will is needed to explain why *these* possibles were actualized, *those* left as *mere possibles*.

Dependence upon the divine free will is, we might note, an excellent reason for using the word "contingent" of all creatures and not merely of generable and corruptible bodies.[15]

Determinate choice of natures. A free will alone could account for the present set-up of the universe or for any previous set-ups.

[14] On physical necessity and some of the implications of "natural minima" and "natural maxima" for the various species, see the interesting essays in *The World of Mathematics*, edited by James R. Newman, New York, Simon and Schuster, 1956, pp. 952–957 (J.B.S. Haldane, "On Being the Right Size") and pp. 1001–1046 (D'Arcy Thompson, "On Magnitude").

[15] See J. DeFinance, S.J., in a book-review, *Gregorianum*, Vol. 43, 1962, p. 174.

Of course, the beings that compose the universe do have natures, and, supposing that the free will that created the universe produces natures A, B, and C, then by the ineluctable law of contradiction, these natures will have the properties A_1, B_1, and C_1 (and not, for example, X_1, Y_1, and Z_1). Free will does not determine what shall be possible, nor what properties pertain to what natures; but among the natures that are possible, it does determine which ones shall be actualized. Consequently, what inevitably follows from the actualization of these determinate possibilities has its origin in the original choice that determines what possible natures shall be actualized in preference to other possible ones.

The being, then, that our reason requires us to admit as the ultimate and uncaused cause of the data of experience emerges from the considerations of the present chapter as not only a cause, a powerful agent, but as an intelligent agent with a free will, in other words, a person.

VI. GOD IS NOT A SUBSTITUTE FOR SCIENTIFIC EXPLANATION

Explanation through final causes not an alternative to nor a substitute for explanation through efficient causes. Finality (or purpose) is not suggested by the metaphysician as an alternative to *efficiency*. Final causes do not substitute for efficient causes. Still less are the two exclusive of each other; they are complementary. Finality is required as the determinant of the specification being shall assume if and when being other than self-sufficient being is effected. It is at least as true to say that a bird has wings *in order to fly* as to say that a bird *flies because* it has wings. The former explanation finds meaning in the existence of wings on a bird; the latter is the explanation of how a bird's motion is accomplished.

"Mechanical" necessity. There are thinkers, however, who realize very well that products require a producer and that events demand causes. But they limit these producers or causes to physical, non-intelligent, and necessarily operating agents. At most, the only intelligent cause they will admit is man. Rather than admit that a divine purpose determined the tendencies and processes of the whole universe, rather than admit that a transcendent, intelligent agent intended the beings and events of our universe, they assert that everything that happens, other than human events, has to happen; it is simply a *mechanical* resultant, the effect of a rugged determinism and of an ironclad *necessity of nature*. Things act as they do because their natures are what they are; whatever occurs is a mere "result" and is not something "intended"; it is the effect of efficient causality, blind, inexorable, but—except for human actions—not traceable to any *intelligent* cause. Such thinkers often insist that even living things are nothing more than complicated "machines." "Mechanical" necessity reigns everywhere in the universe, they claim.

It is strange that the word "mechanical" should have been chosen by such thinkers. They seem to speak as though they considered "mechanical" a synonym for "unplanned," "not designed," or "not directed." But if ever there were something designed, something ordered to an end, something planned, and something the object of whose activity is intended by an intelligent agent and whose forces are therefore directed, then surely a *machine* would be just such a thing. Certainly, to study "mechanical" artifacts will give us a good key to the intelligence of their maker. The more "mechanical" the effect, the more intelligence was exercised by the planner or designer of the machine. The more utility furnished by the artificial organizing of hitherto unrelated parts into a machine, the more intelligence are we justified in attributing to the organizer. Certainly, it would be preposterous to hold that the more perfectly a machine works, the less reason there is for assigning a designer for it or the less reason there is for attributing intelligence to its cause.

"Mechanical," however misused, is not a synonym for "nonteleological." Machines are most excellent evidence of teleology (purpose), of an intelligent designer and a plan. The term "mechanical" therefore is about the last word in the world an anti-finalist (one who denies that there are any non-human final causes) should really want to use to describe the way the universe operates.

"Necessity of nature." Neither is the phrase, "necessity of nature," felicitously chosen by the anti-finalists as an alternative to the thesis of the existence of an intelligent God. The theist is ready, even more ready than the anti-finalist, to admit natural necessities; he freely concedes that *determined* natures do exist. But, he adds, the fact that there exist determined natures, capable of producing determinate effects, is intelligible only if we admit that these natures, being ordered composites, are caused ultimately by a being who has an understanding of the qualities or forces or elements or parts that enter into the composition of these natures, who has control over the actualization of the possibilities of being, and who has freedom to select what concrete things shall exist as the actual natures in our universe.

Certainly, definite natures produce definite effects. A certain type of action necessarily proceeds from a certain type of agent. This is simply an implication of what we mean when we admit that an agent really has a "nature," that is, that it has a principle of *specific operation* consequent upon a "formal" factor in its structure. Certainly, there are *physical laws*; certainly, it is correct to speak of *specific natures* (though the metaphysician should, as much as the positivists, insist that only individuals actually exist as such and that the individual is incommunicable and humanly ineffable). If iron is to exist in a world in which oxygen is also to exist, then rust is inevitable. But neither iron nor oxygen would exist at all were it not for the free choice of a spiritual and intelligent being.

We are back again at our former questions: What is it that specifies *being*, so that it is *this* or *that kind* of being? Granted that *this* or *that* kind of activity must, under given circumstances, flow from *this* or *that* nature or being, and therefore that *this* or *that* effect must necessarily result from the activity of the given natures, still the metaphysician rightly asks: Why are the given natures *given*, and why *these* rather than *those*? An explanation through a non-intelligent agent will tell us *what* has happened and *how* it has happened; but "what" and "how" are not the only questions calling for answers: there is also the "why."

The Scholastic metaphysician will be the first to admit that there is no intellect in beings inferior to man, and that to attribute intelligence to such beings is indeed "anthropomorphic"; but a Scholastic will likewise insist that an adequate (hence a metaphysical, not merely a physical) explanation of the objects that scientists investigate calls for an originating cause endowed with super-human intellect. A person ceases to be human when he has lost all interest in questions of *why*.

Positivistic denial of all intelligibility. Some positivists seem to deny not only final causes but efficient causes as well. They seem to hold that there are no physical necessities and that all "laws" are nothing but "statistical averages." They admit only what they observe, and they observe only succession. They will tell us that we should not say that in these or those circumstances this or that *has* to happen; it does not *have* to happen, they say, it just *does*. But by not admitting even an efficient cause, either free or necessary, of the succession that they observe, such a positivist is rejecting "results" as much as he is rejecting "ends"; he admits "things" or "facts," but he denies the all-important factors: final, formal, and efficient causes.

The metaphysician, on the contrary, argues that it is due to a thing's "nature" *that* it produces such effects as it does, and that it is due to the concatenation of natural conditions that it produces these effects *when* it does. He does not claim that "natural laws" in the subhuman world are moral obligations, but that they are, rather, physical necessities, to ignore or to deny which is—in the opinion of the author of this textbook—to eliminate physical science. But the metaphysician's radical query is not: *"How is it* (or even, *why is it, here and now*) that the natures which exist produce these or those results," but rather: "Why do *these* and *those* natures (among an infinity of other equally possible ones) actually exist, and what coordinates their conditions of operation?"

Inadequacy of a merely physical explanation. These latter questions are as legitimate as the former ones. They call for an answer as much as the others do. Certainly, if four particles are moving away from a common central point, one going north, one going south, one going east, and one going west, if each of them is travelling at a constant rate of ninety miles an hour, and if they meet no obstacles in their paths, then it comes as no surprise to us to learn that after two hours have elapsed the north- and south-bound particles are 360 miles apart, and likewise the east- and west-bound particles. So long as one remains within a *given* closed system of moving particles, any situation is explicable by any previous situation.

Only, nothing at all is *adequately* explained in a *closed* system. To "give" such a system is to give too much; it is to say that events are explained by the natures of things (this we grant), but it is also to say at least implicitly that the natures of things are—despite their composition, complexity, order, determination, and finitude—self-explanatory. With this the metaphysician will not be satisfied. Time explains nothing; an explanation of today's situation merely by yesterday's, and yesterday's by the day before yesterday's, leaves the problem of *any ordered* situation unsolved.

The metaphysician will ask: What accounts for the particles? Why is their number even and not odd? Why do they remain in existence? Why are they going in these precise directions? Why are they travelling with this specific velocity? What is it that keeps them moving? Why is it that their velocity is constant? All these questions are more justified than the almost trivial one that the "mechanist" asks: How is it that the north- and south-bound particles, granting their natures, motion, direction, and velocity, are now 360 miles apart? All the former questions receive satisfactory explanation only if one concedes that no world system can be completely closed, and that there must be a transcendent power that knows the possibilities of being, wills the concrete existence of a definite number of definite types of these possibilities, and has the power efficaciously to produce what it wills. No other explanation will satisfy the mind.

In brief: the whole world system at any particular moment cries out for an explanation—both for its being and for its being a system. The previous chapter showed that the changeable being in our universe calls for an efficient cause; the existence of order in our universe is proof that the maker of its constituent beings is able to produce *a system* and hence is endowed with intellect and free will.

God supplies natures; He does not supply for them. While a theist who believes in the omnipotence of God, in the primacy of the spiritual over the merely material, and in the superiority of the moral order over the physical, will not boggle at the idea of the possibility of a miracle, he does not affirm God's existence only where the physical laws are not at hand to explain an event. For him God is needed if there is to *be anything* at all; an intelligent and free God is needed if the *kinds* of being that exist are to be *these* and not *those* kinds. This does not mean that the theist denies, ignores, or by-passes scientific physical laws, but he does insist that God is needed if any scientific laws are to have concrete embodiment. The theist does not deny the evolution of more advanced species out of less advanced ones; but he does believe that no vague beings exist at all, that whatever exists in the data of experience is specified and has *a real nature*. And he insists that whatever be the virtualities, specific determinations, tendencies, and arrangement of the natural beings that are at any moment in existence, they presuppose at every moment of their existence and specification a supreme, active, intelligent, free creator, conserver, and providential director.

In this regard, God is not one efficient cause, however intelligent, alongside a number of other efficient causes. He is not a coordinated nor a cooperative cause. He is not the supreme physical law, trailed by other and subsidiary laws. No, God is more immanent and more active within things than all their physical laws; but He transcends the physical order completely. God does not *supply for* any *deficiency* in the natural laws; He *supplies* the very beings themselves and all the laws embodied in these beings.

Misconception.   Sometimes the idea is entertained by an atheist that even the theist will quit "postulating" a God once all the laws of nature have been discovered. This idea is based on the naive belief that theists argue for God's existence only in order to account for the exceptions and apparent gaps in natural explanations—to have a being that supplies for the defects of nature, for making forty-nine pounds of potatoes behave as if they really weighed fifty pounds.

Sometimes positivistic scientists talk as if the more complicated the structure of a being, the less need there is of God; as though the more intelligibility one discovers within nature, the less need there is of admitting intellect outside nature as the cause of the intelligibility within nature. It may be the case that, for some shallow thinkers or primitive and superstitious peoples, as scientists discover more and more laws of nature, God becomes more and more remote and superfluous. But if so, we must conclude that they have certainly mistaken the true role of God in the universe.

God is not needed to make simple forces produce complicated effects; complicated effects or simple effects are quite explicable—on the scientific level—by their natural causes, complicated or simple. Again, God is not just a miracle-worker. Hence the evidence for His existence is not just the miraculous. God was never needed as an immediate explanation of hitherto unexplained and even seemingly inexplicable goings on in nature; He is required as an explanation of "Nature."

Anthropomorphic or anthropocentric?   One last point: the finalist is sometimes accused of being anthropomorphic in his teleological interpretation of the universe. The finalist is not anthropomorphic with respect to the universe, but he is certainly, and quite justifiably, anthropocentric. He believes in values, and of the values in the visible universe he believes that man is supreme. He believes that God, the supreme and transcendent value, made the universe *for man*, and that He intends it to be *at the service of man*. The finalist's insistence that things are intelligible does not mean that he considers them endowed with intelligence; when he claims that things are intelligibly ordered in the universe, he is not claiming that they order themselves. Indeed, it is a common thesis (of Scholastic philosophy, at any rate) that "brutes lack intellect," and *a fortiori* there is no intellect in beings lower in the scale than the brutes. What is sub-human is simply not human; that is plain enough. A plant is not a man: a plant does not know, a plant has no intentions, it does not choose. But—the metaphysician will add, to complete the picture —a plant (or a rock, or a brute) does nothing at all to which it is not directed, directed *through* its nature, yes, and *through* its environment, but directed *by* a transcendent intelligent originator and preserver of natures.

LEADING IDEAS of Chapter 3

1. Order is evident in our universe wherever a plurality of parts are related so as to constitute a unified whole.

2. Cases of order are found on all levels of being in our universe: in the mineral world, in the plant world, in the animal world, in the kingdom of man; order exists in the macroscopic world and in the microscopic world.

3. Order, as such, is not a physical element; it is not the object of pure sensation; it is detected only by an intellect, capable of recognizing patterns, relationships, necessity, utility, and beauty.

4. "Parts" are not self-explanatory; being related to something else, they must proceed from something else.

5. The order in our universe is explicable only by an uncaused cause endowed with intellect.

6. A free choice is required to account for the discrepancy between the limitless possibles of "the existible" and the concrete, actual "existents."

7. The definite specifications of being and the selection of the actual patterns and consequent tendencies and laws make us admit that God is not only the intelligent cause of the universe but is also a free cause.

8. Granted the existence of "these" and "those" natures, certain specific effects inevitably follow, but mind and will are required to bring into existence these specific natures from which the action necessarily follows.

9. God does not supply for a deficiency in the laws of nature; He supplies the very beings in nature and the laws embodied in them.

SUGGESTED READINGS for Chapter 3

For Scholastic Exposition:

St. Thomas. S.T. I.2.3 ("The fifth way. . . ."); I.103.1 (*Basic Writings,* Vol. 1, pp. 23, 950–951); *De Pot.* 1.5 and 3.15. (*Power of God,* Vol. 1, pp. 26–33 and 196–205).

Brother Benignus, F.S.C. *Nature, Knowledge and God.* Milwaukee: Bruce, 1947, pp. 83–101 and 494–503.

C. Bittle, O.F.M. Cap. *God and His Creatures, Theodicy.* Milwaukee: Bruce, 1953, pp. 80–104.

M.R. Holloway, S.J. *An Introduction to Natural Theology.* New York: Appleton-Century-Crofts, 1959, pp. 134–153.

For Popular Exposition:

G.K. Chesterton. *Orthodoxy.* New York: John Lane Co., 1909, Chapter IV, "The Ethics of Elfland," pp. 81–118. (*Note:* Chesterton is sometimes accused of "voluntarism" because of this chapter. I do not believe the charge is correct; Chesterton is simply showing a deep appreciation of the presence of God; he has a keen sense of the radical contingency of creatures and of the difference between metaphysical necessity and the physical necessity of the laws of nature.)

For Examples of Order and Teleology:

Wm. Brosnan, S.J. *God and Reason*. New York: Fordham University, 1924, pp. 145–166.
J.A. O'Brien. *Truths Men Live By*. New York: Macmillan, 1948, Chapters 1–8.

On Chance:

H.J. Koren, C.S. Sp. *An Introduction to the Philosophy of Nature*. Pittsburgh: Duquesne University, 1960, pp. 166–176.
B. Lonergan, S.J. *Insight*. New York: Philosophical Library, 1957, pp. 82–139.
Jacques Maritain. *A Preface to Metaphysics*. London: Sheed and Ward, 1939, pp. 141–151.

On Science, Naturalism, and Finality:

Etienne Gilson. *God and Philosophy*. New Haven: Yale University, 1941, pp. 109–144.
C.S. Lewis. *Miracles, a Preliminary Study*. London: Bles, 1952, Chapter 3.

CHAPTER

4

OUTLINE

Creation, or, Being as "Something Given"

I. INTRODUCTION

In *Chapter 2* we explored a proof of the existence of God as the uncaused cause of the data of experience. We did not then specify how God caused the data; we simply used the generic language of production or efficient causality. But, actually, the proof which we gave for the existence of God as the ultimate and unproduced producer, or uncaused cause, of contingently existing beings was implicitly a proof for the existence of God as *Creator*, the absolutely independent and indispensable giver of *being*. We would now like to make this teaching explicit.

II. POPULAR NOTIONS ABOUT CREATION

In our Judaeo-Christian civilization the idea of creation—that the world is made by God out of nothing—is practically taken for granted. It forms so integral a part of our history and tradition that we do not, perhaps, immediately see what a tremendous idea, staggering fact, and "granting" creation really is. Hence, often we do not appreciate its profundity; we do not realize what it actually means to be a creature. We grow up using the words "creator" and "creature" so spontaneously that it is easy for us to think of creation simply as one (the first one) of many historical events in the past, to overlook the real metaphysics of creation, and to fail to grasp the radical relationship linking the creature, even now, to the Creator. We naturally tend to conceive creation like the relation between any other product and its producer. The words "creature" and "creation" have been given secondary meanings; they are often used in ways that take no account of their philosophical import. Even atheists use the terms.

85

Anything that anybody makes is thus imprecisely called a "creature" or a "creation." Especially are artistic products—though made of marble, metal, wood, wire, paint, and so forth—called the artist's *creation*. Fashionable clothes are "the latest creations from Paris (or Rome)." Cardinals of the Catholic Church are "created" by the Pope. Sometimes the word "creature" is so broadened that it simply means a "thing" or "being." One reads translations from Plato where "thing" is rendered "creature," even though Plato's teaching on the origin of our universe is not a doctrine of strict creation but a doctrine of transformation, or better, of the first formation of unoriginated, pre-existent, chaotic matter into an intelligibly structured universe or cosmos. Sometimes people restrict the meaning of "creatures" so that it applies only to living creatures, particularly to animals.

III. PHILOSOPHICAL ANALYSIS OF CREATION

Let us, then, analyze the notion of creation, trying to go beyond its historical to its metaphysical implications. Actively considered, creation is the act whereby God, presupposing no existing subject matter, effects non-divine being. It is His making of something (for example, the universe or a human soul) out of nothing, that is, making it without presupposing anything but His omnipotent Self, and, therefore, not making it *out of* something else. Creation, then, can be called a form of activity, even a form of production: it is God's production of things "out of nothing." Such is creation considered in its starting point or, better, principle. From the point of view of the term produced, creation is the total production of a being, the total dependence of something for all its being upon God. Most formally, creation is the making of a being precisely as a being; creation accounts directly and immediately for the difference between existence and nonexistence.

A. Transformative Causality.

Limited scope of production in our experience. All efficient causality in the realm of our experience is transformative causality. It is called production, yes; but it is better described as the "eduction" of new forms out of the manifold potentialities of some pre-existing composite being. We presuppose the existence of certain beings, beings that have some actual determinate nature but which are still capable of further modifications and are capable even of losing their basic formal determination (their "substantial form") and acquiring so new and so different a one that the being is "essentially" or "substantially" changed, not merely modified. The beings of our experience, therefore, are composed of a determinable subject and determining forms (substantial and accidental). Our causality and that of the other agents of our experience are exercised on these composite beings by changing them. Changing them substantially or essentially is called the "generation" of new beings and the "corruption" of old beings; changing their accidents is "alteration" or "modification."

We bring it about that the old form gives way to the new, rather, that a being comes to exist with a new form. We do not account for the pre-existing composite and changeable being out of which the new thing is made. In a sense, we do not even account for the new composite being. We produce the new thing, yes, but we do not produce it *totally*, through and through; an existing, determinable subject was presupposed to our activity. That subject sustains our transforming activity, and it upholds the new determination after our activity is completed. We produce things, but we produce them *out of other* things. We say that we make *new* beings, but more accurately we make *this* being *become that* being, or we make *this kind* of being *become that kind*.

Non-divine agents not creative. Michelangelo made statues—new realities—but he did not make the stone, metal, or wood that is the intrinsic material constituent of the new statues. He presupposed a subject matter endowed with certain definite actual determinations (he did not even try to make a statue out of water or air); his influence accounts for the fact that at least some old determinations ceased to determine their subject and gave way to other and new determinations. Michelangelo made David, but his activity in making David was "in-formative" or "trans-formative"; it was not strictly "creative." God alone creates. Other agents, all secondary (i.e., non-divine) causes, produce by transforming; they do not produce anything out of nothing, they do not produce the totality of their effects, and they do not make their effects *be* but only *come to be* in *this way* or *that way*.

B. Creation Not Transformative Causality.

A baker makes a cake out of flour, sugar, milk, eggs, baking powder, salt, and other such items. These items are the "ingredients" of the cake; they go to make up the cake; they "go into" the cake; they exist prior to the making of the cake. They are transformed, superficially or radically, in the making of the cake. These items *become* the cake; the cake is *constituted* of them, just as it *was made out of* them. But if something is not "made out of" anything but is totally produced, ingredients and all, then we have a case not of transformative causality but of creation. No items are ever "transformed" into a creature; a creature is not made in or out of any pre-existing substrate(s); if it comes to be at all, it comes out of nothing and comes to be in its totality; it and its ingredients, or constituents, simultaneously come to be. All that it is, its composition and its components, is dependent for its actual reality upon a cause that is not a mere transformer. The product of transformative causality depends for its coming-to-be both upon the efficient cause and upon the material cause. The product of creative causality depends only upon the efficient cause; the material cause is part of that very product.

C. Active Potency and Passive Potency in Inverse Proportion.

Efficient cause of a creature is omnipotent. As with every production, an efficient cause is, of course, presupposed for creation. If ever *nothing whatsoever* existed, there could never have been *anything whatsoever*; if *ever* total nothingness, *forever* total nothingness! There is required, therefore, an efficient cause for creation; indeed, that cause must be omnipotent, for it must be proportioned to the production of non-divine being precisely as being, and being, as being, is not confined to these or those limits and specifications.

Ordinarily, the more that is contributed by the material subject on which an agent works or which he transforms, the less work is needed on the part of that agent. Less expenditure of energy is required, all other things being equal, to turn a spherical mass of clay into an oval than to turn it into a cube. The sphere is more proximately disposed for acquiring the oval shape than the cubic shape. Modern prefabricated homes are more easily set up than homes "built from scratch." Modern "cake mixes" make the baking of a cake easier than was the case when grandmother was a girl—or so the TV commercials promise. On the other hand, an artist's virtuosity is often best shown when the matter on which he works is most recalcitrant, when by itself it is only remotely disposed for the form that the artist educes from it. In such a case, more talent or skill is required on the part of the agent. The supreme talent is that which requires no previously existing subject matter but which simply makes the total being.

D. Creation Not Necessarily a Newness.

New beings have a first moment.   In speaking of transformative production, we rightly speak of its term as something "new," as having a beginning and even a first moment. A being that comes into existence through transformation is a being that exists within time, one that has been preceded in time by some other being, the being namely out of which it was made; it is one whose existence has been preceded by its own non-existence. It is "new" in contrast with the something "old" out of which it proceeded.

"Beginning," as a point of time and as an extrinsic source. Sometimes even creation is described as though it were the production of "new being," the only difference from transformation being that in creation what is produced is *totally* new." But the word "new" would seem to indicate that what is produced by creation was at some time nonexistent or at least was not always existent, and while this last may be true history, it is not essential to the notion of a creature. Whenever production is transformative production, the result is always something "new," but this is not necessarily true of creation. Whenever there is a creature, there is an outside origin or source from which the creature depends, but to say that a creature is "totally produced" or that it is produced out of nothing does not necessarily imply that it has a "beginning" in time. Age and dependence are disparate notions.

A creature is certainly dependent—most radically dependent, dependent in its very being—but it is not necessarily preceded by its own non-being. It has a "beginning" in the sense of a source, an extrinsic principle, to which is due the fact that it exists at all; but this does not imply that a creature, of metaphysical necessity, is preceded temporally by a period of non-existence, that a creature has a "beginning" in time. We must not read into the essential structure of things what is merely accidentally true of them. The universe began to exist—that is (revealed) history! The universe is universally dependent in its existence—this is metaphysics! No contradiction here!

Creation and finite duration in the past. It is not necessary that the world *have begun* to be; a product existing from all eternity would not seem to be a contradiction. In this sense, a created thing is not necessarily *new*. In fact, if "to be something new" implies that there "used to be something old preceding the something new and partially entering into its constitution," then it is wrong, even from the existential point of view (of history and faith), to speak of a creature as "something new."

When we say that a creature is made out of nothing, we do not imply that its duration in the past is finite. We do not mean that it has being after not having being; we simply mean that whatever, whenever, and so long as it has being, it is through radical dependence upon the efficient causality of God, the giver of being, as such. Since the word "new" suggests that nonexistence of a thing preceded, temporally, the existence of that thing, the word should not be used, philosophically, in describing a creature, as a creature. Instead of describing creation as the production of something totally new, we should say that it is the production of a thing in its totality. The fact that the thing exists for a long while or only for a short while, for seventy-nine years or eternally, is irrelevant.

Certainly, if something had a first moment, if something came into being, and if something has existed for a finite duration, it is a creature; but we do not have to say that only if it had a first moment, only if it came into being, and only if its duration is finite, is it a creature. A creature is a creature, even if created from all eternity.

Misconceptions. Many modern writers, however, seem to think that a reason, indeed the *only* reason, why theists hold that the world is created is that "nothing can be eternal." These writers equate "Everything needs a cause" (already a false proposition!) with "Nothing can be eternal." They conclude, logically enough, that if there is a real creator, then He cannot be eternal either; so the theists' arguments are judged to be floundering in total chaos and confusion.

But the argument for God's existence—and what for us amounts to the same, the argument for creation—is not an argument that says, "Nothing can be eternal." Indeed, the argument at least implicitly insists that something had to be eternal or else there is nothing at all existent at any moment whatsoever. This is outstandingly true of St. Thomas's famous "Third Way" for proving the existence of God.[1]

On the other hand, the argument for God's existence is not an argument that says, "Whatever is eternal is uncaused, self-explanatory, or self-sufficient." If a being is real, yet unproduced, then it must be an eternal being; but if a being is eternal, it does not follow that it is unproduced. Professor W.T. Stace does not appreciate the theist's position, for he writes: ". . . There is no reason to suppose that there must have been a first cause, since the chain of causes might go infinitely backwards into infinite time; and . . . if there is a difficulty in conceiving an infinite backward time containing an infinite series of causes, there will be exactly the same difficulty in conceiving an infinite backward time containing only one infinitely prolonged cause, namely God." [2]

God's will and created duration. The duration of the world is the being of the world, and this depends upon God's free will: if He chooses that the world be existent from all eternity, the world is indeed existent from all eternity; if He chooses that it have a first moment, then it has a first moment. In either case it has a causal origin, and that is what the problem of creation is. We cannot, merely by examining the nature of the data of experience, prove what God's free will actually determined regarding the problem of "temporal beginning," not, at any rate, unless we can show that "to be a creature," that is, "to be totally dependent in one's being," and "to be

1 St. Thomas, S.T. I.2.3, *Tertia via*; and C.G. I.15.
2 W.T. Stace, *Religion and the Modern Mind*, Philadelphia, Lippincott, 1952, p. 219.

always existent (to be an eternal being)" are absolutely contradictory notes.

If such a contradiction could be shown *positively*, then reason would be correct in arguing that the world had a first day and that its past duration, however long, cannot be infinite or indefinite. Such an argument would not only prove that the world is created, but that time had a beginning (not only in the sense of an "origin" or a really distinct cause or an "external beginning," but also in the sense of a "first moment" or an "internal beginning" as well). Genuine theists do not stake the proofs for God's existence or the fact of creation upon a proof of the impossibility of an eternal world, even though some occasionally phrase their arguments awkwardly, and some do think that, besides proving that the world is created, reason can also prove that its past duration is finite.

If one could definitively prove the impossibility of an eternal world, if one could show with metaphysical conclusiveness that the data of experience have all ultimately had a first moment of existence, a "beginning of time," then one would thereby have a proof (*another* proof, that is) for the fact of creation. But it is not necessary to take this approach in order to have a proof for creation. Nor is it the approach we have taken.

E. Aristotle and the "Eternal World."

A paradox.   Modern atheists, in general, think that the only argument theists have for God's existence is that "the world cannot possibly be eternal; it must have, therefore, an extramundane cause for its first moment." Yet, paradoxically, the most renowned of the pagan theistic philosophers had actually argued: "The world *cannot* possibly *not* be eternal; it is necessarily eternal." We are referring to Aristotle, who argued to the need of God, not by (certainly, not merely by) a physics of time, but by a metaphysics of dependence. This dependence, however, as presented by Aristotle (here we are following a common interpretation of a difficult question), is a dependence in *motion* (that is, change) and not a dependence in *being*. Thus Aristotle, although admitting the need of God (the Prime Mover) is ignorant of the Creator. Aristotle seems to take *being* for granted; he philosophizes about the causes and conditions, intrinsic and extrinsic, of change. The only way for a being to be effected is for it to be effected *by* a mover *out of* a pre-existent mutable material composite. He equates "efficient cause" with "mover" and explains, ultimately, not *the being* which is changeable but *the change* in the being. His notions of God, therefore, were not the purest. But he certainly cannot be called an atheist.

Eternal Mover for eternal motion. Like the modern atheists, however, Aristotle confused the notions of "the eternal," "the necessary," and "the utterly uncaused or self-sufficient." Holding for the necessity of matter, he held for its eternity; holding for its eternity, he seems to admit that it is uncaused. He does not teach a doctrine of a created universe. At least part of the world (the material substrate) has no efficient cause. Still, even for Aristotle, the world needs God, a Pure Act, not to account for being as being, but to account for the changes that beings undergo. The motion of the world, its changes, are eternal, like its matter. Motion needs a mover; eternal motion needs an eternal mover. Eternal motion also needs an eternal matter. This eternal matter is eternally mobile and eternally being moved. The composing of matter and form, or the "educing" of form from matter, always has an efficient cause, a generator, a transformer, a mover. But the matter itself does not seem, in Aristotle's system, to require an efficient cause. Matter is, for him, a positive necessity in the world, but also a positive unintelligibility; it is real, it is really determinable, it is a real component, but precisely as real it is unproduced and independent.

The true metaphysical argument for God goes beyond the Aristotelian argument. Whatever is determinable needs an efficient cause for its *being determinable* as well as for its determination. The data of our experience not only need a mobile substrate and a mover to account for their changes, they also need a Creator to account for their being and for the being of their substrate.

But at least Aristotle had the intelligence to see that the age of the world is not the primary metaphysical problem. Whether the world was produced in such a way that it began its existence—and that with it time began some ten billion years ago, more or less— or whether the world was eternally produced, the metaphysically important point is that the world is *something produced.* Now, it is precisely as *produced,* and not directly because its *duration* is *finite,* that the world basically calls for a creator. Aristotle called for a divine transformer; but it is a Creator—not merely an ontological First Mover—that is really needed.

Aristotle's criticism of Plato. Plato, in his dialogue *Timaeus*, holds, it would seem, that the universe originated when the Demiurge in-formed a pre-existent but formless matter (itself unoriginated) into an intelligible cosmos. Thus the universe or cosmos had a beginning. Plato insisted, however, that it will never have an end. Aristotle challenged this doctrine.[3] If the universe is never going to end, this is because it is incorruptible; if it is incorruptible, it is ingenerable; if ingenerable, yet existent, then it has always existed and never came to be (for Aristotle, there is no way in which a being can be made except through generation). Aristotle insists that the matter of the universe can never have been in a mere chaotic condition; it is eternal, yes, but eternally united with some form. Succession in forms is possible in—even characteristic of—the central section (the terrestrial part) of the universe; but wherever any kind of matter exists, it exists united with form. It is not possible for chaos ever to have existed or for matter ever to have been without some form.

In this sense, for Aristotle the universe is necessary and necessarily eternal. Matter is eternal, and species also are eternal (that is, they have no origin as species). Only individuals within a species have an origin, and this origin is through generation out of some pre-existent individual. Not admitting creation, Aristotle was forced to hold that there always have been generations and corruptions occurring, that there never was and never could be a first generation, and that there cannot be a first moment to time—nor a last. Whatever is new, indeed whatever is made at all, is made out of something old, some being whose matter was a prerequisite of the new being and is now a constituent of the new being. Aristotle's philosophy of the origin of the universe is a philosophy of eternal generations but not a philosophy of creation; it is a philosophy of change, wherein "origin" necessarily means only the coming-to-be of new substances out of old ones.

[3] Aristotle, *On the Heavens*, Book I, Chapters 10–12 (R. McKeon, *The Basic Works of Aristotle*, New York, Random House, 1941, pp. 421–428).

IV. PROOF OF CREATION

Contingent being is totally caused. Why do we claim that the universe is "created"? Not merely *produced*, but *produced through creation?* Quite simply, because it is *made by God.* Actually, the evidence that the universe is produced at all is evidence that it is created out of nothing and that its ultimate constituents are made, for there could be nothing, no ultimate constituents, from which *the whole* of produced being could have been made. The universe is caused—the individuals are caused, the species are caused, the material and formal constituents of the beings that together are the universe are caused. Hence the adequate cause for the universe can only be an uncaused cause, capable of producing being, as such. That the world is in need of a cause is shown from its contingency; its contingency is manifested to us in various ways, among them mutability. Necessary being is necessarily immutable. Mutable being is contingent being. Contingent being is caused being. Not all being can be caused being. Existent being that is not caused is absolutely necessary being; being that is absolutely necessary cannot possibly not exist, it cannot cease to exist, it cannot have come into being, and it cannot undergo change in its actual being. The universe, teeming with change, therefore with mutability, is contingent, not merely in its being constituted as this and that, but in its very being, comprising something rather than nothing. A being that can undergo change does not have to be what it is; a being that does not have to be what it is does not have to be at all.

Elemental "ingredients" must be caused. Were it not for the action of Michelangelo, the statue of David would not have come into existence. But the marble that served Michelangelo would still exist: it did not depend upon Michelangelo's action. Michelangelo made the marble statue, but he did not make the marble. The marble that became the statue used to be chemical elements (for example, calcium and carbon) existing in some other condition than that of marble. Just as the statue was made out of the marble, the marble was made out of these elements. The forces that made the marble out of these elements did not make the elements, any more than the maker of the marble statue made the marble. Perhaps the chemical "elements" themselves were, in their turn, made out of something still more "elemental," still more primitive, something sub-sub-sub-atomic. The note that strikes the attention of the metaphysician (though not that of a physicist or a chemist as such) is that *they are made.* They are not produced ultimately out of unproduced ingredients; they are *simply, unqualifiedly* produced. In his intellectual analysis of material substances, the metaphysician sees that ultimately there has to be something which is *simply made,* that is, something made but *not made out of* something else. Such an ingredient (or ingredients) will be the ultimate determinable substrate of the corporeal world. It will be elementary indeed, very far from perfection; it will be as close to nothingness as anything of our universe can possibly be. But, for this very reason, the metaphysician must insist that it—this primitive matter—needs a cause. If it does not, nothing does.

Unless there is some primeval ingredient(s), irresolvable into more primitive one(s), we have no products. But a primeval *ingredient* cannot be self-explanatory. An ingredient is a *part,* and a part does not explain itself nor its union with other parts; it is unintelligible of itself and therefore cannot exist of itself. It is rendered intelligible by the cause that makes it and makes it be an ingredient of something. A self-explanatory ingredient would have to be absolutely necessary in its reality; if it is absolutely necessary in *its* reality, it is absolutely incapable of being an ingredient of some more complicated entity, and it is incapable of being determined, directed, utilized, or in any way changed by any outside force.

Matter is created. If the universe is caused by God, but not through creative activity, then God made the universe not out of nothing, but out of something; He presupposed a pre-existent substrate, a something which He did not cause and which is independent of Him in its being, its reality, and its intrinsic nature, something unmade, self-existent, and necessary—yet a something which God can manipulate, control, direct, modify, and determine, a something out of which He can make all the effects of the world. But this is a contradiction. In slightly different words, matter must be created, that is, produced totally, or else be self-existent, self-explanatory, necessarily existent, immutable, and incapable of receiving determination or of being a part. Now if matter, that most indeterminate, that least perfect, and that most unintelligible of all that in any way is real, can be self-explanatory and can exist simply of its own very nature, despite its radical weakness and imperfections, then anything goes! If matter is self-explanatory, thus satisfying the inquiring intellect of man, no man should seek the explanation of anything else. Surely there is no need of a cause of perfect things if even imperfect things can be self-sufficient. If self-existent matter is meaningful, no questions about anything are meaningful. If matter is self-explanatory, *a fortiori* all else is.

Necessary existence is something absolute.   If a certain thing, X, cannot exist without having either the mode or quality Y or Z and yet is not determined by its own very nature to have Y rather than Z (or, conversely, to have Z rather than Y), then that thing, X, is certainly not, of itself or by reason of what it is in its very essence, determined to be existent; rather, it is indifferent to existence and non-existence. It is not, therefore, necessarily existent; it is not self-existent. If it exists at all, it contingently exists. It would be impossible for such a thing to be self-determined to exist, i.e., to exist by right of its own essence, and yet not also have, by right of that essence, the determination without which it cannot possibly exist, namely the determination Y (or, alternatively, the determination Z).

Matter's indifference to existence.   Now, any given matter in the universe is not of its very nature or essence in motion nor in a state of rest, for it can exist in either state. It is likewise indifferent to having this or that size or shape. Again, it can be the matter of non-living beings or of living beings; it can be the matter of any of the elements, or (if you mean by ultimate matter the elements themselves) this matter can be the substrate of the various species of beings, living and non-living. However, matter cannot exist without some determinate size, shape, and state of rest or motion (and, if in motion, without a determinate direction and velocity); it cannot exist without being either in a living or in a non-living being and without being a constituent either of this or that individual and species. Matter cannot exist without being determined in these respects; yet it does not owe to its own essence alone the individual and specific determinations that it actually has at any given moment. Matter is therefore fundamentally, radically indifferent to existence; it does not exist by right of its own essence. That it exists is due to some third reality, not to itself nor to any of its determinations, but to an extrinsic agent that makes the matter *be* and also—directly or indirectly, immediately or mediately—makes it have *this* rather than *some other* determination. In short, if matter exists, this is due to the fact that it is created.

An objection. Possibly, one might think that matter could be self-existent yet not have, of itself, the determination (whether *this* or *that*) with which it is, as a mere matter of fact, found in the data of experience. Perhaps it necessarily exists and necessarily has *some* state of motion or of rest, *some* size (any size—this large one or this smaller one), also *some* direction and velocity, and *some* specific qualities (whether of the living order or of the non-living), but perhaps it does not of absolute, essential necessity have the *particular individual* state, size, shape, direction, velocity, and specification with which it does actually exist. Can we not conceive it as necessarily existent, and even necessarily determined, only, determined *disjunctively* or *indifferently* to *either* Y *or* Z?

Answer. On further examination, we realize that in the real order no reality can exist of its very nature without having its modes or qualities determined according to their ultimate individuation. No reality can be *partly* absolutely necessary. If a being is partly dependent, then basically it is totally dependent. A thing cannot be *half*-created and *half* "necessarily existent." If a given determined reality has a cause for the union of its components, then the very components themselves are not self-explanatory but require a producer. If a subject requires a distinct formal cause, it and its form require a distinct efficient cause. Not only the fact of union and education and composition, but the reality of the components themselves call for an outside explanation; the composite needs a cause of its being, not merely of its being composite. Both matter and its direction, both matter and its state of motion, both matter and its size, shape, quality, and species—all need an outside explanation. It is not possible to conceive, truly and objectively, a reality as *existing of necessity*, yet *indifferent* to this or that matter or mode or quality or species of existing. For an absolute cannot be essentially related to anything else, as everything so related is caused.

V. THE ESSENCE OF CREATION: THE MAKING OF BEING AS BEING

Formal notion of creation. Earlier we described creation according to its two "terms" or extremes: nothingness is the term "out of" which a creature is made, and "the total reality of a being" is the term "into which" a creature is made. Let us now amplify the idea of creation according to its formal, or essential, note. We therefore say that creation is *the making of being as being.* This, of course, is not in contradiction with the statement that creation is the production of the totality of a being, nor does it mean that God, when acting as a creator, produces something which is utterly indeterminate. The utterly indeterminate does not exist. It means, rather, that whereas other causes do not so much *make* the effect as *make it come to be,* whereas they make *this* being become *that* being, the Creator makes beings *be.* Other causes make their effects according only to some particular aspect that presupposes some substrate; God makes effects according to their most universal aspect, the aspect of being —and this cannot possibly have a substrate.

Making a being, and creating a being. The being, David (i.e., Michelangelo's statue of David), is of course David. Since Michelangelo made David, and since David is something real, or "a being," therefore Michelangelo made "a being" when he made David. David is also configured marble; therefore Michelangelo, who made David, made configured marble. Yet the marble itself, as marble, and even the configured marble simply as having *some* configuration at all was not the formal term of Michelangelo's activity. The being, the marble, and some configuration—all existed prior to and independent of Michelangelo's activity. But Michelangelo did make *this* configured marble block *become that* configured marble block. Due to the influence of Michelangelo's causality, a block of marble, instead of *remaining this* being (A), and instead of *becoming that* being (B = Moses, or Hercules, or Niobe), *became this other* being (C = David). We can say that since he made David and since David is a being, then Michelangelo made a being. Only, we cannot say that he "created" a being. For he did not make a being *as a being.* He took an already existent determinate being and simply made it come to be determined some other way—it already had the note, "being," and this note cannot be effected *through transformative causality*, whether by Michelangelo or by any other cause. Being, as such, is effected not by transformative but by creative causality.

Could Michelangelo have produced a statue insofar as it is a being, insofar as it is distinct from nothingness, he could have made any kind of being at all. Small statues, large statues, rude statues, exquisite statues—all were excluded from Michelangelo's scope of activity *unless their being already existed* as marble or wood or bronze or some other suitable material. A porphyry statue was harder for Michelangelo to make than a Carrara statue, but any statue at all would have been impossible for him if there had been no pre-existent matter at his disposal. Michelangelo could make something artistic out of just about everything; but he could not give ontic status, basic being, to anything. Michelangelo did make beings when he made statues, yes; but he did not primarily or basically or essentially make the "being" of these beings. Their being is God's contribution; it is what the Creator does. It is not the *thisness* of *this* being nor the *thatness* of *that* being that prevented it from being *created* by Michelangelo; it was as a *"being"* that it escaped him. A creature could not have been produced by Michelangelo, not because of the *kind* of being which the creature would be (though there are limitations even on this score, since the effect of transformative causality cannot be more perfect than the forces effecting the transformation), but fundamentally because of the very *mode of production* which is creation. We depend upon the collaboration of some sustaining substrate when we produce anything. There are no collaborators in creation.

Creative causality and creatures' causality. The Creator makes the "being" that is found in all beings, substrates, and forms. He makes the reality of whatever is real in all constituent elements, substrates, agents, and activities. But for God's activity no reality would be real at all. God's omnipresent operation, accounting for the being which constitutes whatever is real, to the extent that it is real, is not the negation of creatures' causing. Only, God and creatures cause in very different senses. God is a transcendent cause, causing everything that is and requiring no substrate out of which He would create.

A finite cause can only make a thing come to be some other thing; it always presupposes something. Further, the limits to its active power and the limits to its subject's receptive power are not determined merely by being what they are; they are determined by the outside influence that makes them be, an outside influence that controls the universe and that determines that there shall be beings and what basic species of beings there shall be. The specific texture of the universe at any given moment is truly "given"; it is the term of God's deliberate choice, His infinitely Providential order of willing and permitting.

The dynamic nature, the active powers, indeed the very activities of created agents are themselves something real, existent, and participating in being; they are, then, as such, as having being, and for as long as they have it, the direct effecting of God. We and all other finite agents are but the secondary causes, the caused causes, of whatever it is that we effect. *What a thing is at the present moment* is due, in some sense, to its constituent elements, to some past activity of "generators," and to the specific natural laws here and now operating through the beings that are the natural universe; but *that it exists at all* is due to God's direct and immediate activity. This is not a case of "God makes the protons, we make the electrons; together God and we make atoms." God makes the entire reality, and we make the entire reality—but, plainly, in two very different senses.

Example. Just as Michelangelo could not make a marble statue that was not marble, we cannot make a produced being that is not a being. But when Michelangelo made his marble statue, the formal term of his activity was this configuration, David, or more accurately, the coming-to-be of this configuration. When we produce any determinate being (and indeterminate beings cannot exist), the formal term of our activity is the coming-to-be of the determination. But if God were not making being, the formal term of His operation, there would be nothing out of which mere transformers could make anything else; there would not even *be* any transformers. Without Michelangelo's action, marble would not have become David—but it would still be marble. Without God's action, marble would not even be marble; it would be nothing at all.

Our primary and essential influence is on the *kind*; only secondarily and accidentally do we produce the *being*. God acts in the reverse fashion: what He essentially and primarily produces is the entity of any datum, accounting for the fact that it exists at all. Only secondarily and accidentally does He account for the *kind* of being which here and now exists, for the *individual thisness* that here and now determines what is existing. *Being* is the formal object of God's (creative) activity; *determination* is the formal object of our (transformative) activity.

Amplification.   Let us illustrate this with a further example. We say that "the visible" is the formal object of sight; it is what determines sight; it is what sight primarily and essentially terminates in. In the concrete world "the visible" always has further determinations. The actually visible is a certain subject, determined by a definite color. For example, if "the visible" is a red hat, we say that the red-colored hat is visible because of its color, or redness. In the concrete, the colored hat and the red hat are the same; the redness of the hat is the color of the hat. But it is not precisely because the hat is red but because it is colored that it is "visible." Otherwise, dyeing the hat purple would make it invisible. Similarly, every being is this or that specifically and individually determined being; but God is making it according to the aspect of being, and other causes are accounting for the specific and individual determinations. There is no distinction between the red and the colored in what is colored red; there is no distinction between the determination and the being in a determined being. Still, it is its being, and not its having this or that determination of being, that is the formal reason why any non-divine being is said to be a creature and is a term of God's immediate, direct, and indispensable causality.

If a milliner dyes a red hat purple, he primarily and essentially makes something purple, only secondarily and accidentally does he make something colored—the purple hat already had color when it was red. If a transforming cause makes *this* being become *that* being, it primarily and essentially accounts for the new determination, but not for the being; the newly determined being already had being prior to having the new determination. Being, then, is not the formal object of transformative production, even though in every production being is produced. The being in every production is the formal term of God's activity.

False notion of transformation. Agnostics sometimes accuse metaphysicians of fooling themselves into thinking that they have a special meaning in mind when they use the word "creation," whereas they are really anthropomorphic and are conceiving creation simply as transformation. Anthropomorphism is always a danger; but it is not the only danger: sometimes its opposite is a danger. Curiously enough, so we believe, there is a temptation for metaphysicians, in unguarded moments, to conceive all production, even transformation, as creation. Sometimes we talk as if "producing a form" were creating the totality of a particular reality out of nothing. Let us analyze transformative causality more carefully.

A transformer does not first effect a new form and then unite it with its subject. A transformer is quite dependent in the exercise of its activity on some previously existent and determined being— its subject matter, or substrate, the material cause of the object which will be called its effect. A transformer "makes a form" only insofar as he or it transforms a subject matter. The intrinsic term of transformative action depends in its very coming-to-be not only on its active principle (the efficient cause, the transformer), but also on a passive principle (the material cause, a real but passive substrate or subject).

Michelangelo, for example, did not first make some configuration, David, and then proceed to join it to marble; he made David precisely by sculpturing the marble, immediately and directly "educing" David *out of* the marble. Medicine does not produce a separate reality, health, with which it then in-forms a sick person and thereby cures him; rather, medicine heals by acting directly and immediately on the patient. Healing is an activity, but an activity in a recipient. Creation is an activity, but not in a recipient; it is a total giving. Transformative causality is always the application of active potency to something that has some passive potency; it is not the producing of a separate form and the subsequent uniting of that form to a suitable subject. Otherwise, transformative causality would not differ from creation. The causing of a new form, and the uniting of it intrinsically with its sustaining subject, are one and the same activity or process, caused by the collaboration, according to their respective natures, of the transformer and the subject matter.

If a form were produced separately and, after its production, were united with its subject—or even if both the production of the form and the uniting of it with its subject were simultaneous (as happens in the production of the human soul)—such a production would not be the production of something *out of* something else, it would be the direct production of the form out of total nothingness; it would be creation. When a transformative cause exercises its activity, the form which it educes from the potency of the presupposed subject depends upon that subject even in its coming-to-be and not merely in its subsequent existence in that subject. It itself does not "become" except insofar as its subject becomes differently determined, and it has no being in itself but only in the subject. The waving of a flag is not the co-existence and compenetration of an inert rag and certain vacuous undulations. The "pins and pin-cushion" image of the "act-potency" or "form-subject" relationship cannot be exorcized too strongly. But the exorcist does not have to be an agnostic.

VI. CONSERVATION, OR THE PRESERVATION OF CREATURES IN BEING

Limitations of causes of coming-to-be.   Since our activity is confined to effecting the *coming-to-be* of *this* being *as this*, it does not account for the *permanence* of this being; it is not what *preserves* this being with its acquired thisness. We cause coming-to-be; we do not cause being. To cause being is to create. To cause continued being is to continue to cause being; it is to conserve or preserve being with the same power with which being is created.

The moment a builder puts down his tools, his building, his causality, ceases; his effect, likewise, to the precise extent that it is his effect, ceases to be. His *building* (the "building" which is the coming-to-be or the process, and not the *building* which is the finished structure, e.g., the Empire State Building), lasts no longer than his activity. Indeed, the reality of an act of producing and the reality of a coming-to-be are merely different ways of expressing one and the same reality. One and the same act actuates the active potency of the agent (action) and the passive potency of the patient (passion). The agent is active by reason of his nature, his powers, and his skills, but the action itself is in the patient; it is the coming-to-be of some newness in a pre-existing subject in dependence upon the acting agent. Dependent already upon the Creator for its existence and for the laws of its specific nature, it submits to the exercise of the specific laws of another nature acting upon it, the net result being some individual transformation—some further specifications—blended together in the patient or subject. The qualities in wood, mortar, glass, steel, etc., now exercise their specific forces, physical and chemical, under new circumstances; the builder was responsible for the fact that these forces have come to be under the new circumstances. That is precisely his process of building, and it is this building process, not the finished structure nor its permanence, which is what is attributable to the builder.

The *painting of the picture* is due to the artist; the *painting which is the picture* is due to the nature of paint and canvas, and ultimately to the source of all natures, God. In buildings, in paintings, and in all things artificial and natural, God is the cause of their *being real*, and He is the cause of their *remaining real* and of their being active. What would otherwise be only separate paint and canvas—what would be non-existent as a picture—is made a picture by the artist's craft. What would otherwise, as a being, simply not be at all is made a being by the creative craft of the Supreme Artist.

Identity, in the concrete, of creation and conservation. No being can ever *become* an absolutely necessary being; what is absolutely necessary can never *become*, it can never have been non-existent, and it can never change. To come to be, or simply to exist as something capable of change, is to be not intrinsically necessary. This lack of intrinsic necessity is as long-lived as is the changeable being. If a being begins to exist, or simply if it is a product (perhaps an eternal product), then so long as it exists it *is a product* (*is being produced*), and so long does it have an actual producer.

By now, therefore, the reader should be coming to realize that God's creative action and His conserving or preserving action are, from the metaphysical point of view, one and the same action, that of causing being, or, making something be. We said "from the metaphysical point of view," because from the historical point of view, based on divine revelation, one can distinguish between the *de facto* beginning of the universe at a definite moment a finite time ago, its "creation," and the keeping of the universe existent through all its subsequent moments, its "conservation." Even for the metaphysician, creation does not necessarily imply subsequent maintenance nor previous non-existence. Conservation, however, implies that the conserved being *has been* in existence and that it *will have* some subsequent duration.

The chandelier hanging from the ceiling by a chain cannot, with the mere passage of time, dispense with the chain and still remain hanging. This is true no matter how old the chandelier is or how long it has been hanging from a chain. Where a cause is the cause of a thing's being in existence, then so long as the effect remains existent, its cause is exercising its causation; should the cause cease to exercise this, then the effect would cease to be. Hence creatures, whose being is caused by God, whose existence is His product, and who owe to God all of the reality whereby they are existent rather than non-existent, are dependent upon God so long as they exist, so long as they are real—whatever be the vicissitudes they undergo in their duration. Produced reality can never become unproduced reality; dependent existence can never become independent existence; caused being can never become uncaused being. Existence that was produced in the past, if it is still extant, is existence that is still being produced; it is being caused here and now, just as it was in the past. Its production is a continuous creative activity.

This is not at all to deny that creatures have a true substantiality, a true inner consistency, belonging to them as substances which are adequately distinct from God. Adequately distinct—yes; but totally dependent! Their substantiality is substantial, but it is the substantiality of *creatures:* nothing can make any creature be uncreated; no being can make a thing become independent of God. A creature's being, as a reality, is its very own, but it pertains to it as to a creature, hence pertains to it through the uninterrupted activity of an outside creative influence. Self-sufficiency in being is not a perfection that can be given.

While other things are making a changeable being *become what it becomes,* and while its constituent ingredients are making it *be what it is,* something is also making it simply *be,* accounting for its existing, and causing it to be instead of not to be. It is being produced precisely as a being, so long as it is what it is; it is being produced as a being even when (as undergoing change) it becomes other than what it is. It does not exist by some independent right; it exists because God is caring for it, keeping it in existence, preserving it, sustaining it, and conserving it as a contingent, mutable, existent, and dynamic reality.

Preservation, not stagnation. Divine conservation of creatures does not mean that God fossilizes them; God's conservation is not supernatural formaldehyde. Creatures do not stagnate in their being: their dependent, preserved being is a being which is active and passive; creatures exercise activity, and they suffer from the forces of their environment. That they and their activity and passivity are real throughout all the vicissitudes of their hectic and checkered career is due to God the creator-conserver. God does not make a being which then, independently of Him, persists in its being and acts on other beings and suffers from their actions; rather He makes beings, He makes perduring beings, He makes enduring beings, He makes acting beings—all with one ineffable, eternal, omnipotent, free act, the act of existentializing the contingent, mutable, dynamic universe.

"Generated" beings are still "created" beings. Creation and conservation, then, are one and the same thing in the creature; they are its relation of immediate dependence in actuality upon the Creator. We thus see why we, and all the things that exist today, and not just the beings mentioned in the first chapters of the book of *Genesis*, are truly called "creatures." Sometimes we like to contrast the production which is *generation* with the production which is *creation*. But this is to take the historical or the physical perspective —not the metaphysical—and it runs the risk of making us lose our sense of the immediacy and totality of creation. In the *physical* perspective, the *first* individuals of the various species were *created* out of nothing (or, at least, at the moment of creation a plurality of distinct beings was immediately created—however primitive, still they were determinate, specified); while all *subsequent* individuals (and species) have been *generated*, or evolved, from these. The deeper or *metaphysical* perspective, however, is that though we of today are *generated*, we are *also created*: we are—rather, we *were*—generated by our parents, and we *are created* by God.

Our origin, through generation from our parents, does not exclude our origin through creation from God. Our soul, since it is a spiritual substance, is immediately and totally created by God—but that is not the full story of our creaturehood. After all, nothing can be half-created; a being is totally a creature, or not at all a creature. God certainly is the immediate cause of our soul, and He is the immediate cause of the basic matter composing our body; He is also the mind and will that is prefiguring and determining the basic laws that are governing, even constituting, nature in its various species. But more fundamentally, He is the cause of the being of whatever is real in and about us, matter no less than form, body no less than soul, changes and activities no less than permanence and power, to the extent that these *are real* and not nothing.

Creation as history and as metaphysics. In the historical order, where the universe, including some definite primitive species, did have a "first moment," the beings that came to exist at that moment have, we might say, an "historical" priority to the title "creature"; but, metaphysically speaking, all non-divine realities, whenever they exist and whatever their immediate origin, are creatures, and no one being or group of beings or first of a series of beings has a "metaphysical" priority to the title "creature."

We of today are creatures, not merely indirectly and remotely, on the score that we are descended from Adam (after all, even Adam was not immediately and totally created in the "historical" sense— for his body was made *out of* some pre-existent matter); we are not creatures precisely because our *matter*, in the quite remote past, and our soul, in the more recent past (the moment of conception, or not much later), were immediately made by God. We are creatures because all our reality, as real, is immediately dependent upon God and is being caused by God; our being is our *being caused* by God. We *are*, we exist; but we *are made*: by our parents out of something, and by God out of nothing. We did not, and do not, contribute to our being; we *constitute* it, if you will (better, it constitutes us), but we did not, and do not, *contribute* it; it is a *God-given gift*.

We of today are not merely *generated* beings but are also *created* beings—for we would be nothing whatsoever except for the transcendent activity of God, who is even now causing the reality of all that is real in us and who is accounting for why the constituents of which we are made are not nothingness, why the parents who generated us were not nothingness, why, when we were being generated, the passive potencies in our substrate or ingredients and the active potencies both in our substrate and in our parents were not nothingness.

Because creation is necessarily immediate, we can say that though we descend, *as generated beings*, from our first parents, we are not, *as creatures*, "descendants of other creatures." Creatures cannot be descendants; creatures can have no descendants. Generated offspring have progenitors, but creatures have no father—save only One, Our Father Who is in Heaven!

VII. CREATUREHOOD AND RELIGION

It is the lack of a real sense of creaturehood—the loss of a sense of contingency—that explains, in large part, the atheism and irreligion of contemporary society. Religion has its basis, not in a cringing fear of facing life alone nor in a depreciation of man's true worth, but in the straightforward acknowledgment of creaturehood and the honest and unaffected admission of the radical dependence upon God of our very selves, as well as of the constituent elements of the universe as a whole.

Man is a metaphysical animal; consequently man is a religious animal. Religion—natural religion (as distinct from positive religion based on revelation)—is the spontaneous response of man to his appreciation of what it means to be a creature, radically dependent in the very roots of its being. Adoration of the Creator is the first duty of rational creatures and the natural reaction to the vision of the Alpha and Omega of all being. Sin is the refusal to acknowledge one's status of creaturehood. Denial of the transcendent cause of being ends invariably in man's deification of himself or in deifications even more degrading.

Let us add here, by way of concluding this chapter, a few extracts from an essay in which Father Mersch gives a penetrating analysis of genuine religion:

. . . Our relation to God . . . is a real relation by supreme right: it expresses, in us, that which make us be. It is an indestructible relation. God will always be distinct from us; and with respect to Him our being will always remain an *esse ad*. It is likewise a total relation, affecting not

merely some modality of our being, but absolutely all that we are. . . .
For beings which are not necessary, existence is only something borrowed.
To hold to their reality is then, for them, first and foremost, to cling
to the cause of their reality. . . . We finite beings are, essentially, a
relation and a tendency. And this attitude is not intended to be content
with a few manifestations; some few acts lost in the midst of others; still
less is it intended to surge upward for a moment and then to rest satisfied. The religious aspiration, law of our being as being, relation of all
our reality with the only Necessary Being, should subtend all our other
aspirations. It is *the* aspiration, the unique and perpetual tendency.
Religion in man is all of him.[4]

LEADING IDEAS of Chapter 4

1. Not only does *change* need a cause that induces it, a *changeable
being* requires a *cause of its being*. The cause of being, as being, is a
creator.

2. When a thing is not made *out of* something else but is totally
produced, ingredients and all, this is not transformation but creation.

3. The more that is contributed by the material subject on which
an agent works, the less is required on the part of the agent, and vice
versa.

4. To be produced out of nothing does not necessarily imply "to
have had a beginning in time"; a *product* existing from all eternity does
not seem to be a contradiction.

5. Christians accept from supernatural revelation the fact that the
world has not existed from all eternity; but revelation does not settle the
question of the abstract possibility of a non-divine being existing from
eternity.

6. Aristotle did not argue to the metaphysical doctrine of creation;
he argued that our mobile world is eternal and needs an eternal, im-
moble Mover, or Pure Act, to account for its motion.

7. There can be no *ultimate* pre-existing constituents out of which
the whole of produced reality could have been made.

8. It is not possible for a reality (e.g., matter) to exist of absolute
intrinsic necessity and yet be indifferent to this or that manner or mode
or quality or species of existing.

[4] Emile Mersch, S.J., "Religion, Christianisme, Catholicisme," *Nouvelle
Revue Théologique*, t. 56, 1929, pp. 11, 16, 23.

9. Created causes do not make beings, *as beings*, but determine the coming-to-be of *this* being *out of that* being.

10. Where a cause is the cause of a thing's being in existence, then so long as the effect remains existent, its cause is exercising its causation; God is conserver of all non-divine beings as well as their creator.

11. The lack of a real sense of creaturehood, the loss of the sense of contingency, explains in large part the atheism and irreligion of contemporary society.

12. Natural religion is the spontaneous response of man to his appreciation of what it means to be a creature.

SUGGESTED READINGS for Chapter 4

For Scholastic Exposition:

St. Thomas. S.T. I.44; I.45.1–5; I.46; I.104.1 and 2 (*Basic Writings*, Vol. I, pp. 426–432, 433–442, 447–457, 962–966); *De Pot.*, 3.1–5, 13, 14, 17; 5.1–3 (*Power of God*, Vol. I, pp. 78–111, 185–196, 219–235; Vol. II, pp. 75–97).

L. Bright, O.P. "Creation, a Philosopher's Point of View," *The Downside Review*, Vol. 76, n. 244, Spring 1958, pp. 150–160.

C.B. Daly. "The Knowableness of God," *Philosophical Studies* (Maynooth), Vol. 9, 1959, pp. 102–109.

On the Non-eternity of the World:

C. Bittle, O.F.M. Cap. *God and His Creatures*. Milwaukee: Bruce, 1953, pp. 72, 74, 312–314.

Wm. Brosnan, S.J. *God Infinite, the World and Reason*. New York: Fordham, 1943, pp. 78–83.

F. Copleston, S.J. *History of Philosophy, Vol. II, Mediaeval Philosophy, Augustine to Scotus*. London: Burns, Oates and Washbourne, 1950, pp. 263–265, 366–368.

Fernand Van Steenberghen. *Ontology*, translated by M.J. Flynn. New York: Joseph F. Wagner, 1952, pp. 240–243.

Aristotle and Creationism:

Etienne Gilson. *The Spirit of Medieval Philosophy*. New York: Charles Scribner's Sons, 1940, Chapters 3 and 4.

Francis X. Meehan. *Efficient Causality in Aristotle and St. Thomas.*
Washington, D. C.: Catholic University, 1940, pp. 41–57.

On Creaturehood and Religion:

André Bremond, S.J. *Religions of Unbelief.* Milwaukee: Bruce, 1939, pp.
108–130 (Chapter 6).
Frederick Copleston, S.J. *Aquinas.* Baltimore: Penguin, 1955, pp. 122–
124.
M.C. D'Arcy, S.J. *The Nature of Belief,* rev. ed. St. Louis: Herder, 1958,
pp. 163–192, especially 188–189.

For Spiritual Inspiration:

Emile Mersch, S.J. "Religion, Christianisme, Catholicisme," *Nouvelle
Revue Théologique,* t. 56, 1929, pp. 5–23. Most of this essay is found
translated by Daniel F. Ryan, S.J., in E. Mersch, *Morality and the
Mystical Body,* New York, P.J. Kenedy and Sons, 1939, pp. 3–18.
C.S. Lewis. *Reflections on the Psalms.* London: Bles, 1958, Chapter 8.
L.M. Régis, O.P. "Prayer," *Cross Currents,* Vol. 7, 1957, pp. 41–55.
(The original French appears in *La Vie Spirituelle,* n. 407, June
1955, pp. 563–589).

PART TWO

THE NATURE AND TRANSCENDENT ATTRIBUTES OF GOD

CHAPTER

5

OUTLINE

114

How We Come to Know Something about the Nature of God

I. THE PROBLEM

Just as we do not directly know God's existence, so too we do not directly know God's essence, or nature, and perfections. We came to know that God exists by arguing from the data of experience. It will likewise be through arguing from the data of experience and analyzing their metaphysical condition that we shall arrive at whatever philosophical knowledge it is possible for us to have respecting the nature and perfections of God.

But the very fact that the data of experience need an outside explanation forces us to acknowledge that God, to be really and truly the ultimate and adequate explanation of the data (and, therefore, not in need, Himself, of any outside explanation) must be utterly different from the data of experience. He must "transcend" the data of which He is the ultimate and self-explanatory source; His perfection must "go beyond" that of the data of experience, and it must be something that is utterly different from anything that by reason of its very nature needs an outside explanation. But since the data of experience constitute the objects whose knowability is proportioned to our human intellects, and since God must transcend these proportionate objects, a serious difficulty arises: Can we really and truly have any objectively valid knowledge of God's nature and perfections?

II. THE "TRIPLE WAY" OF DIONYSIUS

Early attempt at a solution. One of the earliest attempts to describe technically how we know God is contained in the treatises

"The Divine Names" and "The Mystical Theology," supposedly written by Dionysius the Areopagite. Who the real author of these early Christian writings is, is one of the unsolved mysteries in the history of Western culture, but his influence has been tremendous, not only in philosophy and dogmatic theology, but also in spiritual, and especially mystical, literature. This influence, it is probable, was due not so much to any clarity and cogency in the writings themselves, as to the authority that was attributed to the "Dionysian" doctrines by ecclesiastical writers, who for centuries held, uncritically, that the author of the works in question was no less a personage than the Dionysius who is mentioned in the *Acts of the Apostles* as a member of the Athenian Areopagus (*Acts* 17:34) and who, supposedly, was converted by St. Paul to Christianity and eventually was made first bishop of Paris (where, to this day, there are many reminders of "Saint Denis").

Affirmation, negation, eminence. The pseudo-Dionysius says that we know God by affirming everything of Him, since He is the cause of all things. We also know God by negating everything of Him, since everything we know is a creature, and God is no creature. Finally, we "know" God by "unknowing" Him, simply admitting that He is beyond all affirmation and all negation. All this knowledge constitutes the "three-fold way of knowing God," *scilicet*, the "way of affirmation," the "way of negation," and the "way of eminence."

Are these three meant to be three discrete "ways" of knowing God, or are they but three stages of one elaborate process of knowing God? In practice, later philosophers have, reasonably enough, combined the "three ways" into one complex way, which we shall try to describe.

III. ANALOGICAL KNOWLEDGE OF GOD

First step. Apprehending the data of experience and reasoning to their adequate explanation, we go on to affirm that God must possess whatever perfections exist in these data. This is the first step in the process of coming to know what God is. A cause cannot give what it does not have; hence God, as cause of the perfections of the data of experience, must Himself possess these perfections, at least in some manner. Such is the way of "affirmation," the way of "causality," or the "positive theology."

Second step. Yet the mode in which perfections exist in creatures is a mode which of its very nature has to be excluded from the adequate cause of these perfections. This adequate cause must be a totally uncaused cause, a necessarily existent being. Hence what God possesses, He must possess in a mode or way that is not found in any of the data of our experience. We can form the conception of the mode in which perfections exist in God only in a negative manner, by denying divine possession of the imperfection (e.g., the contingency, finitude, composition, multiplicity, and mutability) that is necessarily involved in the concrete perfections of the data of experience. Such is the way of "negation," the way of "remotion," or the "negative theology."

Third step. Finally, after we have excluded from God the imperfections characteristic of the data of experience, we extol the remaining perfection. But this must be correctly understood, else we become anthropomorphic. God is not the mere superlative term of a comparison with human or other creaturely perfections; He is not the mere infinite magnification or prolongation, in the same line, of a contingent perfection; His perfection is of a transcendent order, incomprehensible to our powers of knowing. This third step (which might be considered simply as an explicitation of the second) consists in recognizing that God's perfection is utterly positive and of such a nature that of itself it absolutely excludes mutability, limitation, composition, contingency, and any and every thing else that would be a mark of self-insufficiency or a sign of an imperfect mode of existing.

Resultant knowledge. As a net result of this "threefold way," we have "analogical ideas" about the nature and perfections of God, ideas that are truly predicable of God, describing exclusively divine properties. These ideas, partly positive and partly negative, partly representative and partly significative, partly absolute and partly relative, are certainly not adequate nor proportioned to God as He is in Himself, but they are not, for all that, false ideas nor mere symbols, but perfectly true ideas which greatly extend our knowledge of God (while falling infinitely short of an adequate representation of God as He is in Himself). Analogical knowledge steers between the Scylla of Agnosticism and the Charybdis of Anthropomorphism. We avoid, that is, the bleak conclusion that the human mind can know nothing whatsoever about the nature of the ultimate cause or causes of reality (the agnostic position), and yet we do not fall into the contrary error of thinking that all reality is completely intelligible to us humans and that to represent God as though He were merely a supremely perfect human being is to have correct and adequate knowledge of Him.

IV. PROPER KNOWLEDGE OF GOD

Do analogical concepts give us, properly speaking, a knowledge of God? Frequently, "analogical knowledge" is used in contradistinction to "proper knowledge." This contrast could lead one to think that we do not, properly speaking, have any knowledge of God, or that "analogical knowledge" is knowledge simply through metaphors and symbols. To forestall such a conclusion it is appropriate to make certain distinctions respecting the phrase "proper knowledge," especially as this phrase is related to a being, God, that is not an object of our ordinary experience.

An ambiguous question. The question, "Do we have any *proper* knowledge of God?" can have several meanings. It may be equivalent to asking, "Do we have a comprehensive, adequate, and exhaustive knowledge of God?" "Do we intuit the Divine Essence?" "Do we abstract our concepts of God directly from God Himself?" "Is our knowledge perfectly proportionate to what God is in Himself?" If these are the ways in which the question is taken, then our answer must be negative: "No, we do not have any *proper* knowledge of God."

Negative, but significative, knowledge. None of our notions—not even those that are the most sophisticatedly philosophical—are perfectly proportioned to anything divine. In this sense we do not have any proper knowledge of God. God is infinitely perfect, transcending all that we can possibly conceive. But the very reasonings that make us conclude to this proposition—the very arguments that force us to deny that our notions of God are perfectly proportionate to God—also insinuate that we have some conception of the respects in which God is unlike creatures. Judgments about these particular differences are negative judgments and therefore furnish us with no intellectual *representation* of what God is; at the same time they do furnish us with quite specific negations, and these give us *significative concepts*, or at least the elements of significative concepts.

Significative concepts play an important, but not an exclusive role in the process of our acquisition of analogical knowledge. We can signify God's transcendence by the use of negations, e.g., by denying temporality of His duration, by denying multipliability of His nature, by denying composition of His being, or by denying limits of His perfection; but we cannot represent these transcendent perfections by any completely positive, proportionate concepts. Even though an idea we have may signify God's infinity (and not explicitly signify, e.g., His simplicity), this idea is not perfectly proportioned to the divine infinity; even though an idea we have may signify God's eternity, it does not positively represent, in perfect proportion, God's own eternity.

Positive response. On the other hand, the question, "Do we have any *proper* knowledge of God?" may be equivalent to asking, "Do any of the concepts that we have truly represent something that is in God?" "Are any of our propositions about God meaningful statements, statements of literal truths, not merely nonsensical affirmations or—at most—figurative expressions?" "Do we have any notions that are correctly predicated immediately of God?" "Do we have any notions that are predicated only of God?" To questions like these, we must answer, "Yes, we do have, in this sense, *proper* knowledge of God."

To deny such knowledge would be equivalent to saying that all the words that we apply to God are at best merely metaphorical expressions, symbolic terms without any positively known foundation or basis; that we know nothing that is literally true about God; and that nothing that we traditionally predicate of God is predicated according to its strict definition, its formal meaning. Metaphors and symbols are simply meaningless unless they contain some basis, some positive content that is literally true. One knows nothing about happiness if all he knows about it is that happiness is a bluebird.

Agnosticism. The agnostics, of course, even when the question is taken in the second sense just described, say, "No, we do not have any proper knowledge of God." A contemporary form of Agnosticism is held by certain modern philosophers known as "Logical Empiricists" or "Logical Positivists." For these, the knowable is only that which in principle is verifiable by someone's direct experience. One of them tells us:

> In sophisticated religions . . . the 'person' who is supposed to control the empirical world is not himself located in it; he is held to be superior to the empirical world, and so outside it; and he is endowed with super-empirical attributes. But the notion of a person whose essential attributes are non-empirical is not an intelligible notion at all. We may have a word which is used as if it names this 'person,' but, unless the sentences in which it occurs express propositions which are empirically verifiable, it cannot be said to symbolize anything . . . there cannot be any transcendent truth of religion. For the sentences which the theist uses to express such 'truths' are not literally significant.[1]

The position of the agnostics and positivists is most arbitrary and unreasonable. For, even though we do not abstract any of our notions of God directly from God, and even though God is not a proportionate object of our human intellect, still we are intelligent, reasoning beings, we can argue to the existence of a cause from its effects, and we can know of that cause such perfection as must be postulated if it is to explain the given effect. We can argue that the positive formal content of at least some of the perfections whose notions we abstract from the data of experience is literally applicable to God, and that it positively represents the perfections positively found in Him. God has to be a *being*, He has to be an *active agent*, He has to have *intellect* and *will*—or the universe around us simply does not make philosophical sense!

True, there are many other notions which are abstracted from the data of experience and which contain such formal content as to indi-

---

[1] A.J. Ayer, *Language, Truth and Logic*, 2nd ed., London, Victor Gollancz, 1951, pp. 116–118.

cate incompatibility, if taken literally, with the Supreme Being and ultimate source of all; but then we argue that God's own perfections are such as positively to exclude such formal content.

In both cases we are speaking properly of God.

In the first case we represent God through concepts of perfections common to God and to all, or at least to some, non-divine beings. Examples of such concepts are: being, life, power, knowledge, and will. These representative concepts, precisely because their content is common to God and to creatures, do not represent God *as He is in Himself*, nor even God *as He differs from creatures*; they are properly applied to God, but they are also properly applied to creatures, for they are proper to *being, as such*, or at least to *living being, as such*, or to *spiritual substance, as such*.

In the second case—where our predication consists in excluding from God qualities whose formal content (because it is formally, i.e., of its own essential nature, related to the contingent mode of existing) is incompatible with the supreme, necessarily existent being— what we say in such predication is perfectly true, namely that God is not, e.g., finite, composite, nor measured by time; since such statements are true, then we do have some concepts (negative concepts, including the denial of some positive characteristic of the data of experience) that, although they do not represent God's positive perfection, nevertheless signify it. And so we should admit that the significative ideas that we have, e.g., of God's infinity, simplicity, and eternity, do properly apply to God. It is true and proper language to say that God is infinite, is simple, and is eternal. In these cases we are speaking formally, and not metaphorically, about God.

And when we combine these negative concepts with the positive perfections that are properly predicable of both God and creatures (e.g., goodness, wisdom, and power), effecting such combinations as "infinite goodness," "eternal wisdom," and "omnipotence," then with the resultant negativo-positive concepts we have reached the climax of the process of forming our analogical knowledge of God. These negativo-positive concepts constitute the fullest, and the least inadequate notions at our disposal for conceiving God's nature and perfection. The negative, but still significative, concepts, based on negations of creaturely characteristics, and the negativo-positive concepts (partly significative and partly representative) are applicable to no other being but God, and in this sense, namely that they are predicable exclusively of God and directly designate God and not anything non-divine, they are—very much so—*proper* ideas of God. Indeed, they signify God's very *properties*, precisely because they are predicable of no caused being and yet must be predicated of the Uncaused Being.

Thus we not only have proper knowledge of God, we also have some knowledge of what is strictly and incommunicably God's, His very properties. The terms we use to describe God—some of them, at any rate—are truly, literally, formally, and non-metaphorically predicable of God; hence we do have "proper knowledge" of God.

V. DIVISION OF PERFECTIONS: PREDICAMENTAL, TRANSCENDENTAL, TRANSCENDENT

To appreciate better the norms that determine which perfections are attributable "properly" to God and which are predicated of Him only metaphorically, we must make some further distinctions. The perfections of which we humans may in some way or other form a concept, and endow with a term or name, may conveniently be divided into "predicamental perfections," "transcendental perfections," and "transcendent perfections." The first apply properly only to creatures; the last apply properly only to God; the intermediary ones apply properly both to creatures (at least, to some creatures) and to God.

A predicamental (or "mixed") perfection necessarily includes imperfection. A transcendental (or "pure" or "simple") perfection does not necessarily include imperfection, neither does it necessarily exclude imperfection. A transcendent (or "simply simple" or "strictly divine") perfection necessarily excludes imperfection (some authors invert this terminology and call the transcendent perfections "simple" and the transcendental ones "simply simple").

Examples. As examples of predicamental perfections we may list: extension, weight, color, sensation, learning, and desire. Examples of transcendental perfections are: being, life, power, knowledge, intellection, freedom, love, and happiness. Examples of transcendent perfections are: infinity, eternity, absolute immutability, omniscience, omnipotence, and utter simplicity.

PREDICAMENTAL PERFECTIONS	necessarily include imperfection	predicable properly only of creatures
TRANSCENDENTAL PERFECTIONS	do not necessarily include, do not necessarily exclude, imperfection	predicable properly both of creatures and of God
TRANSCENDENT PERFECTIONS	necessarily exclude imperfection	predicable properly only of God

VI. ORIGIN OF OUR IDEAS OF THE THREE TYPES OF PERFECTION

A. Predicamental Perfections.

These are known by us through a simple process of abstraction from the data of experience. The very nature of these known perfections, however, is such as necessarily to imply that their possessors, if existent at all, are contingently existent; for predicamental perfections cannot be self-existent but can exist only if they are caused to exist by some power distinct from themselves. We cannot conceive them according to their true, formal nature without implicitly conceiving them as pertaining to a contingently existing subject. For simplicity's sake we shall call the process of obtaining the concepts of predicamental perfections "predicamental abstraction," admitting, of course, that sometimes prolonged analysis and reflection are required if we are to discover the contingency implicit in that formal content and thus to come to know these perfections precisely *as predicamental*.

B. Transcendental Perfections.

These, too, are known to us through direct abstraction from the data of experience (we are speaking now solely of the *direct* knowledge of *what is* transcendental, not of the *reflex* knowledge *that it is* transcendental). As concretely existing in the data of experience from which they are abstracted, transcendental perfections are, as a matter of fact, embodied in a subject that is contingently existent; but there is nothing in the formal or essential nature of perfections of this kind that demands that they exist only in contingent subjects.

Any perfection whatsoever in the data of experience, *if* it is conceived *precisely as* qualifying a *contingently existent* subject, will of course be conceived as something caused, as something imperfect, as something predicamental. It will be abstracted with "predicamental abstraction," and we shall be dealing not with a transcendental perfection but with a sheerly predicamental one. But there are certain perfections in the data of experience that are not necessarily conceived precisely as qualifying a contingently existent subject, despite the fact that the beings from which we derived our concepts of them are contingent beings.

Creaturely modes not always immediately evident. Contingency, finitude, and even imperfection are not necessarily the most *immediately evident* characteristics, nor the first-known qualities, of the data of experience. "Contingency" is a refined notion acquired only after some reasoning. There may be need of a long while before a person becomes aware that the data of experience are "finite." It requires more than simple abstraction to come to know individual data as intrinsically "composite" and to know their varieties of composition. Just because our concepts are derived from beings that are contingent, finite, material, and composite does not force the content of all these concepts to represent only aspects that are, and according as they are, formally contingent, finite, material, and composite.

Perhaps I did derive my concept "wisdom" from a venerable statesman or from an experienced teacher or from a wise old grandfather—from beings, in other words, whose wisdom, however impressive, is nonetheless contingent, finite, and human (and, in some cases, accompanied with a beard). Still I do not, by "wisdom," necessarily mean "*human* wisdom," "*derived* wisdom," "*contingent* wisdom," or "*finite* wisdom." From the data of experience I can derive the notion "human wisdom" (doing so through predicamental abstraction); but I can also derive from that data the simpler notion, "wisdom." I can, and sometimes do, prescind the idea from the human and imperfect aspects of the wisdom that I find in the experience.

I shall not be conscious that I am prescinding a concept from imperfection, if I am simply conscious of the perfection. It requires reflection to know a "transcendental" *as* "transcendental"; but the positive formal content of the transcendental perfection must be in my conception without the concrete admixture of imperfection found as a matter of fact in the actual data of experience, else I cannot even ask meaningful questions such as: "Is there any wisdom not acquired by reading?" "Is there any love unmingled with desire?" "Is there any being that is not extended?" "Is there a cause that is not a caused cause?" Even an atheist should admit that it is legitimate to raise this last question.

The process, then, of obtaining notions of what are transcendental perfections is the process of "transcendental abstraction," and it furnishes us with notions of perfections that can properly and without correction be applied to God. It will not furnish us with notions that are exclusive to God, but these latter notions could not be formed at all unless it were possible for us to make "transcendental abstraction" of the "pure" or "transcendental" perfections. "Human wisdom," certainly, is not literally or properly predicated of God; but "wisdom" is, and it is a positive notion, though (unlike "omniscience") not exclusive to God. "Transcendental abstraction" will be the object of a special study, at the close of this chapter.

Subdivisions of transcendental perfections.   There are two subdivisions of "transcendental perfections." There are those that are co-extensive with *being*; these are formally possessed by absolutely every being, God included. And there are other transcendentals (such as life, knowledge, love) which are not co-extensive with *being* but do transcend the higher species and genera and are not confined by a superior limit beyond which their formal content would forbid them to go. Both types are "pure" in the sense that they do not essentially demand matter or finitude or contingency. In our treatment, "transcendental perfection" is taken to include both subdivisions.

Transcendentals proper to God and to creatures.   Transcendental perfections are correctly predicated both of God and of creatures. Every being whatsoever, from God to a microbe and on down to the most insignificant inanimate reality, is "good"; moreover, every being whatsoever is "true." Human beings are really and truly intelligent; God is not the only intelligent being. God is spiritual but is not the only spiritual being. Intellectuality is found wherever spiritual substance exists. God is free, but all intellectual substances are free, and it is not necessary that a being be uncreated in order to be intellectual.

The transcendentals are not exclusive to God, even though they pertain primarily to Him and only secondarily to other things (for they belong to God essentially and to other things only through participation, as receivers of God's bounty). Terms that are common to God and creatures are still "properly" predicated of God; but they are also properly predicated of beings that are not God and, therefore, they are not exclusively divine and do not describe to us God *as* God. Nevertheless, they have an extremely important role to play when we are forming more precise notions (the transcendent ones) of God and when we come to predicate of Him something that is at least partly positive and at least partly representative, and not totally negative nor merely significative.

C. Transcendent Perfections.

Not known by mere abstraction. Exclusively divine perfections are known to us only analogically. Our concepts of them are not derived from the object—God—of which they are the concepts, nor do these concepts positively represent God according to His own unique mode of being. Although our knowledge of these perfections presupposes abstraction of some positive transcendental note (at least the note *being*), they are not known to us merely by that abstraction. We have to do more than abstract, or prescind, from the imperfections accompanying the transcendental perfections when these are concretely realized in the data of experience. We have to add a negative judgment, separating or excluding from God the imperfection of contingency with which the positive transcendental note is materially joined in the data of experience.

The process of elaborating conceptions of the transcendent perfections is certainly not independent of experience, but it does not consist merely in an abstraction of a note from the data of experience. We make a transcendental abstraction, obtaining such notes as "being," "power," and "wisdom," and after reasoning to the impossibility of such transcendentals existing only in a predicamental way, we conclude that they must also exist in a transcendent way.

Guarantee of their validity. The guarantee of their objective validity is similar to that of the validity of our knowledge that God exists. We argued that, if we examine the data of experience, we must admit that at least some beings are produced beings, and some are producers. We then reflected on this fact and on the absolute nature of being, product, and producer, and we had to conclude that, if a being exists which is a product, then there exists some being as its ultimate producer and which is itself not a product but unproduced—otherwise there would be no beings at all in existence. Similarly, we argued that the order in the data of experience calls for a Creator endowed with what we mean by wisdom, and that, though the wisdom we know of in the data of experience is itself ordered and hence imperfect and contingent as a being, still there is no formal necessity for wisdom to be imperfect and contingent; we concluded that the Creator must have an uncaused and perfect wisdom—otherwise there would be no adequate and ultimate explanation for the order of the universe (including the contingent and imperfect wisdom of the data of experience). The arbitrariness, so to speak, of the actual *specification* of existing beings—whereas "being," as such, does not in itself call for *this* rather than *that* specification—argues to the existence of a real free will and power as the determinant of what shall exist and what shall not: an imperfect will or a dependent power would not be an ultimate explanation. "Uncaused wisdom," "perfect wisdom," and "utterly independent power and freedom" are "transcendent perfections"; they are strictly incommunicable and exclusive to the ultimate source of our universe. They are properly predicated of God, but they are not directly derived from God nor through a process of mere abstraction.

VII. HOW THE VARIOUS KINDS OF PERFECTIONS EXIST IN GOD

A. "Virtual" Existence in God of Predicamental Perfections.

God does not possess them formally. Of the positive contents that are presented by the perfections found in the data of experience, some of them are "pure"; they do not essentially or formally, simply by reason of their quiddative nature, include any imperfection. These are the "transcendental perfections" and will be discussed in a few moments in Section B. Other perfections, in their formal nature and not merely in their actual mode of being, include an admixture of imperfection, at least implicitly. To understand what they are is to realize that they contingently are. These are the so-called "mixed" perfections, or the "predicamental perfections." God does not possess these predicamental perfections *formally* or literally, according to their strict definition; if He did, He would be necessarily imperfect and contingent and therefore incapable of being their ultimate explanation.

Virtually and eminently. "To have pre-existence in the power of an efficient cause is not to have pre-existence in a more imperfect manner but to have it in a more perfect manner; although to have pre-existence in the potency of a material cause is to have it in a more imperfect manner." [2] Since God is capable of producing the predicamental perfections, He can be said to possess them *virtually*; because the manner in which God can produce them (and their effects) transcends the order of our experience, it can be said that God possesses the predicamental perfections not only virtually but also *eminently*.

This latter expression would be very misleading, however, if it amounted to saying, for example, that God is infinitely extended and sentient, and that He *reasons* to things in an infinitely perfect way.

In other words, some of the qualities of the data of experience are, by reason of their formal nature itself, known as necessarily finite, contingent, and dependent in their perfection and mode of

[2] St. Thomas, S.T., I.4.2, c.

existence. A thing, for example, cannot literally be blue and yet self-existent. If it is blue, it is extended or quantified; if it is extended, it is material and hence has passivity, dependence, and contingency as its mode of being. God, the pure act, the independent and necessary being, cannot literally be blue. He is the ultimate origin of blue things; He can produce the effects that blue things *as blue* can produce (i.e., cause certain light-waves to impinge on the retina); but God is positively immaterial in His mode of being (i.e., He is spiritual) and therefore cannot be material and hence cannot be literally, or formally, blue. Blueness cannot be a true form in God. Yet God is powerful, infinitely powerful, and able to make—indefinitely—blue things. He possesses blueness within the infinite gamut of His power; blue things exist and operate only if He wills their existence and operations. Since blue things exist in His power, that is, in His "virtue" (Latin: *virtus*, power, active force possessed in a stable manner), we say that blueness exists in God *virtually*.

B. "Formal" Presence in God of Transcendental and Transcendent Perfections.

An inconsistency of Agnosticism. A position taken by many agnostics is that none of the expressions that we use of God is capable of being sufficiently purified so as to be properly, i.e., *formally*, applied to Him. All of our expressions, they claim, are symbolic, symbolizing only the causality of God. "God is good" and "God is wise" are expressions that tell us nothing of what is positively true of God; they merely signify that God is the cause of (finitely) good things and of (relatively) wise beings or *acts as if* He were good and wise. In short, all of our predicates, in this view, are necessarily conceived as predicamental perfections and are to be attributed to God *only virtually*; there is nothing that can be attributed by us to Him formally.

The position is overly modest; indeed, it contains at least one glaring defect. Of one who insists that we know God only as He *virtually* contains the perfections of the data of experience, we would like to ask the question: Is God at least *formally the cause* of these good things and of these wise beings, etc., or is He *only virtually* that cause, and not formally, not literally, not properly? When one says that "God is wise" means only that "God is the *cause* of wise beings," does one mean that God is what we properly designate as a "cause," or does one mean only that "God is *virtually the cause* of wise beings," that is to say, "God is the *producer of the cause* of wise beings"? And if nothing that we can conceive can be conceived except predicamentally, and hence if nothing is predicable by us of God literally but, at best, only "virtually," are we to interpret the last-quoted proposition as meaning: God is the *effecter of the producer* of the cause of wise being? And then is the "effecter" to be taken only virtually, signifying the "*maker of the effecter* of the producer of the cause of wise beings"? And is this "maker" not to be understood "formally" but only "virtually," so that it does not signify literally one who makes the effecter, but "one who is the cause of a being who makes an effecter" and so forth?

Words have simply lost their meaning when even the word "cause" is said to be predicated not formally but only "virtually." To say that God is only "virtually" a cause gets us nowhere—fast! Either we have the ability to know something that is formally true of God, or it is utterly meaningless for us to say anything about Him, even that He exists or that He is the cause of what exists. It would be just as meaningful, in such a view, to say that God is an effect as to say that He is a cause, or to say that He is a stone as to say that He is a mind.

But if "cause" (active power) is formally applicable to God, why not "being"? Why not "wisdom"? Why not "goodness"? Why not "will" and "love" and "happiness" and "freedom"? There is as much need for us to admit these qualities in the transcendent source of the *ordered* universe as there is need to admit the existence of a being having such active power, that is, of a being who is the cause of the *existence* of the ordered universe.

The transcendentals. These truly and literally exist in God. They are *formally* possessed by Him. Since they do not involve the imperfection of being necessarily related to contingent existence, they may be literally predicated of God; they may be *formally* possessed by Him. Of course, since these perfections, which in their formal content are common to God and to creatures, are had by

God in His own unique, infinitely perfect way, transcendental perfections exist in God not only *formally* but also *eminently*. And since God is able to communicate these transcendental perfections to His effects and is able to produce the effects of which these transcendental perfections are capable, He can of course be said *also* to possess the transcendental perfections *virtually*. In this context "virtually" and "formally" are not mutually exclusive. We have a more perfect notion of God, however, when we know Him as "formally" possessing wisdom than when we know Him only as "virtually" wise.

The transcendent perfections. These exist *formally* in God. Indeed, they are the perfections that *par excellence* describe God, for they take us as far as we can go in philosophical knowledge and describe, as accurately as it is possible for our natural faculties, what is divine. We should not say that the transcendent perfections are possessed by God *virtually*, since they are strictly incommunicable and cannot exist as caused perfections. For they are either the expressly divine modes of being (for example: eternity, infinity, utter simplicity), or are positive transcendental notes formally qualified by such modes (for example: infinite love, omniscience, eternal goodness, immutable justice). Neither should they be said to be possessed by God *eminently*, for this term would add nothing. These perfections precisely *constitute God's eminence*. It is no real help to philosophical language to say that God is "infinitely infinite," "eternally eternal," or even "infinitely eternal" or "eternally omnipotent," and so forth. God is transcendent; there is no need to say, and no advantage in saying, that He is transcendently transcendent.

	POSSESSED BY GOD		
PREDICAMENTAL PERFECTIONS	virtually	eminently	not formally
TRANSCENDENTAL PERFECTIONS	virtually	eminently	formally
TRANSCENDENT PERFECTIONS	not virtually	not eminently	formally

VIII. ANALYSIS OF THE PROCESS OF TRANSCENDENTAL ABSTRACTION

Because transcendental abstraction seems to be the hurdle at which the agnostics balk, and because it is nonetheless of key importance in the process of forming proper concepts of God, i.e., in our coming to know anything that is *formally* in God, we must now go into some detail concerning it.

Sensing and understanding.   In substance we are simply trying to show that humans have a capacity for *understanding* the data of experience and for grasping and communicating *meanings*. Not all of our knowledge is sense-knowledge. The intellect finds in the data of experience, which affect us first through our senses, aspects which do not affect the senses. The eyes see two things which are similar; the mind sees their similarity, and it may even know why they happen to be similar. We have intellectual knowledge of what affects the senses, but intellectual knowledge is not sensation. We have phantasms of triangular shapes, but no sense can tell us whether—and why—the three angles involved in any triangle are equal to two right angles. There are intelligible notes even in the sensible qualities of things, but not all intellection is an understanding of what a *sensible thing* is, for it can as well be an understanding simply of what a *thing* is.

Our human condition as substantial units of matter and spirit brings along certain intellectual risks. We live in danger of thinking of every perfection as predicamental. The agnostics and Logical Positivists have simply succumbed before the danger. A predicamental perfection, as we saw earlier, is one whose formal content, or nature, includes, at least implicitly, a necessary relationship to contingent existence. Now, obviously, if our concepts include notes incompatible with necessary existence, or with self-existence, they cannot be properly applied to God. Hence words and concepts indicating matter, passive potentiality, finitude, imperfection, or contingency are all predicable only of non-divine beings. If they are applied to God at all, this will be through symbolism or through figurative usage. And if we are guided by our imagination and phantasy instead of by our intellectual operations, or if we use our intellects only to grasp—in an abstractive and universalizing fashion—the sensible aspects of things (quantity, shape, greenness, etc.), then we shall be forced to think and speak of God in terms that can apply to Him only figuratively or metaphorically.

Metaphors need a basis in a literal predication. It is meaningless to claim that the words and concepts we form are even figurative, unless we have a true and proper concept of some basic nonmetaphorical perfection that we intend to signify. If "being" simply means "purple mouse," then certainly God is not a "being." If "being" is only "sensible being," again God is not a "being." If "being" is we-know-not-what, then it is impossible to say whether or not God is a being, whether or not He even exists. Agnosticism about God's nature is, in truth, not very far removed from atheism. The foundation of our symbols and metaphors about God must be something literally and properly predicable of God, and it must be known as such by us; else our symbols are not even symbolical, for they will not be symbolizing anything, and our metaphors are not even metaphors, for they will be figures of speech that are nothing but speech with nothing figured at all.

Danger of mere sensism. The danger we have been discussing —of thinking of every perfection as predicamental, as having no aspects but sensible ones, whether these sensible aspects are judged to be accessible also to intellectual knowledge or not—comes from our tendency to read into our concepts too much of what affects our sense-experience, to read into them the images of their accompanying phantasms, and to fail to use our understanding to attain what is intelligible, but not sensible, in the data furnished us originally by our senses (including the imagination and memory).

Accompanying all our concepts are phantasms. These phantasms are produced by a sense-faculty and necessarily represent material conditions (e.g., extension, color, configuration, weight, succession). But our human cognoscitive faculties are not confined to knowing merely the sensible aspects of reality. "The knowable" is not the same thing as "the sensible." All objects, even the most sensuous of them, have intelligible aspects that can be grasped by our intellect. We must not think of the intelligible aspects of reality as merely vague representations of sensible aspects. The intelligible note "being" is not a mere oblong blur; the note "power" is not the image of Atlas's muscles. We must not think that whatever we can signify we can also represent and even picture.

Phantasm and intellectual representation. If we signify something merely by negations or exclusions, we are not representing it; but neither must we hold that whatever is represented is necessarily only what is imagined. Positive notes are needed for representative ideas, but the human intellect—and not merely the human imagination—is capable of representing these positive notes. An intellectual representation, however, is not at all a mere vague shadow of a phantasm: it is a penetrating insight into the quiddative aspects of an object; it is the intellectual grasp of positive notes; and it is an act of *understanding*, of coming to know the ontological structure of the object imagined, and of detecting certain absolute and necessary relations in that object.

Example. There is a world of difference between *seeing* a wagon wheel (as a result of certain light rays impinging on the retina of the eye) and *understanding* a circle, knowing what a circle is, and intellectually "seeing" its inner nature (the relationships of line, center, distance, radii, etc.). The eye sees a wagon wheel or a hoop, and this sensible image may be stored up more or less accurately in the sense memory or in the imagination. But the intellect understands a circle —positively so—and this intelligible grasp—of quantity, surface, circularity, line, center, radii, and their mutual relations—is an intellectual representation of the intelligible aspects of the circle concretized as the hoop. This act of understanding is not a vague, elusive imitating of the phantasm. For shifting imagery and for vagueness, look not to the idea but to the phantasm! What the intellect represents is permanent, definite, applicable to any existing circle, and a definitive criterion for judging how closely or how remotely existing configurations (e.g., a hoop) come to being circular. The phantasm, however, with its fuzzy edges and wobbly configuration, is perhaps verifiable in no existing circle whatsoever.

The understanding of necessary properties and relations. An existing piece of wood, triangular in shape, painted brown, weighing half a pound, and used as a paper-weight, has a great number of aspects according to which it can be known—intellectually as well as sensibly. Capable of being seen, felt, smelt, and tasted, it can also be known as something existent, substantial, material, wooden, triangular, and heavy. Each of these latter aspects is an intelligible note terminating, or capable of terminating, an apprehension on the part of the human knower. Just because it is wooden does not keep it from being triangular—nor, on the other hand, does the "woodenness" demand that it be triangular. We understand that the combination is a coincidence, a contingent event. Just because it is triangular in shape does not keep it from being substantial; just because we know it is something brown does not prevent us from deriving from it the less determinate but nonetheless knowable note "something colored," and even "something existent."

Each of these quiddative aspects has some property or related quality necessarily belonging to the subject in question (the paperweight) precisely because of the particular nature of the quiddative aspect that is being considered in the paper-weight. Thus, because the paper-weight is triangular, the angles are equal to two right angles; because it is bounded by plane sides and has an appropriate center of gravity, it can stand upright on a smooth surface; because it is heavy and comparatively impenetrable, it is capable of exercising a certain causality on certain other objects; because it is something real—a being—it cannot be itself and not itself at the same moment under the same aspect. It is not precisely because it is wooden that it obeys the law of contradiction—wooden things, of course, do obey that law and are, therefore, not simultaneously non-wooden things —nor because it is something material, nor finite, nor contingent, but because it is a being. As wooden, the paper-weight obeys certain other laws, e.g., the chemical laws governing dry cellulose; but it obeys the law of contradiction because it is a being.

The various aspects, therefore, in the objects of our experience have their own necessary concomitant relationships or properties, and at least some of these necessary relationships and properties are detectible by the human understanding. Otherwise, we should never have *understood* anything, we should never have had any acts of knowing except our sensations—and this belies experience. We see the wooden triangle lying on top of the paper, we see the paper which is staying on top of the desk, and we simultaneously feel the wind that is blowing; but we not only see and feel all this, we also understand—from our knowledge of the nature of relative weights and momentum and friction—that the wood, because of its heaviness and friction (and not precisely because it is wooden nor because it is triangular) is keeping the paper from being blown away.

Applications to God. Let us apply this analysis to some of the terms that we predicate of God. Any perfection that exists in a creature, whether that perfection in itself is a predicamental one or a transcendental one, exists with the creaturely mode of existence, to wit, contingency; although whatever exists in creatures also exists in God (the predicamental perfections virtually, the transcendental ones formally), it does not exist in God according to the creaturely, or contingent, mode of existence. The predicamental perfections are produced perfections or simply do not exist at all; it is impossible that they should exist except as products. Their mode of being enters into the very intelligible structure of their specific reality. A being endowed with eyesight is necessarily a material being, hence mutable, hence contingent. God cannot be contingent; therefore God cannot be literally endowed with eyesight. If we say that God "sees" all things, we are speaking metaphorically.

Use of metaphors in speaking about God. Religious writings abound in symbols and figurative language. Sacred Scripture is constantly using metaphors: "He that planted the ear, shall He not hear?, or He that formed the eye, doth He not consider?"; [3] "Have pity on me, have pity on me, at least you my friends, because the hand of the Lord hath touched me."; [4] "In Thy anger Thou wilt tread the earth under foot." [5] Metaphors are extremely useful and can be readily justified, but they would be totally useless unless they presupposed some underlying literal meaning which we would be able to understand. In the case of God, this underlying perfection must not be predicamental but transcendental. We may wish to affirm that God has a direct, immediate, and intuitive *knowledge* of all things past, present, and future. To accentuate this fact, to make it strike others in vivid fashion, and to emphasize the reality of this knowledge, we symbolize God's act of knowing by the word "sees." We do not mean to attribute a visual sense to God, nor do we mean that God has two eyes (or even one eye), optic nerves, retina, and

[3] *Psalm* 93: 9.
[4] *Job* 19: 21.
[5] *Habacuc* 3: 12.

so forth; but we do mean—and we mean this literally—that He has an infallible comprehensive awareness of the nature and existence of all that is, and that He is certain of the past, present, and future. Since we tend spontaneously to consider that we ourselves are most certain of what we *see* present before our very eyes, we illustrate God's knowledge with metaphorical terms and say "God sees" or refer to "the eye of God."

"Knowledge" and contingency. God does not literally "see," but He does literally "know"; for knowledge is not the sort of perfection that is existible in contingent beings only. At least, this is not implied in what we mean by knowledge (unlike the implicit meaning, "related to matter and contingency," involved in "visual knowledge"). Hence there is no evidence, in the nature of knowledge as such, that a being endowed with knowledge is necessarily a contingent being. We can understand what knowledge is without judging whether the knower is dog, man, angel, or God. We do not mean here to affirm that we can understand the positive possibility of a concrete "knowledge" that is in no wise contingent; all we insist is that if there is knowledge which is contingent, the contingency is due to a factor which is not essential to, nor contained in, what we understand and mean by "knowledge."

"Knowledge" and "learning." But even on the level of intellectual knowledge we might be inclined to slip into errors, e.g., to confuse that which is characteristic of *human* intellectual knowledge with what is essential simply to *knowledge*. "Knowledge" is one thing, "learning" is another, even though we frequently use the words as though they were synonyms. Still, a process and its term (its end result) are not altogether identical. We may say that such and such a man has a vast amount of "learning," meaning that he has acquired a great fund of knowledge. But the "learning" is really the process of acquiring the knowledge, whereas the knowledge itself is not the process but the thing acquired. It is not necessary, however, to conclude that no being has any knowledge who has not undergone a process of learning.

Figurative language has habituated us to use what are processes and what are terms of processes interchangeably. Yet a little reflection will convince us that we do not have to consider knowledge as a term of a process at all. You do not have to go to school to acquire knowledge; it often helps, but it is not absolutely necessary. If someone answers perfectly the many subtle questions on a TV quiz program, we tend to say that "he surely knows a lot" (or has a good prompter!), even if we consider the items of his information of little value except as a means of winning TV prizes. But whether the quiz program genius went to school or not; whether he had a private tutor or not; whether he got his wealth of knowledge from books, by private investigation, or through telepathy; whether he was born already knowing it (endowed with innate ideas) or gets infused knowledge from some unidentified source—still, so long as he answers the questions correctly, we would say, in all these cases, that he is manifestly in possession of much knowledge. The origin or source of that knowledge is one thing, but it is not the actual knowledge itself. Whether the person had to learn it the hard way, whether he learned it the easy way, or whether he never learned it at all but simply always knew it, we still are entitled to say, literally, that he has knowledge.

To know is one thing; *to have acquired knowledge* is another. The one is transcendental; the other is predicamental. If a knower has acquired his knowledge, that knower is not a self-existent being and hence is not God. Our admission of this fact is not based on any arbitrary or *a priori* grounds; we are not arguing from a bias (as though we already know in advance that God has a knowledge that is unacquired, and so make the claim that it is not necessary for knowledge, as such, to be something acquired). We are arguing from an analysis of what precisely it is that we mean by being a knower and what we mean by knowledge. The analysis is possible prior to knowing God's existence. It is possible even to an atheist.

"Knowledge" predicable of God.   If we have purified the notion, we should be ready to concede that it is not a predicamental perfection but a transcendental perfection and that it does not have to be excluded from God merely by reason of its own nature. That God actually is a knower is argued to from the order and intelligibility of the universe—facts which demand the existence of an intelligent producer. God's way of knowing, and God's knowledge itself, must certainly be transcendently superior to that of creaturely knowers, but our proper notion of "knowledge" does not have to be emptied of its literal meaning and turned into a vacuous symbol in order to be predicated of God. It applies properly, though not exclusively, to God. The same is to be said of the other transcendentals (e.g., life, will, freedom, happiness) that we apply to God.

"Transcendent knowledge." To make "knowledge" or "wisdom" not only properly predicable of God, but also predicable as an exclusive property of God, we must transform it by the addition of some negation, a negation which absolutely excludes the contingency to which, in its "impure" state, it is subject. By denying the contingency and imperfection by which knowledge is accompanied when it is found in the data of experience, we are qualifying it with something that separates the formal content, "knowledge" or "wisdom," from its created subjects and that signifies the transcendence of its uncreated subject. Reasoning on the impossibility of an ordered universe existing as a result of an agent that has only predicamental wisdom, we judge that wisdom or knowledge must exist, in its literal meaning but in a transcendent mode, in the ultimate cause of the universe.

There may not be very many positive and negativo-positive notions that we can correctly form about God; still, "the least that can be known about the noblest realities is more desirable than the most certain knowledge about the lowest types of beings." [6]

LEADING IDEAS of Chapter 5

1. Since the adequate explanation of the data of experience must "transcend" these data, and since the objects whose knowability is proportioned to our human intellect are precisely these data, a problem arises: what validity have the concepts that we form of God?

2. As First Cause, God must in some way possess the perfection found in His effects, but He Himself cannot possess it as an effected perfection, nor in any manner that would imply contingency.

3. We have no "proper" knowledge of God in the sense of knowledge directly proportioned to God as He is in Himself; we do have some "proper" knowledge of Him in the sense that we can understand in a literal and not merely in a metaphorical sense many terms predicated of God.

[6] St. Thomas, S.T., I.1.5, ad 1m.

4. A "predicamental perfection" includes in its formal content, at least implicitly, an admixture of imperfection, and so can exist in God only virtually, not formally; a "transcendental perfection" does not include in its formal content an admixture of imperfection, and so can exist in God formally as well as virtually; a "transcendent perfection" positively excludes all, even implicit, admixture of imperfection, and so can be found in God formally, indeed is found exclusively in God and is predicable of God not only properly but even as a strictly divine property.

5. Though the "transcendental perfections" (e.g., being, activity, knowing, willing) are first known by us from the data of experience, where they are verified in a predicamental manner, still we can abstract from such modes; the resultant concepts give us whatever positive and representative knowledge we have about God, even though reasoning, not mere abstraction, is required if we are to know that we must, and therefore can, predicate them of God.

6. Sometimes, for rhetorical purposes, we predicate predicamental perfections of God; in such cases, these are to be taken as metaphors or symbols and presuppose our knowledge of their foundation in some transcendental or transcendent perfection that is literally predicable of God.

7. The human intellect grasps, even in the data of sensible experience, intelligible aspects and necessary relationships, some of which do not formally include imperfection; these when qualified by the "negative attributes" (those that describe God's excluding of the modes of creaturely perfections) give us our best descriptions of God, the "negativo-positive attributes" such as omnipotence, infinite goodness, omniscience, eternal wisdom, and immutable happiness.

SUGGESTED READINGS for Chapter 5

For Scholastic Exposition:

St. Thomas. S.T. I.12.12 and I.13.1–6 (*Basic Writings*, Vol. I, pp. 109–110 and 112–122). *De Pot.* 7.4–7 (*Power of God*, Vol. 3, pp. 18–46).

D.J.B. Hawkins. *The Essentials of Theism.* New York: Sheed and Ward, 1950, pp. 90–98.

M.R. Holloway, S.J. *An Introduction to Natural Theology.* New York: Appleton-Century-Crofts, 1959, pp. 172–227.

G.H. Joyce, S.J. *Principles of Natural Theology.* London: Longmans, Green and Co., 1934, pp. 236–275.

C.G. Kossell, S.J. "Principles of St. Thomas' Distinction between the

Esse and *Ratio* of Relations," *The Modern Schoolman*, Vol. 24, 1946–47, pp. 33–35.

Expositions on a Popular Level:

R. Knox. *The Hidden Stream*. New York: Sheed and Ward, 1953, pp. 34–44.

C.S. Lewis. *Miracles*. London: Bles, 1952, Chapters 10 and 11.

E.L. Mascall. *Words and Images, a Study in Theological Discourse*. New York: Ronald, 1957, pp. 106–108.

On Problems Arising from Modern Linguistic Analysis:

W. Norris Clarke, S.J. "Linguistic Analysis and Natural Theology," *Proceedings of the American Catholic Philosophical Association*, Vol. 34, 1960, pp. 110–126.

C.B. Daly. "The Knowableness of God," *Philosophical Studies* (Maynooth, Ireland), Vol. 9, 1959, pp. 90–137.

M.J. Charlesworth. "Linguistic Analysis and Language about God," *International Philosophical Quarterly*, Vol. I, 1961, pp. 139–167.

A Passage to Evoke Discussion:

W.T. Stace. *Religion and the Modern Mind*. Philadelphia: J.P. Lippincott, 1952, pp. 221–222.

CHAPTER

6

OUTLINE

OUTLINE (continued)

A. "God Is Pure Act"; "God Is Pure Actuality"

B. "God Is Perfect"; "God Is All-Perfect (Omniperfect, Absolutely Perfect)"

C. "God Is Perfect Being"; "God Is Subsistent Being"; "God Is Being Itself"

V. *Misconceptions Concerning the Infinite*

A. "The Infinite" Not the Same as "The Incomplete," "The Indefinite," "The Indeterminate"

B. "The Infinite" Not the Same as "The All"

OUTLINE (continued)

God's Transcendent Perfection— the Divine Infinity

I. GENERAL INTRODUCTION TO THE DIVINE ATTRIBUTES

Anything that is literally and correctly predicable of God may be called an "attribute of God." Thus we are accustomed to list among God's attributes eternity, omniperfection, goodness, infinity, knowledge, power, infinite power, immensity, infinite perfection, omnipotence, omnipresence, omniscience, etc. Or, expressing the situation with adjectives and adverbs instead of with nouns, we say, for example, that God is eternal, wise, powerful, all-perfect, infinite, immutably just, infinitely good, etc. But if we are to appreciate the real meaning of the various attributes applied to God, we must make certain distinctions and amplifications.

Some of these attributes are conceived by us in a strictly positive fashion through abstraction ("transcendental abstraction," we called it in the previous chapter) from the data of experience. Attributes that we conceive in purely positive fashion are not exclusive to God, nor are they strictly attributes of divine being as divine; they are properties of being as being, or of spiritual being as spiritual, and so forth.

Some others of the attributes that we predicate of God strictly do nothing but describe God's *manner* (or *mode*) of existing, God's way of having, in the concrete, whatever it is that He has; rather, they tell us that God's mode of possessing a perfection is not the mode that characterizes, in this or that way, the data of experience. They attribute to God, for example, non-contingency, non-dependence, non-finitude, and non-causedness. Such attributes we call "negative attributes." They are, assuredly, exclusive to God; in fact, they imply God's transcendent mode of possessing perfection; but they furnish us with no positive representation of God.

145

The best predications of all combine the pure, or transcendental, perfections with a mode that negates the imperfection of non-divine reality; these combinations effect the "negativo-positive" attributes (e.g., omniscience, omnipotence, eternal knowledge, and infinite love).

A. The Negative Attributes.

The data of experience manifest the contingency of their being in many and various ways; for example, they are finite in whatever perfections they have, that is to say, they have limitations and imperfections. They are composite (being a "subject" determined or actuated by various forms or perfections). Their natures are multipliable within their species. They are mutable. They are measured by time and space. When analysis has revealed ways or modes that characterize the data of experience precisely *qua* contingent, then we know we are confronted with modes that cannot possibly be literally predicated of the being who is the ultimate explanation of the data, for modes that imply contingency and dependence implicitly aver that the subjects they modify are beings that are caused or produced. The necessary existent cannot be characterized by such modes of being. We are forced to conceive Him with concepts which presuppose the judgment that His nature is a positive reality whose very perfection positively excludes the modes or manners of being that characterize the data of experience *qua* contingent.

Contingent Mode That Is Excluded	Resultant Negative Attribute of God
FINITUDE	INFINITY
COMPOSITION	SIMPLICITY
MULTIPLIABILITY	UNICITY
MUTABILITY	IMMUTABILITY
TEMPORAL MEASURABILITY	ETERNITY
SPATIAL MEASURABILITY	IMMENSITY

Importance of the negative attributes. These negative attributes (we have listed six of the main ones, but the list is not exhaustive) are extremely important in our effort to learn something about God's nature or essence. These negative ways of describing God are the means we have for keeping our ideas from being anthropomorphic; they guarantee us that we are not reading human terms and creaturely perfections into what is strictly divine. The negative attributes do not, except in an extremely general fashion, tell us *what* God is; rather, they tell us—in a negative manner—*how* God is *whatever* He is; they tell us some of the ways in which God transcends the data of experience. We know from them simply that God is so perfect and so positively perfect in what intrinsically and positively constitutes Him that His perfections cannot be, for instance, finite, mutable, composite, multipliable, or measured in terms of time and space.

The negative attributes, obviously, are enough, if proven objective, to enable us to distinguish God from all that is not God. By them, therefore, one excludes the very possibility of pantheism, the pseudo-philosophy that teaches that all reality is substantially divine and constitutes but one being: God. The negative attributes, however, are not conceived by us through notions derived directly from God (even though they apply only to Him). They are known by us through factitious ideas, involving in their formation the important process of negative judgment.

Introductory proofs of the negative attributes. As a sort of first perspective, and in order to indicate where we shall be going in the present chapter and the four subsequent ones, we here present in extremely condensed form arguments establishing these six negative attributes. The elaboration of the meaning and proofs will come later.

1. Whatever is finite is caused;
   But God is not caused;
   Therefore God is not finite—but *infinite*.

2. Whatever is composite is caused;
   But God is not caused;
   Therefore God is not composite—but *simple*.

3. Only when a nature can be conceived as prescinding from individuality, hence, as indifferent to this or that individuality, can it be conceived as multipliable;
   But divine nature cannot be conceived as prescinding from individuality;
   Therefore divine nature cannot be conceived as multipliable —but is *unique*.

4. Whatever is mutable is composite;
   But God is not composite;
   Therefore God is not mutable—but *immutable*.

5. Whatever is measurable by time is mutable;
   But God is not mutable;
   Therefore God is not measurable by time—but is *eternal*.

6. Whatever is measurable circumscriptively by quantity is material, and whatever is measurable definitively by quantity is finite in power;
   But God is not material, nor is He finite in power;
   Therefore God is not measurable by quantity either circumscriptively or definitively—but is *immense*.

B. The Positive Attributes and the Negativo-Positive Attributes.

The positive attributes of God are those perfections that can be predicated directly and formally of God and are properly conceived by the human mind without the need of making a negative judgment excluding this or that note or imperfection. They are the "transcendental perfections" discussed in the preceding chapter, and they tell us something positive about God. They tell us, for example, that God is good, true, beautiful, wise, free, and happy.

How positive attributes are made strictly divine. So long as these predicates are not qualified by one or other of the negative attributes—implicitly or explicitly—then these predicates, though correctly, properly, and formally predicable of God, are common to God and to (at least some) creatures; hence they are not predicable exclusively of God, as strictly *divine* properties. Not only God, but every being, is good. Not only God, but every being, is true. Not only God, but every spiritual substance, is free. But if a concept—"goodness" for example—is qualified by the term "infinite" or "uncreated" or "subsistent," then the result—"infinite goodness," "uncreated goodness," "subsistent goodness"—is a strictly divine predicate; it is an exclusive property of God; it is an attribute of God and only of God. "Infinite goodness" is correctly predicated of God, and it contains something quite positive in its content, but it does not represent God in an entirely positive manner, since it is qualified by the negatively conceived mode, "infinite." It is, therefore, the sort of attribute that most deserves the name "divine attribute," since it is not merely something that gives us some positive knowledge and can be *correctly* predicated of its subject, but something that is characteristic of, *exclusive* to, that subject; it is a property and not a merely logical accident of God. Only God is "eternally wise," "independently powerful," etc.

We can now turn to our detailed presentation of the "negative attributes," the attributes that express the divine transcendence over the characteristics of the data of experience. And first, the attribute "infinity," which expresses God's transcendent perfection in general.

II. MEANING OF THE STATEMENT, "GOD IS TRANSCENDENTLY PERFECT"

Difficulty in the phrase. Although by reason of our Judaeo-Christian background we are used to admitting the fact of God's infinity, it is not easy for reason, unenlightened by revelation and faith, to establish the fact. Indeed, there is even great difficulty in clarifying precisely what we are affirming when we say that "God is perfect," or "is all-perfect" ("omniperfect"), or "is subsistent perfection," or "is pure actuality," or "is being itself," or "is infinite," or "is infinitely perfect."

This last phrase ("God is infinitely perfect") is, in our opinion, the one that stresses most the transcendence of God and is the most accurate and significant when discussing the transcendent perfection of God. But we shall not be quibblers over mere expressions; in the present textbook all the phrases we have just used are ultimately intended to signify the transcendent perfection of the Being Who is God. Just what do we mean, however, when we say that "God is transcendently perfect"?

Meaning.   We mean that God's very being has no imperfections in any line at all and no limits in any order at all. We mean that God has all actual perfection in the highest degree, or rather, that He has it beyond all degrees, beyond all comparisons, and that He has it without any limits, so that in His case nothing in any line or order of excellence is, or can be, lacking. His perfection is His being, and His being is inexhaustible. If He is good (and "every being is good"), then He is good without limits. If He is true (and "every being is true"), then He is infinitely true. He not only has beauty; He is beautiful beyond all bound. He is not merely just and merciful and loving; no element whatsoever of perfect justice, mercy, and love is, or can be, absent from His consummate being. He is not merely patient; His patience simply cannot be exhausted. He is not merely wise; there is absolutely nothing knowable that He does not know, and He exhausts the intelligibility of all that is knowable (He is "omniscient"). He not only has power; He is powerful without limits, all-powerful ("omnipotent"), infinitely powerful. He is utter reality, reality without limits. Infinitely perfect in every line of being, endowed with every perfection that is "existible," He is— in one concentrated phrase—Infinite Being.

We mean by God's transcendent perfection the actuality of in-exhaustible richness or "nobility" or excellence; we mean the meas-ureless intensity of perfection. No finite intensity, no matter how many times multiplied, will commensurate or exhaust the infinite; it simply will never reach it. Indeed, it will never even approximate it, no matter what the intensifications given it. There simply is no terminus to the divine perfection. It is full, complete, and perfect— yes; but it is not bounded, there are no norms or measures for it, and it has no limits. There is no non-being at which the divine per-fection would finally terminate. Non-being is infra-being, not ultra-being. There are no upper limits to being, no finite "maximum" be-yond which perfection would suddenly become non-being.

We cannot grasp the positively infinite—not because it is too hazy and vague and indefinite, but rather because the positively infinite transcends the finite powers of our human intellect. We cannot gaze upon the noonday sun. This does not mean that the sun is hazy or vague or indefinite, but that its inherent brightness surpasses our visual powers.

Implications of omnipotence. Being omnipotent, God is the virtual and eminent equivalent of all the perfections in the data of experience, for whatever exists in creatures exists eminently in their creative cause. This statement presupposes, of course, something that is explicitly proved only in the following chapter, namely, the uniqueness, the non-plurality, of the uncaused, or necessarily existent, being. But if we do admit that there is, and can be, only one uncaused being, then we must admit that all other realities are caused by Him, therefore that He is "formally" endowed with power and with whatever else is needed to account for their being, and that He contains at least "virtually" and "eminently" all the perfections of all other things and is, therefore, "omniperfect."

This implication furnishes the foundation for some beautiful metaphors which are of help to the religious imagination in its ascent to God. Leonard Lessius (died 1623) does not fail to capitalize on these perfections that are virtually and eminently possessed and gives us a vivid realization of the infinite beauty, wealth, and grandeur of the God Whom we ourselves shall possess in Heaven. He writes:

(God) is the immense ocean of being. In Him there are infinite worlds, infinite species of angels, one excelling the other, on and on through infinity; infinite nations of peoples, infinite species of animals, infinite natures and varieties of plants, of minerals and precious stones. There is an infinity of gold and silver in Him; there are infinite pearls of rarest size, and every description of precious stones. There are infinite species of colors, of paintings, of harmonies, of fragrances, of savors and delectable objects of the flesh and the senses; infinite regions and cities, and fields and forests, and groves and gardens; infinite fountains and hills; infinite rivers and seas, infinite palaces and temples, infinite furnishings of every kind and of inestimable price. In Him finally are contained an infinite abundance of all that the mind can conceive that is precious and beautiful and splendid and delectable. All these things and an infinity of others that no created intellect can grasp, exist in the essence, wisdom and omnipotence of God, and shine before His mind in such a manner that He can with a single sign of His will produce them outside of Himself in all conceivable multitudes and splendors. Hence it follows that whoever possesses God possesses at the same time all those things and enjoys them in God in a most exalted manner.[1]

III. INTIMATIONS OF WHAT IS MEANT BY "GOD IS INFINITELY PERFECT"

Commonplace personifications. Some intimations of the meaning of the phrases that we apply to God in order to describe His transcendent perfection can possibly be furnished us when we recall that even in our more ordinary ways of speaking we sometimes "substantialize" a creaturely perfection (or defect), we "personify" it, and we attribute infinite intensity to it. We spontaneously use figures of speech to give rhetorical emphasis. We use "hyperbole" and "personification." Thus we refer to the "living truth." We say, "Now, there's Progress for you!" We say that this or that picture is "consummate art" or that such or such a person is "the personification of holiness," "holiness itself," or "walking sanctity." We find that some things are "sheer delight" or "pure joy" (not: "they contain a pure joy," but: "they *are* pure joy"). We find a friend so wonderful that we call him "goodness incarnate." In the other direction, and in our bleaker moods, we style some situations "utter confusion" (not: "the situation is confused," nor: "the situation contains some confused and confusing phenomena," but bluntly: "the situation itself *is* utter *confusion*"). We refer to the statements of people whom we dislike as "utter nonsense" or "*being* sheer stupidity" (not just: "*containing* something stupid").

We do have some inkling, therefore, even apart from philosophical and theological training, of what one is trying to express when he speaks of God as "Pure Actuality," as "Sheer Reality," as "Being Personified," as "Being Itself."

[1] L. Lessius, S.J., *The Names of God*, New York, The America Press, 1912, pp. 8 and 9 (we have slightly altered the translation of T.J. Campbell, S.J.).

IV. EXPRESSIONS THAT ARE EQUIVALENTS OF, OR ALLIED TO, "GOD IS INFINITELY PERFECT"

There are a great number of words and phrases that, for all practical purposes, are synonymous with, or certainly allied to and explicative of, "infinitely perfect." Thus God is called "pure act," "pure actuality," or "subsistent existence"; He is said to be "perfect," "omniperfect," "absolutely perfect," or "all-perfect." Let us pause a while on a few of these expressions.

A. "God Is Pure Act"; "God Is Pure Actuality."

This means that God is nothing but perfection, the complete fullness of perfection. He has no potency, no capacity, for further perfection, not because He has "capacities" which happen to be already filled (God is a source, a fountainhead, not a basin!), but because He positively excludes potency and receptivity. He is not constituted of a potential subject that is actuated by perfection (though, of course, our judgments and propositions necessarily make Him a grammatical subject with logical predicates or attributes). He is utterly simple and perfect. He is independent, self-sufficient, subsistent perfection, subsistent actuality, and a subsistent act of being. He is subsistent existence—not an existent specified to such and such a level, that is, an existence collocated by its essence to some particular realm within the indefinite gamut of the existibles. For He is not limited to only a part of what "being" can be; He is, rather, the unreceived fullness of being; He is Being. He is perfect actuality (actuality that is of itself perfect); He is perfection that is of itself actual.

B. "God Is Perfect"; "God Is All-Perfect (Omniperfect, Absolutely Perfect)."

That is to say, God has all the perfection possible. He has all the perfections of all beings and has them to the fullest degree possible. He is "infinitely perfect"; if one so wishes to express the matter, He has the fullest degree possible of perfection; more strictly, He has perfection in an inexhaustible degree, indeed, He has it beyond the realm of comparisons and measurements, for He is outside the order where it is meaningful to speak of "degrees" and "measures." He has a limitless intensity, an intensity not measurable in any finite terms at all. His perfection and any creaturely perfection are not commensurable, no matter how much the creaturely perfection is increased or intensified or multiplied.

For God to be measurable by a finite but indefinitely applied measure of creaturely perfection (that is, for God to be measured by a ceaseless application of a creature's finite perfection) would mean that at least a part of God's perfection is commensurate with a part (or with the whole) of the creaturely perfection in question. But God has no parts to His perfection; He is transcendently perfect. He is not just more perfect than creatures with respect to the ("transcendental") perfections that, through analogy, we attribute both to God and to creatures. God is not just more perfect being than the data of our experience; He is not just more wise than they are, He is not just more holy. His being, His wisdom, and His holiness belong to a different realm; they are immeasurably superior to the being, wisdom, and holiness of the data of our experience. God is not just a more perfect being than any being of experience nor just a *de facto* or relative *maximum*. He is Perfect Being, a *de jure maximum*; He is supremely being, Supreme Being, an absolute that is beyond measurement.

C. "God Is Perfect Being"; "God Is Subsistent Being"; "God Is Being Itself."

God is not merely a perfect *kind of being*. He is not merely perfect in a certain line of being, order of being, or level or degree of being, but is perfect in the very note "being," itself.

Various contexts of "perfect." The word "perfect" is of course used in many contexts. But its ordinary usage is to indicate that the subject it qualifies is *complete*, is fully actual, and has no further potency or capacity for being actuated *with respect to some particular quality under consideration* or *with respect to some particular order* in which the subject is said to be perfect. A thing is perfect in a certain order when nothing is lacking to it with respect to what is possible in that order.

Thus we speak of a perfect crystal, a perfect bloom, a perfect day, a perfect statue, a perfect marksman, or a perfect executive. We say that John got a "perfect grade" in the algebra test. In this case we obviously do not mean that John knows all that is to be known about any subject whatsoever, nor even all that is to be known as regards algebra; we mean simply that in the particular area with which the test was concerned, John manifested a complete knowledge, and so his score was "perfect." We even speak of a perfect nuisance, namely, a complete, total, unqualified nuisance; a nuisance unmingled with anything attenuating its nuisance value; a sheer, unmitigated, unvarnished nuisance. We speak, too, of perfect crimes, e.g., the perfect murder. Sometimes, in order to accentuate the completeness of the being in question, we go outside its order or species to describe it. Thus, the gentleman whose opinion we despise is "a perfect ass." Or, on a nobler level, we call our neighbor's child "a perfect angel." We say that this or that is "perfectly obvious," "perfectly sober," "perfectly ridiculous," "perfectly harmless," "perfectly wonderful," or "perfectly delicious."

"Perfect being" and "perfect kind of being." Commonly, the order in which a being is "perfect" is a restricted order, is one of the sectors (one of the indefinite multitude of sectors) of reality or being. When this is so, then the "perfect being" in question is only relatively perfect. It is not absolutely perfect; it is not perfect precisely in the order or line of "being." If someone calls it *"a* perfect being," he would mean that it is a perfect specimen of its *kind of being,* but not that it is *perfectly being,* for it is not complete (fully actual) with respect to all the perfection open to "being." A crystal may very well have all the molecules it should, and have its correct structure and configuration; it is thus "a perfect crystal." If it is called "a perfect being," the meaning is that it is "a perfect crystalline being." Similarly, a flower may be a perfect being, that is, a perfect flower. But neither the crystal nor the flower is all that a being can be, even though each is all that an individual of *its type of being* can be. The perfect crystal and the perfect flower are the best that a crystal and a flower can be; they are complete, perfect specimens in the order of crystalline being and floral being; *they are per-*

fect kinds of being, perfect in their genus or species; but neither of them is *perfect being*. They have *some* being or some of the perfection of being; they do not have *all* the possible perfection of being.

No existing being other than God has "being" in its fullness; nothing but God, uncreated being, is completely and perfectly being or has all that can possibly be had by a being ("being" can be uncaused—but only in one case!). Things other than God "participate in" being ("have a part of" being); they have being as a *datum*, something given them, parcelled out to them, conferred on them. But God has—indeed, is—the plenitude of being; He is being not through "participation in" it but through identity with it. He is being; He does not receive being. The supreme degree of being, the zenith in being, cannot be a "datum," something received.

Sense in which "being" admits no degrees.   There is, of course, a sense of the word "being" which does not admit degrees. When we ask the question, "Does X exist in any way at all?" ("*An est?*"), or "Is X real in any way at all?" the answer must be either "yes" or "no"; no intermediary, no compromise, is possible. No thing can be half-existent; nothing real can be midway between "existing" and "non-existing." A composite being, and even a principle that is a constituent of a complete being, is real—yes or no; it is not half-real. Something may really be half or part of a composite being, but it cannot in itself merely *half-be*. "To be in any way at all" and "not to be in any way at all" are contradictorily opposed. In this context God and a molecule are both "beings": both have all that is requisite for being called "a being." Neither are mere concepts nor mere possibles; neither are non-existent.

In this sense—where "It is a *being*" (meaning: "it exists" or "it is real, extramental, not just possible, and not just conceived by the mind") is an answer to the question, "Does it exist?" ("*An est?*")— the word "being" implies very little, indeed the minimal intelligible determination or perfection or actuality requisite to justify an affirmative answer. It states the factuality of some conceivable subject, and therefore (since no subject can lack all perfection) it implies the possession of at least a minimal degree of perfection. But this does not mean that "existence" is itself only a *minimal perfection*. Existence simply is "perfection"; it may be realized in a minimal degree, but it may also be realized in higher degrees; it is indefinitely open for more and more perfect realization.

Sense in which "being" admits degrees. On the other hand, the more perfect a thing is (or the more perfection it has), the more "real," determinate, and actual it may be said to be. Conceding the real identity of perfection, actuality, and being, then the more perfect a subject (or the more actuality or being it has), then too the more intensely does it share (participate) in being.

In other words, "being" ("existence," "actuality," "perfection") has a minimal sense and a maximal sense. There is the *idea* of being; there is the *ideal* of being. God and God alone verifies, or realizes, the ideal of being; anything real at all verifies the idea of being.

There is but very meager content to "being" in contexts where the statements "Yes, it is *a being*" or "Yes, it has *being*" are simply answering the question, "*An est?*" Clearly, it is not merely in this meager sense that we would say that the being, God, is perfect. For any being at all is "perfect" in the sense that nothing whatsoever "half-exists" or "partially exists."

Still, it is possible to speak of one thing existing more intensely or more perfectly than another. Certainly, we speak of some persons *living* more intensely than others. And we speak of human life in general as more active or more perfect than animal life and of animal life as more dynamic than plant life. If being is existence and existence is perfection, let us not balk at saying that plants exist more perfectly than rocks.

The possibilities of intensification in perfection (in being) are unlimited. "Being" is open; there is no point at which being, by reason of the intensity of its perfection, suddenly becomes (or even verges on becoming) non-being. Now, God has the fullness of the possibilities of being. He is this fullness in the concrete identity of His factuality and actuality. Hence we say that "God is a perfect being," "God is perfectly being," "God is perfect being," and "God is Being Itself."

V. MISCONCEPTIONS CONCERNING THE INFINITE

Here it would be good for us to point out certain misconceptions that would hamper an appreciation of the discussion of God's infinity. Unless God were finite, it might seem that He must be something vague and indefinite, hence something unreal, hence not something at all! Or at least He must be incomplete and imperfect. Or, from a very different approach, if He were really infinite, would He not exhaust the totality of reality, actual and possible, so that it would be impossible for other beings to exist?

A. "The Infinite" Not the Same as "The Incomplete," "The Indefinite," "The Indeterminate."

To the ancient Greeks (admittedly we are oversimplifying a complex situation), our phrase "infinitely perfect" would be a meaningless expression. It would be a formal contradiction; for if a thing were perfect, it would have no unactualized potency, but if infinite, it would (according to the Greeks) have a potency never fully actualized. For the Greeks, what was infinite was indefinite and indefinitely perfectible; what was actual was definite and finite. What was perfect was, of course, not perfectible—at least not in the order in which it was perfect (a perfect athlete might not yet be a perfect scholar) —but what was infinite could never even be perfect, for it would always necessarily lack some actuality possible to it.

Only an imperfect thing, that is, only a being that had some unactuated potentialities, could thus be "in-finite." An imperfect kind of being (a sapling, for example, or a kitten) might become a perfect one (a full-grown tree, a cat); in the normal course of events it would do so. But if the imperfection in question was rooted in an infinite determinability, in a potency that was an indeterminacy without restriction, then that being, *as a being*, was exceedingly imperfect. Material beings, for example, might become perfect specimens of this or that species; but their materiality and their very extension were, or included, passive potentiality that could never be fully actuated.

Without a doubt, some even of the modern meanings of "the infinite" are very correctly associated with "the imperfect." For they signify an infinity rooted in passive potentiality, the infinity of a determinability that can never be totally eliminated. Such an infinity is possible only in an imperfect being.

But an infinity that is rooted in act or actuality is, rather, infinite determination, infinite reality, infinite perfection. Hence if God is going to be styled "infinite" at all, we shall certainly mean that He is infinite with an infinity of actuality, for an uncaused, necessarily existent being can have no passive potentiality at all.

B. "The Infinite" Not the Same as "The All."

When we say that God has all perfections, that He possesses the fullness of being, and that there are no limits in His being, we certainly do not mean that He is numerically identical with all being or has numerically all perfections. Rather, there are no perfections in things which God does not possess virtually and eminently. Even those perfections of creatures which are in God formally (the transcendental perfections) do not exist univocally, but only analogously, in God and creatures.

The infinite perfection of God's being no more prevents the existence of the finite perfection of other beings (creatures) than a teacher's knowledge prevents pupils from learning from him, than supreme authority prevents the existence of subordinate authority, or than necessary existence prevents dependent existence. The teacher communicates what he knows; the pupils receive. Through the process there is effected a multiplication of knowers, but no multiplication of what is known. Knowledge becomes more widespread, but not more intense or richer; there are more knowers, but not more knowledge. Knowledge in the pupils is derivative; being, in the data of experience, is derivative.

Of course, in our example the particular teacher has himself acquired his knowledge. All that we were trying to illustrate is the fact that so long as the imperfect and finite realities are what they are (or, have the perfection they have) because of a gift deriving from a being who possesses the perfection in His own right, then it is not contradictory to have a plurality of beings in existence, even if the Supreme Being should be infinitely perfect. God has all perfection, but He is not all the beings that there are.

Further examples. A person who has supreme authority may delegate some of this authority; he may exercise this authority through deputies. In fact, that is the usual way civil authority, military authority, and ecclesiastical authority are exercised. In the latter case, for example, the Supreme Pontiff entrusts jurisdiction over certain dioceses to the Bishops (we speak here according to a common opinion of Catholic theologians), and the Bishops appoint parish priests, who in turn may delegate some of their jurisdiction to their assistants. The supreme commander in an army has a whole host of officers of varying ranks hierarchically organized under him; they are all, in the literal sense of the French words, his *lieu tenants*: they are "taking his place" with respect to the particular area of authority that has been delegated to them; they are not absolutely autonomous. Or a sheriff may appoint "deputies" to help in enforcing the law, and he does so without losing or diminishing his own authority.

God necessarily exists, but He is endowed with free will and omnipotence. He chooses to multiply beings, which therefore imitate His Being (participate in His perfection) and depend upon Him for their own being. Thus there are effected more beings, but the perfection, *being*, is not increased nor intensified. There are more beings than God, if God creates, but there is not more perfection in a totality or universality consisting of God and three (or three sextillion) creatures than there is in a universality consisting of God alone. God, if He creates, is not the all, but God, whether He creates or not, is all the uncreated, independent perfection there is or can be. But because He is what He is, there can be created and dependent perfection as well.

It may be difficult to see how finite beings can co-exist with Infinite Being, and, in philosophy, we never directly understand the positive infinity of God. But we can come to realize that at least some of the beings that exist (since they are obviously less perfect than others) are finite, that it is not possible for all existent beings to be finite, but rather that it is necessary that at least one being —indeed, that only one being—be infinite. The finite could not co-exist with the infinite unless the finite were derivative from the infinite. The primary instance of being—considered in the ontological order, and not in the order in which we come to know things— is infinite being; all other being is derivative, all other beings are secondary instances or analogs. Infinite Being is the objective prototype of beings; no derivative being can be infinite, and no underived being can be finite.

VI. ARGUMENTS TO ESTABLISH THE INFINITE PERFECTION OF GOD

Recall the skeletal proof we presented earlier in this chapter:

> Whatever is finite is caused;
> But God is not caused;
> Therefore, God is not finite—but *infinite*.

We shall here try to develop, under several different forms, this simple argument. We shall argue that the essential difference between caused and uncaused being, between creature and Creator, cannot be sustained if uncreated being can be finite; that Necessary Being cannot be necessitated to any finite level of perfection; and that no intelligible explanation could be given for limitation in the case of a self-existent being.

A. The Essential Difference between Creature and Creator Cannot Be Sustained if Necessary Being Can Be Finite.

Finite being cannot be self-explanatory. The mind is not satisfied with a doctrine that claims that a *finite* being can be self-explanatory, that a being can be *limited in perfection* yet *absolutely uncaused in existence*. A thing that is limited is not adequately explained merely by the fact that it exists with just so much perfection. This would tell us *that the thing is* and *vaguely what it is*, but would leave us legitimately wondering *why it is, how it is*, and why and how what exists is *only* this particular thing that it *de facto* is.

Self-explanatory finite being (finitude that does not have an external efficient cause) would surely be paradoxical. The fact of an *existent* does not account for the fact that it *exists with just so much and no more perfection*—especially since the mind can see the (abstract, absolute, and *de jure*) possibility of more perfection. We do *not* mean to say (ever!) that the human mind has the power naturally to grasp the positive intrinsic possibility of infinitely perfect being, but only that no conceivable finite perfection exhausts its power. Existence, as such, does not call for *this or that limited amount* of perfection, and any amount that we can conceive leaves an indefinite intensity still conceivable. Perfection is "bounded" only by non-being; that is to say, it is bounded by nothing, it is *not bounded at all*, it is "open." To say that even the most perfect being can only have finite perfection seems to say that there is a moment in the nature of things when the very structure of being, the very intensity of a thing's perfection, would annihilate the thing and reduce it to non-being. To give a certain being more being would be to make it not be at all. Such a being would be so perfect that it would be nothing!

Finitude not determined formally by existence. Finite existence, or, what amounts to the same thing, an existent being whose perfection is limited, must be caused or produced, not because *existence as such* requires an outside explanation but because the existence in question (that of a finite being) is found with less perfection than is compossible with existence as such. Certainly it is not the aspect "existing" that makes us affirm that a certain existent is "caused"; such aspects as "mutably existing," "contingently existing," or (as we now argue) "finitely existing" (that is, "having merely so much perfection and no more, though more is absolutely possible")—it is such aspects as these that puzzle our minds. We are dissatisfied with the very idea of an unproduced finite being. If a being is finite, it must be a produced being.

If determinate limits are to be had, they must be determined by an efficient cause, something that determines for the concrete what is not present in the abstract, just as an efficient cause is needed to determine the fact of existence in the case of a mutable or dependent being which, considered in itself, might not exist at all. If a being is unproduced, there is no rhyme nor reason why it should be finite, why it should have *this* limit rather than *that* possible higher one or *this* determinate finitude rather than *that*. If a being is unproduced, it must pertain to a realm where determinate limits have no place, otherwise this problem of finitude remains forever unanswered. If a being is unproduced, no power—intrinsic or extrinsic to it—can make it finite. "Considered absolutely, being is infinite," says St. Thomas, "since it can be participated in by infinite participants and in infinite ways. If, then, the being of some thing is finite, that being must be limited by something other that is somehow its cause. But there can be no cause of the divine being, for God is a being necessary through Himself. Therefore His being is infinite, and so is He." [2]

Every finite being is a caused being. Hence, if God were a finite being, He too would be a caused being. But, as we know from our proof of His existence, God cannot possibly be a caused being. We must therefore conclude that neither can He be a finite being. This is a negative way of saying that He must be infinite. We do not say that we positively and directly grasp the divine infinity; we only know *that* God cannot be finite. Similarly, we do not see God's own necessary being, but we realize that it is absolutely impossible for all beings to be contingent beings.

Finite being is caused being. The only difficulty about this proof is the opening statement: every finite being is a caused being. Let us see if we can justify this statement; if so, the rest of the argument is entirely valid. Our argument will be of the type known as a *"reductio ad absurdum,"* wherein one shows that not to hold the proposition in question (here: "every finite being is a caused being") is equivalent to defending what is positively unintelligible, absurd, or self-contradictory.

If an existing finite being were not a caused being, then it would be adequately self-explanatory; it would have a natural, essential, and absolute exigency for existing. It would exist simply because it is what it is; it would exist because that is its nature. But if this natural exigency is had in a certain being whose perfection is finite to, let us say, the finite degree, 10, then surely such an exigency must be had by any other being that has perfection to this same finite degree, 10. We cannot possibly imagine, nor can our intellects furnish any reason whatsoever in explanation of why, if two beings are equally perfect—both having perfection to the degree, 10—one of them, X, is self-existent, intrinsically necessary, self-explanatory, essentially existent, and uncaused, whereas the other, Y, is not self-existent or necessary but rather is contingent and caused.

It is an absurdity to admit that although both of these two realities have perfection of 10 degrees, X nevertheless contains the tran-

---

[2] St. Thomas: C.G. I.43, n.8 (translation slightly adapted from that of Anton C. Pegis, *The Truth of the Catholic Faith*, Garden City, N.Y., Hanover House, 1955, Vol. I, p. 167).

scendent attribute of self-existence and Y does not. This would be like admitting the possibility of identical twins who would be identical in all respects save one, namely, that *only one* of the twins *has parents!*

A *fortiori*, self-existence should belong to any being that has more than 10 degrees of perfection; it should belong to any being that is more perfect than X. We could even argue that beings that have X's perfection in a less intense degree than 10 should be self-existent, for two finite degrees do not differ from each other enough to furnish, by their mere finite difference of perfection, any intelligible explanation why the one, X, should demand self-existence and the other one, Y, should not. An intrinsically necessary perfection and a contingent perfection differ as night and day, indeed infinitely more than night and day. They simply do not belong to the same order; their different existential condition cannot be accounted for merely by some finite, and therefore relatively small, difference of intensity in the possession of the same perfection.

Existence and essence must be proportionate. Let us word this argument in a slightly different fashion. Finite difference in the order of essence (quiddative perfection) cannot account for a radical, transcendent difference in the order of being (existence). It would be impossible for the Creator to give a creature "everything but" self-existence. Just as a creature cannot have self-existence, so its essence cannot be perfectly similar to the essence of the uncreated being from whom it has proceeded. Hence, where we know that existence is so radically different in two beings (God's necessary, self-sufficient, independent existence, on the one hand, and the creature's contingent, dependent existence on the other), there we can deduce that the essential or quiddative perfection—to which the existence is proportionate—must be radically, transcendently different.

Finite perfection "A" and finite perfection "B" are not—and cannot be—as quantitatively different as *existential aseity* is qualitatively different from *existential abaleity*, that is, as *uncreated (utterly independent) being* is from *created (totally dependent) being*. In any being, however, essence and existence are proportionate the one to the other. Since a creature's essence must be as different from God's essence as the creature's existence is from God's existence, then God's essential perfection must be more intensively different from the creature's perfection than any difference possible between finite perfection "A," and finite perfection "B." God's perfection must transcend the entire order of finite intensities or degrees.

Finite multiplication not proportioned to necessary existence. Our human minds will not assent to the idea that if such and such a produced being, such and such a creature, or simply such and such a finite being were but *ten times* more perfect than it actually is, then it could and would be equal to God; that it would indeed be divine (for it would be as perfect as God and thus would necessarily exist); that it would, if thus intensified, become an unproduced, uncaused being; that it would become—by this merely quantitative addition to its perfection—necessarily existent and completely independent.

Of course, a mere *ten times more* perfection would not turn the trick—but what about a *hundred times more?* or at least a *thousand times more?* No! No matter how many *times* the perfection is magnified, so long as that magnification is *finite*, it still could not make a thing's existence be necessary. If necessity of existing were compatible with finite perfection, then what is essentially contingent would, by receiving from God a finite magnification of its perfection, become independent of God, for it would become self-existent, necessarily existent! We could justly imagine a collection of finite creatures "ganging up" and, collectively, becoming a necessarily existent totality, no longer needing God, independent of God (because—presupposing that perfection and existence are proportionate—they would have as much perfection as the Divine Nature). This would be to hold that a finite, but uncreated, divine essence demands self-existence, necessary existence; while some other (a created) essence, likewise finite but just as intensively perfect as the uncreated divine essence, would not demand self-existence.

The proportion between essence and existence would no longer hold if we could say that God, who is supposedly finite in essence, nevertheless has an uncaused and necessary existence, whereas a creature, endowed with an essence that is likewise finite, having its essential perfection equal to that of the uncaused, absolutely necessary, utterly independent being, God, has, nevertheless, a mere caused and contingent existence and is utterly dependent!

Whatever it is that constitutes God's transcendence over the data of experience, whatever it is that is the necessary ultimate otherness that separates God from the data of experience, it cannot be merely a perfection that is only ten times greater (or a hundred times greater, or a thousand times greater, or any other finite number of times greater) than the perfection of one (or more) of God's effects.

B. Necessary Being Cannot Be Necessitated to Any Finite Level of Perfection.

Second argument "ex absurdo."   Another way of presenting an argument *"ex absurdo"* for God's infinite perfection is as follows. God is absolutely necessary; whatever He is, He is of absolute, intrinsic necessity. In God there is absolute identity between existence and constituent perfection. God exists simply by reason of what He is. If He is finite, we must agree that finitude is essential to God, that uncaused, uncreated, necessarily existing, self-explanatory being is necessarily not all that being might conceivably be. If the Necessary Being were under any aspect at all incomplete or imperfect, then we must conclude that this lack or this imperfection is a necessary condition of the supreme perfection in virtue of which He exists (it would be a formal contribution towards making Him exist). In the case of divine being, nothing is merely accidental, merely concomitant. God is in no degree indifferent to what constitutes His being. With regard to Him, any possible perfection is either necessarily had by Him or is necessarily excluded from Him.

But if some perfection that is absolutely possible is missing from God, if He is lacking something that absolutely and *de jure* is capable of existing, what is there in God to determine this particular lack? If necessarily existing being necessarily excludes some conceivable perfection, why not all? *What* is there *to determine* the exclusion of *what perfections?* What determines the necessary exclusion of whatever it is that a finite God would be lacking? The reason for this lack would ultimately have to be simply that God is necessarily what He is and that what He is (although the note "being" does not necessarily include limits) is, in His case, necessarily finite,

with the *finitude* simply *self-determined* at *this particular*, arbitrary
level of being.

Our argument and Kant. In his *Critique of Pure Reason*, in the
famous chapter entitled "The Impossibility of a Cosmological Proof
of the Existence of God," Immanuel Kant tries to show that if we
could argue that a necessary being is all-perfect, then we should be
able to argue from the mere concept of all-perfect being to its necessary existence, and that since we cannot legitimately do the latter,
neither can we do the former.

Our present argument for the infinite perfection of God does
indeed argue that "a necessary being is all-perfect"; but it presupposes that we have proved the existence of God, the necessary being,
on some score other than that we have a concept of all-perfect being;
we have proved that existence on the score that not all existing being
can be contingent (and, therefore, caused).

To this day Scholastic philosophers debate whether we can have
a mere concept of the positive infinity of God as something absolutely and positively possible; but no modern Scholastic would concede that we have, of God's possible perfection, such a *notion* (a
mere *concept*) as would justify us in passing directly to the *affirmation* (a *judgment*) of God's necessary existence. For our own part at
least, we would not even claim that we know God's infinite perfection; we merely know *that* God is infinitely perfect.

C. No Intelligible Explanation for Limitation Could Be Given in the Case of God's Perfection.

No efficient cause. To explain the limitation of a thing's perfection, one must attribute this either to something extrinsic to the
thing (its efficient cause) or to some internal cause (inner principle)
of the thing. But God has no efficient cause; He is not produced.
Hence nothing extrinsic to Him can be assigned to explain any
limitation of His perfection. If, then, divine perfection is really
limited, this will be by reason of an internal cause or principle; the
inner constituent(s) of God will be the only explanation of the
divine limitation.

Now, either God is constituted simply and entirely by a subsistent form or else by internal principles or constitutents related as

material cause (recipient subject or potency) and non-subsistent formal cause (act, as determining, or perfecting, a recipient subject).

No limiting potency.   As was demonstrated in the chapter on creation, however, and as will be again shown in the following chapter, if a being is composite, it is a caused being; the union or composition itself is caused, and the very components are caused; for if something existed without an efficient cause, it would not be a component, it would be absolutely independent, and it would not be necessarily related to something else. Now, in the case of God, there is surely no receptive subject, no passive potency for the formal determination or perfection. God is purely act, otherwise He would need an outside cause to actuate His potential principle. Since He is not caused, then He is not composite. He does not have a "receptive subject" nor, therefore, an "actuating form." He cannot have His perfection limited by a potential principle or capacity. His act or perfection cannot be the kind that requires a recipient subject in which to subsist. "The being of God," says St. Thomas, "since it is not received into anything, but is pure being, is not limited to any particular degree of the perfection of being, but contains all being within itself, and thus, just as *being* taken as a universal can extend to an infinity of things, so the divine being is infinite." [3] God's act or perfection cannot be the kind that requires a recipient subject in which to subsist.

Perfection not formally limited.   The only thing left to account for limitation in the hypothesis that divine being is really limited is to say that the perfection itself, the formal element (now not an actuating form but a subsistent form), explains the limitation and is of its very intrinsic nature limited. But, as we have seen in the previous proof (B, above), this perfection does not contain limits. Certainly the abstract notion prescinds both from limitation and infinity. The abstract notion itself cannot, of course, be self-existent. Hypostasized abstractions are absurd. It is only the perfection in the abstract order that prescinds both from finitude and infinitude, from the modes "created" and "uncreated," and so forth. Such a perfection, as *abstract* (therefore, as a concept), cannot exist in the extra-

---

[3] St. Thomas: *De Pot.* 1.2 (our translation slightly adapted from that of the English Dominicans).

mental order. Hence, it cannot be the reason why the concrete existent has or does not have finite perfection. We are left without any explanation of concrete limitation unless we hold that the concrete form of the necessarily existent being (essentially identical with its actuality) necessarily demands finitude and, indeed, this particular individual degree of finitude. We argued against this absurdity above (B).

In brief, a perfection exists in a limited mode if it is received into a subject, or even simply if it is produced by an efficient cause; but where it necessarily exists, exists simply by reason of itself with no efficient cause to produce and limit it and no quasi-material cause or recipient subject to sustain and contain it, there can be no satisfactory explanation, no intelligible *raison d'être*, of limits at all. Such a perfection must be unlimited.

D. Sketches of Other Proofs.

Other proofs for God's infinite perfection could be derived from the consideration of God as creator of all things, the "giver of being." Presupposing what the next chapter will explicitly prove, namely, that there can exist numerically only one necessarily existent being (that is to say, that a being that exists of absolute, intrinsic necessity must be utterly unique), it follows that all other beings that exist are made by the necessary being. God is not merely creator; he is creator of *all* existent non-divine being. God must, therefore be all-perfect or omniperfect, at least relatively so, in the sense of containing virtually and eminently all the perfections that are *de facto* found in non-divine beings and that *de jure can* exist in non-divine beings.

On another score it can be shown that God the Creator, precisely because He is the *giver of being*, is not merely *relatively* all-perfect but *absolutely* all-perfect. He is not just the cause of why *this being* is *this*, or why *that being* is *that*; He is first and foremost the cause why this or that being *exists at all*. He is their cause, their proper cause, precisely inasmuch as they are produced *being*. This or that contingent being needs a cause for why it is this or that, but it also, more fundamentally, needs a cause to explain why it exists at all; it is according to this aspect that God is the First Cause of all things and is precisely a "Creator" and not a mere "transformer."

God is the cause of produced being as produced being. He must, therefore, be capable of producing any and every thing that is producible, any and every thing that is neither God nor a formal contradiction. On this score, then, God, as Creator, as cause of being, must be infinitely perfect; He cannot Himself be merely an active being of this or that specific type; He must be beyond all species and genera of being; He must be Transcendent Being, Being without qualification, Being Itself.

Further arguments, at least suasive ones (which some authors with time and talent might perhaps convert from suasive into conclusive), may be derived from the desire of man for perfect happiness, a happiness that he can never attain from any finite good, and also from the ability of the human mind to increase its knowledge indefinitely, to know ever more and more.

LEADING IDEAS of Chapter 6

1. The "positive attributes" are the transcendental perfections common to God and creatures; the "negative attributes" are exclusive to God but merely tell us, in a negative fashion, of God's mode of existing; the "negativo-positive attributes" are exclusive to God but include notes that have representative and not merely significative value.

2. There are as many "negative attributes" predicable of God as there are aspects of contingency to be negated.

3. That God is Pure Act (Pure Actuality) means that His perfection excludes all admixture of potentiality; God's perfection is subsistent, and it is not received in any limiting principle nor caused by any extrinsic agent.

4. That God is All-Perfect (Omniperfect) means that He has all the perfections of all beings, with an intensity not measurable in any finite terms at all.

5. God is not merely a *perfect kind* of being, He is Perfect Being; He has the fullness, the inexhaustible richness, of perfection (act, actuality, being).

6. God's infinity is not to be confused with incompleteness, indefiniteness, or indetermination; neither is it the same as "the all."

7. The co-existence of the infinite with the finite is paradoxical, but unless there were an infinite being, no finite beings would exist at all.

8. The essential difference between caused and uncaused being cannot be accounted for by a mere finite difference in intensity of perfection.

9. In the Necessary Being, there is nothing to necessitate a level of perfection that would be finite; neither could anything extrinsic to God render His perfection finite.

SUGGESTED READINGS for Chapter 6

For Scholastic Exposition:

St. Thomas. S.T. I.4.1 and 2; I.7.1 (*Basic Writings*, Vol. I, pp. 37–40 and 56–57); C.G. I.28 and 43 (*Truth of the Catholic Faith*, Vol. I, pp. 135–137 and 165–170).

C. Bittle, O.F.M. Cap. *God and His Creatures, Theodicy*. Milwaukee: Bruce, 1953, pp. 226–231.

Wm. Brosnan, S.J. *God Infinite and Reason*. New York: America Press, 1928, pp. 49–74.

D.J.B. Hawkins. *The Essentials of Theism*. New York: Sheed and Ward, 1950, pp. 64–76.

That the Infinite God of Philosophy Is Personal:

J. Danielou, S.J. *God and the Ways of Knowing*, translated by Walter Roberts. New York: Meridian Books, 1957, pp. 52–93.

On the Co-Existence of the Finite and the Infinite:

L. DeRaeymaeker. *The Philosophy of Being*, translated by E. H. Ziegelmeyer, S.J. St. Louis: Herder, 1954, pp. 319–321.

Dom R. Williams. "God Distinct from the Universe," *God, Papers Read at the Summer School of Catholic Studies, Held at Cambridge, July 26 – August 4, 1930*, edited by the Rev. C. Lattey, S.J. London: Sheed and Ward, pp. 80–81.

On the History of the Question of God's Infinity:

W. Norris Clarke, S.J. "The Limitation of Act by Potency: Aristotelianism or Neoplatonism," *The New Scholasticism*, Vol. 26, 1952, pp. 167–194; "The Meaning of Participation in St. Thomas," *Proceedings of the American Catholic Philosophical Association*, Vol. 26, 1952, pp. 147–157.

Leo Sweeney, S.J. "Infinity in Plotinus," *Gregorianum*, Vol. 38, 1957, pp. 515–535 and 713–732. "Divine Infinity 1150–1250," *The Modern Schoolman*, Vol. 35, 1957–58, pp. 38–51.

CHAPTER

7

OUTLINE

I. *Introduction*

II. *Meaning of Simplicity*

III. *Simplicity as a True Perfection*

IV. *The Simplicity of God*

V. *Arguments to Establish the Divine Simplicity*

VI. *Plurality of Our Concepts Regarding God's Perfection*

VII. *God's Unicity: Introductory Remarks*

VIII. *The "Unique Uniqueness" of God*

IX. *Polytheism and Dualism*

X. *Arguments to Establish the Divine Unicity*

God's Transcendent Unity—
the Divine Simplicity and Unicity

I. INTRODUCTION

In this chapter we want to show, briefly, that God is not made up of parts; that the divine nature can exist in only one being; that God, therefore, is not composite and that He cannot be multiplied. These two characteristics describe for us God's transcendent unity and bear the names "simplicity" and "unicity" (or "uniqueness").

Unity, or oneness. We learned in General Metaphysics that unity or oneness is a property of being: "Every being is one." "To exist," "to be" (or "to have being"), and "to be *one* thing" are really the same. "A being," insofar as it is *one*, is defined as that which is undivided in itself and divided from everything else. A thing's oneness, therefore, includes a double aspect: the unity which is the thing's self-identity, and the unity or oneness which is the division (separation, distinction) of the thing from everything else.

Application to God. God is perfectly being, therefore He is perfectly one; He is perfectly undivided in Himself and perfectly divided or separated from all that is not Himself. As *perfectly* undivided in Himself, He is not merely (like most units) not actually divided, He is altogether indivisible; He has no plurality of constituent principles; He is non-composite; in a word He is *simple*. The divine nature, as *perfectly* separated from all that is not itself, is not merely distinct from every other nature but excludes the very possibility of its own numerical multiplication. Nothing else can exist that would be perfectly similar to the Being Who has divine nature. Indeed, nothing is specifically or even generically similar to God. Divine nature can exist in only one existent. Unlike created natures, uncreated nature is unmultipliable or absolutely *unique*.

	UNITY or ONENESS	
	UNDIVIDEDNESS IN SELF	DIVISION FROM ALL ELSE
CREATURES HAVE	unity of composition	a universal, specific nature, which is contingently this individual (commonness of nature)
GOD HAS	unity of SIMPLICITY	a necessarily existent nature, necessarily this individual (UNICITY of nature)

Figure 3.

We shall first discuss the divine oneness taken in the sense of a unity of *simplicity* and then the oneness which is God's *uniqueness* or *unicity*.

Paradox: God, "all-perfect," yet "absolutely simple." It probably comes as a surprise to a person who has just heard a disquisition on God's infinite perfection and inexhaustible richness to learn that God is absolutely "simple." The paradox needs explanation. Still, the very fact that we saw, when discussing the infinite richness and omniperfection of God, that this could be expressed by the simple phrase "Perfect Being" or "Being Itself," should make us surmise that infinity and simplicity are not incompatible attributes and that to say that God is simply perfect is also to say that He is perfectly simple. But what we seek is *understanding*, not a catch phrase.

II. MEANING OF SIMPLICITY

Variety of meanings. If unity or oneness is a perfection, then surely (all other things being equal) the kind of unity which is simplicity is a very great perfection. However, we use the word "simple" in a variety of ways and apply it to many non-divine, imperfect things. We often refer to something as "simple" if it is relatively easy to understand, if its structure and function are obvious, or if its relationships are readily apprehended. This will usually be the case if the thing has but few parts; the fewer the parts the more "simple" we say the thing is. We call elementary or primitive things "simple." We speak in this way of the elementary, or grade-school, courses in arithmetic and spelling; we say that such subjects are "simple." Primitive machinery and crude instruments we call "simple." Most of us would consider an old-fashioned well on a farm (a hole in the ground, a chain, a pulley, and a bucket) a quite "simple" device for obtaining water.

Sometimes we call people "simple." This is not always a compliment. A person is simple, in the bad sense of the term, if he has not much intelligence, also, if he is naïve or easily misled. Yet "simplicity" can be a virtue. Sometimes we refer to a person as "simple" when we mean that he is honest, candid, not hypocritical and devious, plain-spoken, childlike, and single-minded. However, in the present section on God's simplicity, although we are referring to a perfection, we are not referring primarily to a moral perfection but to an ontological one. We are referring to the lack of composition in the constitution of God's being. God's internal unity is complete; it is the most perfect type of internal unity or self-identity possible. It is the unity of a whole that has no parts.

Composite unity of mutable beings. Every being is one, that is, it has unity or self-identity; every thing is what it is and not something else. To the extent that a thing exists, it is undivided in itself; it is assuredly not doubly itself nor in contradiction with itself, but rather is identical with itself. However, despite its being *actually one* thing, it may still be quite *composite:* its total reality may be constituted out of a number of parts, and it may itself be a *virtual plurality* of other and distinct beings. Indeed, the unity that we find in the data of experience is proved, upon investigation, analysis, and reasoning, to be a composite unity or a unity of composition.

Mutable beings are composite beings; they are what they are through being composed of potency and act, of a determinable principle or passive "subject" and one or more determining principles or actuating "forms" (one substantial form and a plurality of accidental forms, in the case of each individual material substance).

Again, when we consider material data, their very extension or quantity makes them a virtual plurality of distinct beings. Mutability is a sign that a thing is not altogether indivisible. So long as it is what it is, it is itself; but its composition enables it to become other than itself. Neither quantified beings nor even merely mutable beings are "simple" ("indivisible") beings. Their perfection as beings, like their perfection as "one," is quite remote from that of a being that is substantially, accidentally, and integrally indivisible.

Difference between unity of composition and unity of simplicity. Internal oneness or undividedness, therefore, may be a unity, or indivision, of simplicity, and it may be (as in the data of experience) a unity of composition. Unity of simplicity is a unity without parts; it is not only *indivision* but also *indivisibility*. Unity of composition is a complex unity, consisting of a plurality of parts related to each other and only thereby forming a whole. Both kinds of unity include undividedness; but whereas unity of composition is divisible, the unity of simplicity excludes divisibility. Not only is an indivisible being actually only one being, it is so one, so identically itself, that it is not even potentially a plurality; it cannot under any circumstances cease to be itself, nor become other than itself, nor undergo even any accidental change. The unity of a composite being is a changeable or divisible unity and is less perfect than would be indivisible unity. A unity constituted of parts is necessarily a dependent unity: it is contingent upon some outside cause. This is not necessarily true of a simple, or indivisible, unity.

God is a being; therefore, He has unity. But God's unity, like His being, must be most perfect; hence it is not a unity of composition. It is the unity, not constituted of parts, of a being that is totally, adequately, and immutably itself; it is the unity which excludes composition; it is the unity of perfect simplicity.

III. SIMPLICITY AS A TRUE PERFECTION

A difficulty. It is likely that most people find at least a superficial difficulty in seeing how the negation or exclusion of composition from a being is a perfection. Hence it is not immediately clear to them that it is a perfection for God to be "simple." An impressionable mind might spontaneously be disturbed upon first hearing

William James's gibes against the philosophers' doctrine of the divine attributes, particularly the attribute of simplicity. For example, in a very famous series of lectures, James has stated:

If . . . we apply the principle of pragmatism to God's metaphysical attributes . . . I think that even were we forced by a coercive logic to believe them, we should still have to confess them to be destitute of all intelligible significance. Take God's aseity, for example; or his necessariness; his immateriality; his "simplicity" or superiority to the kind of inner variety and succession which we find in finite beings, his indivisibility and lack of inner distinction . . . and the rest. . . . Candidly speaking, how do such qualities as these make any definite connection with our life? . . . I must frankly confess that even though these attributes were faultlessly deduced, I cannot conceive of its being of the smallest consequence to us religiously that any one of them should be true. Pray, what specific act can I perform in order to adapt myself the better to God's simplicitly? [1]

"Simplicity" can be meaningful. The impressionable mind might unreflectingly assent to James's statements. But if one is not content with remaining on a superficial level, much less the level of mere rhetoric, he will find that the divine simplicity, admittedly a rather abstruse notion, can still be very "vital" to his religion; he will realize that God could not be God at all were He a *composite being* instead of being "simple." Even remaining on the popular level, we can, to some extent, see that simplicity—the exclusion of composition from one's ontological make-up—might very well, at least in certain respects and in certain cases, be a perfection and that the more "one" a thing is, the more perfect it is. We warn our friends, for example, at times of stress not "to go to pieces"; we encourage them to "pull themselves together." In other contexts we warn them not to "dissipate" their energies; we deplore the "disintegration" of character, or of mind, or of health. "Going to pieces," "pulling oneself together," "dissipation," and "disintegration" are not even possible where a being is utterly simple. In the case of a simple being, we truly have a case of "all or nothing."

Need of distinctions. Still, one can recall many cases in which composition and complexity are rather to a thing's advantage, or at

---

[1] Wm. James, *The Varieties of Religious Experience*, New York, Longmans, Green and Co., 1907, Lecture 18, pp. 445–446.

least to the advantage of other and better things, and therefore composition and complexity are in some sense, at least in some cases,
perfections. We may possibly have a tendency even to generalize
and to think that the more complex any thing is, the more perfect
it necessarily is. Thus, if a machine has a great number of correlated
parts, we are much more impressed by it than we are by less complicated machines, and we think it much more excellent than the
simpler ones. Modern electronic machines, with their thousands of
tiny parts, do very complicated things, and we cannot help but
marvel. As usual, some distinctions are called for. We cannot, without more ado, just say bluntly that "simplicity" is better than "complexity"; the problem is not that simple!

Perhaps it is true in the majority of cases of complex entities
(whether natural or artificial) *in the visible (material) universe*,
complexity does make for the perfection of the thing. Still, we
have merely to remind ourselves of Rube Goldberg's cartoons, and
we shall quickly realize that not every complicated contraption is
*eo ipso, by reason of its sheer complexity and the multiplication of
parts*, a thing of excellence. Certainly, if a thing is composite but
has its component parts in very poor order with respect to one
another and with respect to the end or purpose of the thing, the
complexity will tend to be a disadvantage and not a perfection.

Again, if, as sometimes happens, a machine can be constituted
with relatively few parts, which, nevertheless, can do what a much
more complicated machine can do, and if the simple machine can
do its work just as easily, just as excellently, just as speedily, and just
as cheaply as the more complicated machine, then we tend to praise
the simpler machine and judge it all the better for its simplicity.
There are fewer parts to wear out, fewer relationships to break
down. A skilled craftsman spontaneously practices an economy of
means; he dispenses with many of the instruments and props that
an amateur requires. And concerning the physical sciences, Albert
Einstein is quoted as saying: "The grand aim of all science is to
cover the greatest number of empirical facts by logical deduction
from the smallest number of hypotheses or axioms." [2] Hence the
ideal of achieving a "unified field theory."

[2] Lincoln Barnett, "The Meaning of Einstein's New Theory," *Life*, January
9, 1950, p. 22.

All other things being equal, simplicity adds an excellence and a nobility; thus it is a perfection or, at any rate, an excellent mode in which to have whatever perfection one has. Still, no mutable, and therefore finite, being can be absolutely simple (free from all composition whatsoever, real and conceptual). In a created being, if some kind of simplicity can be found as a perfection of it (with "all other things being equal"), it will still be only a "relative" simplicity, infinitely remote from that of God.

God's mode of being (His way of having perfections) is a mode of absolute simplicity. He is infinitely perfect; He has (is) all perfections, but He has them *"per modum unius"*—as something one. He is perfect being, and this without qualification. He is all that being—as perfection, actuality, determination—can possibly be. When we were analyzing the concept of the divine infinity, we referred to the idea of "perfect being." This idea, we hinted, sums up everything that can be said about God: God is Perfect Being. This was not a denial of the richness of His perfection—quite the contrary!

Illustrations. To help us get over our superficial impression that complexity *necessarily* adds to perfection, let us illustrate the point with a few rather clumsy examples, realizing all the while that no case of seeming "simplicity" in the data of experience is at all parallel with the strictly divine negative attribute "simplicity."

If we want plenty of light for a large room, we might insert a number of different light bulbs into the sockets of a central chandelier. We can get the cumulative effect that comes, for example, from a 15-watt bulb, a 60-watt bulb, a 75-watt bulb, a 100-watt bulb, and a 150-watt bulb. We thereby get a much more intense light than we would have if we merely used one or other of those various bulbs. But we could "simplify matters"—as the popular expression goes— and use only two 200-watt bulbs or, still more simply, one 400-watt bulb.

This example is extremely *simpliste*, if you will, and certainly an exacting scientist could point out some differences between the light coming from the several bulbs together and that coming from the single bulb. All we are trying to do is suggest that in some not positively describable way, God, without any addition or multiplication of distinct parts, is the virtual, eminent equivalent of all the perfections that are found pluralized and scattered in the varied data of experience. God, however, is not merely equal to a sum-total of the various finite perfections; He is, rather, an infinite intensity of perfection, transcending the whole order of quantitative addition and qualitative calculation. God's oneness of simplicity includes in its intensity all the perfections that are contained—always in finite degree—in the whole multitude of non-divine beings; it contains all these perfections without any real plurality or divisibility.

This shows a defect in the example we have given. The light of the two 200-watt bulbs or that of the single 400-watt bulb is the equivalent *in the same line* of the light furnished by the five less powerful bulbs. The perfection of the single bulb could be equalled and even surpassed by the adding together of more of the weaker bulbs. But God's simple perfection cannot possibly be equalled by any addition or intensification of finite degrees.

To bring up another crude illustration. Recall how the human intellect is a single power or faculty; yet it still performs not only an indefinite number of numerically distinct operations, but also several rather different kinds of operations: we form ideas (that is, we apprehend meanings, we detect relations, we understand non-sensible aspects of things, we conceive them mentally), we make judgments, and we reason. All of these operations are forms of knowing; but "knowing" is a generic term, and we cannot reduce the operation of judging to that of merely conceiving, nor the operation of discursive reasoning to that of merely judging. In one and the same perfection, namely, our intellectual faculty, we have the virtual, eminent equivalent of several really distinct powers. Again, with our will (our "intellectual appetite") we love, we hate, we desire, we take complacency, we rejoice, or we choose. Even in us not every operation requires a really distinct faculty, nor are the single faculties restricted to performing operations that have only numerical differences.

God's single power has diverse terms. God's creative power is related to beings inasmuch as they are effected or produced beings; God's cognoscitive power terminates in beings inasmuch as they are comprehensively knowable; God's affective power terminates in them inasmuch as they are lovable. We are not trying to explain how God's being *is* His power, and *is* His intellect, and *is* His will; we are not at present trying to prove anything. We are simply trying to eliminate a prejudice some students may have to the effect that a being, merely because it is one substantial being and has no really distinct parts, can be perfect in only one respect and can do only one particular, determinate thing. We are trying to convey the idea that it might not be too preposterous to judge that the infinitely perfect God, without any real complexity or plurality in His constitution, is a creator, a knower, and a lover, and that He is the eminent equivalent, though in a transcendently unified and simple manner, of the myriad varieties of powers and perfections found in His effects, i.e., in the terminations of His power, knowledge, and love.

We ourselves do not need distinct faculties to see yellow, red, or green, etc.; we do not need distinct powers in order respectively to conceive ideas, to judge, and to reason; we do not need distinct powers in order to choose and to love. God does not need distinct powers or perfections in order to create, in order to know and to love, and, in general, in order for us to be able correctly to predicate many different attributes of Him.

IV. THE SIMPLICITY OF GOD

Exclusion of composition. God is simple. This means that the divine nature excludes all intrinsic composition. Intrinsic composition may be that of substance and accident, of matter and substantial form, or of essence and existence. God's mode of being is such as to exclude these three kinds of composition. It also excludes the foundation for a virtual major (conceptual) distinction of genus and specific difference.

God is purely act, without any potential principle or a plurality of acts or actualities. Thus, His unity of undividedness transcends that of all non-divine beings. For even though every non-divine being is "one," is "undivided in itself," still it is not "indivisible." Obviously, integrally composite (extended or quantified) beings are not "indivisible." Their extension makes them divisible *in infinitum*. If a being is a material one, its subject matter can be "divided from" its form, that is, the matter can lose the form that specifies it as *this kind* of being and gain another form specifying it as *that kind*.

At the very least, there is composition of substance and accident in all non-divine beings; they can all be "separated from" (be without) not merely their external effects but even their own internal operations. And in no Scholastic system is the union of essence and existence absolutely the same in the case of creatures as it is in the case of God.

God's perfections identical with God's simple substance. God's absolute simplicity does not mean that God has no thoughts, no operations, or no volitions. Certainly God has these—really and truly so. But these are not distinct realities in Him. He is wise, He is just, He is merciful, He is good, He is truthful. This does not mean that He has acquired moral habits nor even that He eternally has really distinct virtues; He has always been powerful, certainly, and has always been merciful, but power and mercy are really identical with God Himself; they are not accidental forms of the divine substance. Further, His power is His mercy, and His mercy is His goodness, and His goodness is His truth. Divine goodness is divine wisdom; not because goodness is necessarily wisdom (it is not), but because in this case the goodness and wisdom are both *divine*.

V. ARGUMENTS TO ESTABLISH THE DIVINE SIMPLICITY

Expressed briefly the argument comes to this:

A composite being is a caused being;
But God is not a caused being;
Therefore God is not a composite being—but must be simple."

A *composite being is a caused being;* such a being cannot be self-explanatory; it cannot exist of absolute necessity. A composite being is made by the union of parts. Now, either these parts need the union in order to exist at all—and in this case each of them is essentially contingent in itself—or else the parts are contingently united —and this means that the composite unit, the one being that results from the union of the parts, is a contingently existing thing. In either case, the being in question does not exist of absolute necessity.

Imperfect nature of "parts." Again, we may argue that a being whose unity is a unity of composition is a being formed out of parts, therefore, out of imperfect realities; from which it follows that it itself is not an infinitely perfect being. A part, as we saw in *Chapter 4*, is an imperfect reality. To understand *parts* precisely for what they are, to understand them *as parts*, is to realize that they constitute a whole which is not adequately identical with any of the parts. The whole is more perfect than any of the parts; the parts exist only within the whole, and they depend for their completion upon their being within the whole, upon their union with the other parts. The parts themselves are not self-existent; otherwise they would not be related to other parts and to a whole. Parts, precisely because they are *parts*, are relative: they have their intelligibility through relationship to something else, they depend upon something else, they cannot be self-explanatory in their reality. An adequately self-explanatory being or reality cannot be dependent upon or necessarily related to anything extrinsic to itself. A part, therefore, is something relative, something incomplete in itself, something dependent upon something else, hence, quite obviously, an imperfect reality.

God's being excludes real composition. Composition, that is, the union of distinct elements or parts to form one thing, may be of various types. The composition is *real* if the constituent parts are really distinct; it is merely *conceptual* if the parts are formally only distinct concepts of one and the same reality. In all real composition the component parts are related as potency and act are related, that is, they are related as a determinable subject to its determining perfection. The determinable subject may be of itself substantially incomplete; it may, for example, be matter in potency to a *substantial* form which is needed if there is to be a complete substance of a definite specific type. The determinable subject may also be a complete substance (whether substantially simple or substantially composite), but a substance in potency to a number of *accidental* perfections and modifications. Again, in any composite being, all the parts are "potential" relative to the whole, which alone (if we are talking of natural, not artificial, units) is "actual."

Where there is composition, therefore, the components are all imperfect; they are dependent upon each other and upon the whole.

The whole ensemble, the components in themselves and the fact of their union, is dependent upon something other, since neither the constituents themselves nor the ensemble can be self-existent. Something adequately distinct from the whole is required to cause whatever reality it is that the parts (or principles—from the present point of view, constituent principles are as imperfect as parts) have in themselves and also to cause the actual union of the parts. And so, if God were really composite, this would mean that the being which is God would be a plurality of really distinct parts or principles mutually related so as to form a self-existent, necessarily existent reality. The absolute and necessarily existent being would not be pure act; it would contain passivity and also relativity.

God's being excludes composition of genus and specific difference.   God cannot even be conceived as composed of a strict generic note and a strict differentiating or specifying note. For whatever is conceived as composite of genus and specific difference is necessarily conceived as finite. A generic note does not, even implicitly, include the differentiating notes in its conceptual comprehension; neither do the differentiating notes even implicitly include the generic note.

The generic note "animal," for instance, does not include the differentiating note "rational"; otherwise all animals would be essentially human, that is, "rational animals." Likewise, the differentiating notes do not include the generic note. Not all irrational beings are animals: some are plants, others are minerals. And, taking "rational" simply as "intelligent" (as we should take it if we are not to be redundant when we say that a man is a "rational animal"), angels are "rational" but not animals.

Hence generic notes and differentiating notes are necessarily conceived as finite. The being whom we conceive as infinite cannot be conceived at all as constituted of two finite notes, a generic one and a differentiating one. Genus and specific difference are conceived as finite perfections, and they presuppose ontological finitude in the being from whom the generic and differentiating notes are abstracted.

God, then, the utterly indivisible being, is transcendently one—at least in regard to the first of the two aspects of unity, namely, *indivision in oneself*. In a moment we shall turn to the second aspect of unity, *division or distinction from all that is not oneself*. But let us first pause to consider the fact that, although we must judge that

God is simple, we still legitimately apply a plurality of predicates to Him.

VI. PLURALITY OF OUR CONCEPTS REGARDING GOD'S PERFECTION

One concept implicitly includes the others. How is it that in multiplying our concepts that supposedly represent and signify something validly predicable of God, we are not asserting a real multiplicity of God? Our answer is that the various predications we make about God are virtually, *implicitly* identical with one another. Were they explicitly identical, they would be synonymous expressions. But because the *explicit* content of one (for example, divine goodness) is not the *explicit* content of another (for example, divine wisdom), therefore we have justification for a plurality of attributions, even though we know that implicitly there is no real distinction among the attributes themselves nor between God's nature and His attributes.

Logical composition not an infallible sign of real composition. A plurality of concepts is not always a sign of objective plurality or of composition in the object conceived. Whenever we attribute a predicate to a subject, we necessarily have in our minds some sort of composition: we conceive the subject and predicate as forming at least a logical composite (not always with the composition of a genus, strictly so-called, and a specific difference, strictly so-called). The subject is at first conceived somewhat indeterminately, that is, when we are at first conceiving a thing preparatory to relating it as subject to a predicate, we are conceiving it without conceiving this or that attribute (the predicate); then (after judging the relation between the subject and predicate) we conceive the subject as having this or that further determination (here I am speaking only of judgments affirming a quality of some subject, not of the judgments that affirm the existence of a subject).

But such a mental activity, the judging whereby we come to attribute something new to a thing known at first less determinately, such a mental activity (called *composing* by the ancients) does not require that the object itself which we are conceiving should be objectively composite, for we are not affirming that there is real composition. We do not have to say that because our conception is necessarily composite, so too is the reality as it exists in itself. We pluralize words and concepts even when we affirm identity ("Admiral Nelson was the victor at Trafalgar"); the subject is taken at first in precision from some quality which in the real order truly belongs to it, whether through real identity or through real addition. The judgment makes at least an explicit conceptual addition but does *not necessarily* affirm a *real* addition. This is clear from such a proposition as "The measuring-stick I need is one yard long." Again, in the proposition, "This thing's color is green," the color of the thing is grammatically and logically the subject of the proposition: "green" is predicated of it and attributed to it. But we do not mean, in our judgment, that the colored thing has two real, adequately distinct qualities, one of them being color and the other being greenness.

Now, when we predicate attributes of God, we must form grammatical sentences and must still use subjects and predicates; therefore, we still use a plurality of terms and even of ideas; hence we have a logical composite in our minds. But we are *not necessarily* referring to a plurality of distinct realities; we may be simply giving more determinate conceptual expression to one and the same reality. Indeed, if we are predicating of God a strictly divine property, if we are predicating something exclusively of God (e.g., "omniscience," and not merely "wisdom"), then we are, at least implicitly, denying plurality and denying composition.

An analogy.   Perhaps we can say that our process of predicating attributes of God is like inscribing a polygon, with ever-increasing sides, inside a perfect circle. The ends of the lines that we draw truly reach the circle at definite points; similarly, with our predications we truly attain God in some definite respect. But our knowledge is very, very inadequate, and just as the lines of the polygon can never be commensurate with the circle, so our conceptual knowledge will never be commensurate with God. We multiply our concepts of God, just as we multiply the lines of the polygon (and the points in the circle). The more lines we give to the polygon the more closely the polygon comes to representing the circle; but we shall never succeed, even with a myriagon, in equating a polygon with a circle.

Neither shall we ever represent God just as He is in Himself. Our efforts are not altogether futile, nor merely symbolic; for we do correctly state what is verified in God: God *is* intelligent, God *is* free, God *is* wise, God *is* just, God *is* powerful, God *is* merciful. But there is no really distinct element in God which is His intelligence as distinct from His will, His will as distinct from His intelligence, nor His justice really distinct from His mercy, and so forth. Even conceptually, if we conceive God's wisdom precisely as the "transcendent quality" *divine wisdom,* and not as the "transcendental quality" *wisdom,* we are implicitly conceiving the divine justice and the divine mercy and all else that is in God. For the "divine" element in our concept "divine wisdom" tells us that the mode of God's wisdom is such as to include through identity all possible perfections, and that it does so without plurality and composition.

VII. GOD'S UNICITY: INTRODUCTORY REMARKS

Besides the aspect of unity that we have just been treating, namely, the oneness of a thing's *undividedness in itself* (with the transcendent case of God's absolute indivisibility), there is also the other aspect to be considered, the aspect which consists in a thing's *dividedness* (separation, or distinction) *from all that is not itself.* And here, too, God is *one* in a transcendent sense. He is so one that He is identically the divine nature; He is the *unique* possessor of divine nature.

Socrates, Thomas, Napoleon, and so on—each is a possessor of human nature; each participates in, or numerically multiplies, human nature. But divine nature cannot be numerically multiplied. If a being possesses divinity (divine nature), it is necessarily the sole possessor of divinity; it simply is really and conceptually identical with actual divine nature.

Christian *revelation,* it is true, tells us of that most mysterious of all mysteries: the mystery of the Holy Trinity. There are three really distinct Persons Who are really God. Divine nature, however, is not thereby thrice multiplied. It is impossible that divine nature should be numerically multiplied by a multiplicity of possessors. The same Christian revelation that tells us of the three Persons insists on monotheism, the doctrine that there is only one God and that there *can be* only one.

Multipliability of a finite, specific nature into a plurality of individuals. Each experimental datum is a unique individual; God, too, is unique. But the data have a specific nature that is multipliable; they belong to this or that class, all the members of which equally possess the common note, with no one of them completely identified with that note or "exhausting" it in the sense of excluding other participators from sharing in it. The data of experience, however incommunicable they are in their individual oneness or separatedness, do not exclude the multiplicity or plurality of individuals within their species or their genus. The existence of any one of the data of our experience is compatible with the existence of another, specifically similar being. Partners, compeers, and fellow-travellers in the same species and genus are not, and cannot be, ruled out in the case of the data of experience. Unlike *individuals*, all *specific natures* except divine nature are multipliable.

A note on the angels. If we go beyond the data of experience and bring up the question of the angels, then one should at least mention the Thomistic thesis of the unicity of subsistent forms. According to this, each angel "exhausts his species"; there is no plurality of individual angels within one and the same species. Does God's unicity transcend even such a unicity? Yes—for in no case is an angel's nature conceptually identical with the angel's existence; there is at least a quasi-genus, "angelic nature," which is specifically multiplied by each existing angel. Divine nature cannot even be a "quasi-genus."

God transcends numerical multipliability within a species (or even within a genus or quasi-genus). It is not just this individual God that is unmultipliable; it is *divine nature* itself. The specific nature of God and His individual nature are really and conceptually the same—unlike the case of the specific nature (man) and the individual nature (Socrates's) of a datum of experience. Indeed, it is an artifice of language even to speak of the "specific nature" of God. God is simply not in a species; whatever is "specifically" divine is, without further determination, also "individual."

Factual uniqueness and essential uniqueness. When Adam was the only human being in existence, there was a sense in which it was true to say that "human nature is unique." There was a time, then, when only one being had human nature. But it was not impossible, even then, for other humans to exist, and with the creation of Eve, Adam lost his *de facto*, or merely factual, uniqueness as a human being. Eve's coming into existence effected a plurification of human nature; human nature, never *de jure*, or essentially, unique, quickly ceased even to be *de facto* unique. Were human nature *de jure* unique, only one individual human could ever have existed.

Certainly, it is not a mere *de facto* uniqueness that we are attributing to the transcendence of the divine nature; rather, we attribute to divine nature a *de jure* uniqueness. Not only is there only one being who has divine nature, there can only be one being having this nature; for divine nature is essentially, *de jure*, unique. Divine nature is numerically one of absolute necessity—as much so as is an existent individualized nature. Indeed, this is so precisely because divine nature is, as such, individualized, for divine nature as such is absolutely necessary and independent; it is absolutely identical with its act of existence—and existence is only of the singular, the individual.

Absolute natures and multipliability. To conceive "man" is, certainly, to conceive "a being having human nature," but it is not to conceive "this individual man" (Socrates, for example, or Napoleon). "Man" is not "a being having this individual (Socrates's or Napoleon's) nature." "Man" is not identically "Napoleon"; otherwise, if man exists, man must be Napoleon. For a being to be human at all, it would have to be Napoleon; all men would be the one man, Napoleon; that is, only one man would and could exist, namely, Napoleon. "Man" does have a oneness about it—in the *abstract* order, in the mind. "Human nature," considered absolutely, that is, independently of the way it is concretized in the existential order, is one; there is only one "human *species*." But the "oneness" of "man" is, like "man," an abstraction; in the concrete order, "man" is multiplied millions of times in determinate individuals, and it is the existent individuals who are, each of them, unique, incommunicable, and ineffable. But their specific nature can be considered in abstraction from what renders it individual and incommunicable.

Considered abstractly, human nature prescinds from this and that individuation (Socrates's, or Napoleon's, and so forth); "man" is not *this particular* "multiplyee" or participant of human nature. Of course, no abstract nature, as such, can exist; Tom, Dick, and Harry exist, but not mere "man" unindividualized. Nothing can exist with *real precision* from the determinations of the real order from which its abstract note *conceptually prescinds.* Something more than what is contained in the notion "man" is required, and something more than the fact of existence is required, if "man" is to exist as Napoleon, not something that, of necessity, is really, however inadequately, distinct from this real concretized human, but still something that is not conceptually included when we are merely conceiving "man" in the abstract.

But when we take the concept "divine nature" ("necessarily existent nature" or "uncreated, self-explanatory, self-existent nature") and predicate it of a certain subject of existence (an uncreated being whom we name "God"), we should realize that this (divine) nature *is* so identified with the existence in question that we not only can, but must, affirm the unmultipliability of this nature. "Human nature," considered absolutely, *is not identical* with Socrates or Aquinas or Napoleon. "Divine nature," considered absolutely, *is identical* with one and only one individual existent, the one we name—with a proper noun—God.

We cannot, in truth, form a purely "abstract" notion of divine nature; among other reasons, we are not truly conceiving divine nature if we are not at least implicitly conceiving this particular individual existent, God. There is nothing, explicit or implicit, about the quality, "human being," that demands that, if it be existent, it must be the existent Napoleon. There *is* something about the quality, "divine nature," however, that demands that, if it exist, it be God (not: "a god," but "God," "*the* God," "the *only* God"). "God" is a proper noun, like "Socrates" and "Napoleon"; it is not a common noun, like "man" (even though we sometimes make comparisons and contrasts between "God" and "man"—that is, between "divine nature" and "human nature" considered "absolutely"). To have divine nature is not "to be a god"; it is "to be God." C.S. Lewis puts it neatly: "The difference between believing in God and in many gods is not one of arithmetic. As someone has said, 'gods' is not really the plural of God; God has no plural." [3]

The word "god" as a universal. It is true that the word "god" can be used as a "common" term; it can stand for a sort of "universal idea." We say, for instance, that many pagan peoples had a great diversity of "gods"; we call them "polytheists." Even the Judaeo-Christian Scriptures refer to other "gods"—false gods, of course. So long as we are considering merely a certain explicit, formal, conceptual content (e.g., "uncreated being," "uncaused being," "necessary existent"), considering it in itself without attending to its necessary implications, then our concept, "god," appears to be multipliable. But never is it so clear as here that merely to have some concept of a thing is not necessarily to have grasped the inmost ontological essence of that thing. Because of the difference between *explicit* and *implicit* content, we can, in the situation described, not unreasonably ask such questions as: "Is there more than one god?" "Can there be a plurality of distinct, necessarily existent beings, each one of which has its own really distinct divine nature?" These questions do have some meaning. Yet, to raise them is to show that one has not gone very far in his appreciation of what divine nature really implies. He has not yet reflected on what is necessarily involved in the nature of necessarily existent being. Were one to reflect, he would see that divine nature is necessarily singular and incommunicable, and that, therefore, to ask, "Can there be a multiplication of divine nature?" is to show a lack of appreciation of what is implicit when one proves that something exists which must be necessarily existent.

VIII. THE "UNIQUE UNIQUENESS" OF GOD

If a thing exists, *it* exists obviously as *itself*; *it* is incommunicable. As concretely itself, everything existent is unique. *It* cannot be multiplied and still be *itself*. As having individualized natures, any two existents are adequately distinct from each other, however "one" or similar they may be when we abstract from the individualiza-

[3] C.S. Lewis, *Reflections on the Psalms*, London, Geoffrey Bles, 1958, p. 82.

tions. Every individual existent is incommunicable and, therefore, "unique." Hence, if we are going to advocate a certain unicity as a strictly divine attribute, we must accentuate the fact that the way in which divine nature is unmultipliable transcends the way in which the nature of any non-divine being is unmultipliable.

Socrates is necessarily singular, and God is necessarily singular. But the necessity in both cases (though due to existence, or at least to a pre-condition of existence) is a different type of necessity. In God there is essential necessity, for there is perfect identity of His essence and existence. In Socrates, the existence is not of his essence; Socrates contingently exists. Although if there is a Socrates he is necessarily unique, it is a contingent fact that there is a Socrates, that is, that Socrates concretizes "human nature"—other existents can, and do, concretize it. It is not a contingent fact, however, that God concretizes divine nature; no other existent could possibly concretize it; there can be only one *necessarily existing* existent.

"Necessarily existing" does not enter into the concept of "human nature"; we can conceive "human nature" without conceiving it as "necessarily existing." But we cannot conceive "divine nature" without conceiving it as "necessarily existing." Of course, conceiving it thus is not to know that there actually is a God necessarily existing. But in this chapter we are not proving the existence of God; rather, we presuppose that we know that there necessarily exists some un-created nature, and we are simply trying to show that a nature which necessarily exists is unique, that there cannot be a plurality of individuals multiplying that nature. If necessary being is possible, it is possible but once. Whatever can be conceived as "necessarily exist-ing" must be conceived as necessarily unique.

Multiplication presupposes an indifference. Our point here is not merely that divine nature requires individuation (*some* individu-ation, *any* individuation) if it is to be in the existent order—that is true of any nature, divine or not. But of the divine nature we do not say, as we should say of any other nature, that it requires, *dis-junctively, either* individuation A *or* individuation B *or* individuation Y *or* individuation Z. Rather, we say that divine nature requires *this particular* individuation (*scil.,* A), and it excludes the possibility of any other individuation (B, Y, Z).

Human nature, to be existent, requires concretization either in

Peter or Paul or Thomas or Socrates or Napoleon, but it is indifferent to these and other possible individuations. Human nature merely requires, disjunctively, some individuation. Human nature, being indifferent to existence, is indifferent to this and that and the other individual determination. When an individual creature's nature is considered abstractly, it does not have to be conceived as having the particular numerical individuation that it actually does have in the concrete instance from which the thinker has abstracted it. Divine nature, on the contrary, is self-existent; it is existent simply of itself and as such is individually determined. There is nothing abstract about divine nature; it is not indifferent to anything characterizing it in the existential order. Divine nature, therefore, cannot be without the ultimate determination which is *this* individuation. The individual being, God, has a nature that cannot be the term of an abstractive process. Divine nature transcends numerical multipliability; it cannot be conceived as a species or even a genus or quasi-genus (for these are indifferent to *this* or *that* further determination, though requiring further determination). God, thus, is a transcendent case of a unique existent; He is "uniquely unique."

IX. POLYTHEISM AND DUALISM

Non-philosophical position. The doctrine, philosophical and religious, that there is and can be only one divine being is called "Monotheism." The doctrine that does not admit the transcendent oneness and unmultipliability of divinity is "Polytheism." Ordinary polytheism is surely not a profound philosophy nor an edifying religion. It is often considered a mark of primitive civilizations. Yet it is worth noting that even in their golden ages Athens and Rome had many citizens who were polytheists. Indeed, the more "progress" or "culture" that the Greeks and Romans had, the more quickly it seems did they introduce other gods into their pantheons. One may well wonder, however, whether the really cultivated citizens, the serious thinkers, sincerely believed in the divinity of their many gods. Did they really make a distinction among the many super-human powers they personified, or were these various gods only various concepts or aspects of what they implicitly considered one divine transcendent power? At any rate, the more philosophical minds among the pagans, an Aristotle, for example, or a Cicero, seem to have been idolaters through convention rather than conviction; they give the impression that they looked upon the "gods" merely with polite gestures, as symbols of traditional ideals, but not as real divinities.

A philosophical temptation. Polytheism of the crass sort has never been a *philosophical* temptation. Yet throughout the history of ideas there is a philosophical temptation to hold a doctrine of dualism. To account for certain of the data of experience—those classified as evil—a number of thinkers have insisted that there are *two* uncreated beings, two "supreme principles." They have taught that, besides the supreme maker of good things, there is also a supreme and positive source of evil.

This dualistic doctrine received emphatic form in the ancient Persian philosophy of Zoroaster (or Zarathustra). In this doctrine there is a god of light, Ahura Mazda (or Ormazd), and a god of darkness, Ahriman (Angra Mainyu). The two have been in an eternal struggle, though supposedly the god of light and goodness will eventually triumph. The Persians, or Chaldeans, held this view. Their wise men were known as "Magi."

Another form of dualism is Manichaeism, a heresy of the early Christian centuries. Dualistic doctrines are also to be found in the various Gnostic sects of early Christianity. In the middle ages, the doctrine of dualism was to some extent revived by the Albigensians.

Often a dualistic religion, or even a dualistic philosophy, is accompanied by a dualistic morality, a double standard in morals. What is moral law for the ordinary run of mortals is not binding upon the "enlightened," the real knowers (the "gnostics"), the esoterics. These initiates have their own special lights; they are the elite, the *alumbrados*, the "illuminated ones"; they are above sin; nothing they do, however abominable, is blameworthy in their case. Small wonder that they ran afoul of Church and state.

Every few centuries there seems to be an outcropping of thinkers or believers who imagine they can simplify everything and solve the perennial problem of multiplicity and diversity, and especially the problem of good and evil, by postulating *two supreme* principles. Even Plato and Aristotle, as we saw in Chapter 4, were not completely immune from this temptation. From what we have been saying in the present chapter, and from the proof that we are now prepared to give, it should be evident that *two supreme* beings cannot exist.

X. ARGUMENTS TO ESTABLISH THE DIVINE UNICITY

A plurality of gods is *not necessary* to explain the data that need explanation; one omnipotent God quite suffices. A plurality of gods is *not probable*; the unity of the universe seems rather to manifest the plan of a single mind. Finally, a plurality of gods is *not possible*; for divine nature necessarily exists, and what necessarily exists cannot be indifferent to *this* particular individuation—*a* divine being is necessarily *this individual*: God.

Plurality not necessary. The first two arguments are merely to the effect that a plurality of gods is not necessary nor probable. It is not necessary to admit a plurality of beings, each of them endowed with divine nature. Philosophical investigators are usually quite content to have found *what is necessary and sufficient* to account for the data that stimulated their investigations. When they have found what is needed and yet suffices, they stop. This is a reasonable and economical procedure. It is Ockham's razor: "Beings (and explanations) are not to be multiplied without necessity." As philosophers we do not admit more than what the rational evidence calls for. The universe, the data of experience, *can* be adequately accounted for by numerically one divine being, one infinitely powerful being, one uncreated, necessarily existent being; hence there is no reason compelling us to admit more than one.

Plurality not probable. Indeed, more than one god is *not probable*. The order, the harmony—not merely the existence—of the universe would seem to argue to oneness of its designer. It is truly a *uni-*verse, not a chaotic juxtaposition of unrelated entities. Such an harmonious whole would seem to deny more than one ordering Intelligence. At any rate, it is not probable that at the source of the present universe there is a plurality of free-willed beings acting in concert, presenting a united front, and collaborating as one in an eternal pact to make and preserve a universal scheme of providential care and government.

Pushing things to the absurd, we can argue that if more than one god were possible, there is no rhyme nor reason to stop with any conceivable number of gods. How many gods should we admit? Two? Thirty-two? Three thousand and sixty-seven? If there is or can be more than one, then an indefinite number, an infinite multitude, would seem to be possible and even called for. For divine nature necessarily exists; in the case of divine nature, whatever is possible is actual. If divine nature can possibly be multiplied, then it is necessarily multiplied. How manifold can it be? No definite number of gods would seem to be called for; yet every possible deity must exist. It seems improbable that an infinite multitude of gods should exist; if there are many gods, there ought to be some evidence for a plurality, and there is none.

Plurality not possible. However, reasons based on the lack of necessity and of probability of the existence of a plurality of gods are not all that we are looking for. We are interested, still as philosophers, not in the minimal knowledge of God, but in whatever we can find out about Him as a result of investigating the data of experience and analyzing the nature and origin of the universe. Metaphysical investigations will make us conclude not merely that a plurality of gods is neither necessary nor probable, but that it is not even possible. Divine nature is not, and cannot be, multiplied numerically. God, a god, the God, this God—all are absolutely identical. A multipliable nature cannot be had by the being who is needed to explain the world, namely, the necessarily self-existent, uncreated being.

Necessary being not indifferent to individuation. If divine nature were multipliable, then divine nature, of its own formal content, would have to be indifferent to whatever it is that makes a certain divine being (A) be the individual god, A; it would have to be indifferent to whatever it is that makes another divine being (B) be the individual god, B, and to whatever it is that makes another divine being (C), be C. In other words, divine nature would have to be indifferent to individuation, just as "human nature" is indifferent to Tom, Dick, and Harry. Yet nothing can exist without its own individuation; universals, as such, do not and cannot exist in the real order outside the mind. Now, divine nature is not indifferent to existence. Divine nature is necessarily existent; it is really, conceptually, adequately, and convertibly identical with its existence. Hence divine nature cannot possibly be indifferent to individuation, for individuation is either existence itself or an absolutely necessary prerequisite condition of existence. If divine nature were indifferent to existence, or indifferent to an absolutely necessary prerequisite condition of existence, then divine nature simply would not be divine nature. For, either divine nature necessarily exists of adequate inner necessity (*a fortiori*, has all the absolutely prerequisite conditions of existence), or it cannot exist at all.

Let us suppose that divine nature is multiplied into a plurality of gods: A, B, C, etc., just as human nature is multiplied into a plurality of men: Tom, Dick, Harry, or at least as angelic nature is multiplied into Michael, Raphael, Gabriel. We are forced to conclude that divine nature prescinds from the individuation of A (for divine nature is, by hypothesis, found without this individuation in the case of god B); and we are forced to conclude that divine nature also prescinds from the individuation of B (since divine nature is found, by hypothesis, in god A, without the individuation of B), etc. We must forthwith conclude that divine nature, as such, prescinds from existence; for if it did not prescind from existence, then neither could it prescind from the singularity or individuality of A. If divine nature includes necessary existence (and it does, not precisely because it is *this*, but because it is *divine*), it has to include that without which existence is impossible, namely, singularity. But divine nature, the nature of necessarily existing being, cannot prescind from existence.

In short, if there were a plurality of necessarily existent beings, they would have to differ at least in individuality. And yet the essence of necessary being has to have *this* determinate individuality; otherwise it is not absolutely necessary. A plurality of necessary beings involves a contradiction.

"God" would be an existent universal. Putting the argument in another way: If divine essence could be found in many individual gods, then divine nature would prescind from the various individuating notes and would therefore be a universal; and yet, because necessary in itself, it would actually and necessarily exist. It would be a "universal idea existing outside the mind."

God would be caused. If divine nature were multipliable, it would not have individuality of itself; it would have to be determined to singularity by something really distinct from itself. But no being can have divine nature (and therefore be self-existent) if it has its individuality caused by some extrinsic cause.

God is not in a genus or species. Finally, there can be no plurality of *specifically* distinct divine beings, that is, a multitude of beings each of them constituting a separate, distinct species ("quasi-species") under a common genus (or "quasi-genus"): *necessary being*. If a plurality of specifically differing necessary beings were to be possible, the generic note could not contain even implicitly its differentiating notes. No one of the specific differences whereby a plurality of necessary beings would be constituted, could be absolutely necessary to the quasi-generic note, "necessary being." If any specific difference is necessarily contained in the generic note, there can really be no plurality of species. Neither "rational" nor "irrational," e.g., is contained in the note "animal," as such; otherwise, "animal" could not be multiplied by more than one species; the genus and species would coincide. If animality had to have canine form, then only dogs could be animals. Necessary being, even in its least determinate expression, necessarily includes everything without which it could not exist. It cannot be indifferent to a plurality of specific determinations.

Divine being is under all aspects absolutely necessary; otherwise, under that aspect it is caused, dependent, non-divine. Divine being cannot be indifferent to a plurality of specific or quasi-specific determinations; it cannot be a genus, nor a quasi-genus. Divine nature can be only *this* being, namely, God.

LEADING IDEAS of Chapter 7

1. A being is "one" inasmuch as it is undivided in itself and divided from everything else; God, as *perfectly undivided in Himself*, is not only actually undivided, He is absolutely indivisible or simple, and, as *perfectly divided from everything else*, His nature excludes the possibility of a plurality of divine beings.

2. In some particular cases of material reality, composition and complexity seem to be advantageous, a good; but it is not true that a being, as such, is more excellent the more composite it is; quite the contrary.

3. In God nature, faculty, and operation are utterly identical, are Pure Act.

4. Since a composite being is a caused being (the composition is caused, and the components are caused), God, who is necessary and uncaused, is not composite.

5. The divine essence cannot even be conceived as conceptually composite of genus and specific difference; otherwise, it would have to be conceived as finite (since neither genus nor specific difference is conceivable as including each other's perfection).

6. The plurality of our concepts about God does not argue against God's simplicity; for each concept, if truly of God, will implicitly include the concepts of all the divine perfections and the negation of their distinction.

7. Although polytheism is not taken seriously by philosophers, dualism (the doctrine of two supreme principles) is a perennial temptation.

8. All natures except divine are multipliable.

9. Divine nature has not merely a *de facto*, but a *de jure*, unicity; it is impossible that there should be many divinities.

10. Divine nature, considered absolutely, necessarily includes existence, hence individuality.

11. Divine nature, since existing necessarily, cannot be indifferent to individuations, A, B, C, etc.; otherwise it would have to be determined to actual existence (and concrete individuation) by a really distinct or outside cause.

12. A plurality of gods is not necessary: the universe is explicable by one only; a plurality of gods is not probable: the unity of the universe is suasive of the doctrine of the unicity of its Creator; a plurality of gods is not possible: otherwise, divine nature (necessarily existent) would have to be intrinsically indifferent (not necessitated) to a condition of existence, its individuation.

SUGGESTED READINGS for Chapter 7

For Scholastic Exposition:

St. Thomas. S.T. I.3 and I.11 (*Basic Writings*, Vol. I, pp. 25–36 and 85–90); *De Pot.*, 7.1–3 (*Power of God*, Vol. 3, pp. 1–18).

Wm. Brosnan, S.J. *God and Reason*. New York: Fordham University Press, 1924, pp. 97–99.

A. Dulles, S.J., J.M. Demske, S.J., R.J. O'Connell, S.J. *Introductory Metaphysics*. New York: Sheed and Ward, 1955, pp. 192–203.

G.H. Joyce, S.J. *Principles of Natural Theology*. London: Longmans, Green and Co., 1934, pp. 304–313.

On Simplicity in Creatures:

Walter Farrell, O.P. *A Companion to the Summa*. New York: Sheed and Ward, 1941, Vol. I, pp. 58–59.

On Persian and Manichaean Dualism:

George Ring, S.J. *Gods of the Gentiles*. Milwaukee: Bruce, 1938, pp. 61–83.

Etienne Drioton and others. *Religions of the Ancient East* (Vol. 141 of the *Twentieth Century Encyclopedia of Catholicism*, edited by H. Daniel-Rops). New York: Hawthorn Books, 1959, pp. 117–137.

J. Lebreton and J. Zeiller. *The History of the Primitive Church*. New York: Macmillan, 1949, Vol. II (Books III & IV), pp. 1009–1016.

On the "Illuminati" and Similar Sects:

Wm. Thomas Walsh. *Characters of the Inquisition*. New York: P.J. Kenedy, 1940, *passim*.

For Spiritual Inspiration (and apt answer to Wm. James):

D. von Hildebrand. *Transformation in Christ*. New York: Longmans, Green and Co., 1948, Chapter 5, "True Simplicity," pp. 57–85.

Raoul Plus, S.J. *Simplicity*. Westminster, Md.: The Newman Press, 1951, *passim*.

CHAPTER

8

OUTLINE

God's Transcendence over Change—
the Divine Immutability

I. INTRODUCTION

Divine immutability already established. The negative attribute immutability is one of the first that we come to know in our philosophical study of God. In fact, we have already proved that God is immutable, namely, when, in the proof of God's existence, we showed that the mutable data of experience—*precisely because* they are *mutable*—are not self-explanatory and therefore require another being as their explanation, that is, some being really distinct from them, to cause them to exist, some being, ultimately, that is not itself in need of any other being but is self-sufficient and self-explanatory. This other being must therefore be unlike the data of experience in the precise respect in which these are not self-explanatory; and so, in the case of mutable beings, their ultimate cause must be an immutable being.

Moreover, what exists of absolute necessity is absolutely immutable; for whatever is in any way really mutable is not absolutely necessary and hence not adequately self-sufficient in existence. Conversely, mutable beings are caused beings; not all beings can be caused; therefore, some immutable being must exist.

Why further discussion? We do not, therefore, need to spend much time on the proof of God's immutability, since it is already contained in the proof for His existence given in *Chapter 2*. But we wish to discuss more fully the meaning of this attribute, in order to eliminate certain misconceptions that tend to render the "*immutable* God of philosophy" somewhat unreal and impersonal to undiscerning minds.

II. DIVISIONS OF CHANGE

Change, in general, is the transition from one state of being to another, from the state of potentiality to that of actuality. The divisions of change may be seen from the following chart:

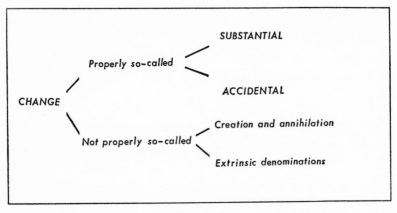

Figure 4.

Real change requires pre-existing passive subject. Real change, change properly so-called, always demands that under the change abide a pre-existing real subject, a substrate that first supports the old form and then supports the new one. This subject or substrate of real change must be passively indifferent to the various forms by which the power of an outside agent (a "mover") actuates it. Change properly so-called happens only when a previously existing being is transformed, is "moved," so that it becomes intrinsically different.

Divisions. Real change—*intrinsic* to the being *of which it is predicated*—may be substantial, and it may be accidental. Accidental change may be of the spiritual order (new spiritual qualities: for example, new ideas, new volitions), or it may be of the material order (in the line of quantity or of material qualities). In all cases of real intrinsic change, composition—the union of a passive, determinable principle and an actual or formal determining principle—is required.

A. Substantial Change.

Substantial (or essential) change is an intrinsic change that affects the very substance of a thing. It occurs, for example, when a living thing dies, or when food is digested and becomes part of the living substance of the being that has digested it. The food in this case is not annihilated, but it has ceased to be what it hitherto was. It has lost its own substantial form and has been incorporated into another substance.

B. Accidental Change.

Besides substantial changes, there are also accidental changes. Obviously there is a great difference between merely getting sick and dropping dead, even though both events are intrinsic changes. A man when healthy and the same man when sick is not quite the "same," but he is still human; though there are accidental differences, he has undergone no essential change, no change in species. A dead man, however, is no longer a man at all; a cadaver is really a heap of disparate chemicals, rapidly decomposing into simpler kinds; if it is still called a "human" body, this is only by a (clearly justifiable) figure of speech.

Examples of true accidental change. True accidental changes are intrinsic changes, even though they do not transform the species; they are changes in quantity (either augmentation or diminution) or changes in quality. They are extremely common. A man becomes feverish, he suffers from chills, he gets sunburned; a tree's leaves change their color, its fruits ripen; changes take place in the shape and configuration of living and non-living bodies. Spiritual changes, too, are among the data of our human experience; they consist in the acquisition or in the loss of some intellectual knowledge or some volition.

A word on change of place. With regard to change of place, or local motion, a defensible view is that although changes of place are most obviously happenings in the data of experience, they are not, precisely as "changes," truly intrinsic to any of the beings in motion. Change of place is, in this view, an "extrinsic change." Still, local motion would not be occurring unless it were preceded by, accompanied by, and followed up by intrinsic qualitative changes (and perhaps even quantitative changes) in the thing that is moving locally. A body at rest will not begin to be in local motion unless it receives an impetus from some other being or is given some gravitational attraction that it hitherto did not have. Changes in molecular cohesion, modifications induced by friction, alterations in energy and in inertia—all kinds of changes may occur when a body moves locally.

At any rate, it seems to us that local motion can only be predicated meaningfully of quantified beings, of extended bodies; and extension, as such, involves potentiality, divisibility, hence contingency. An extended being cannot be self-existent. God, therefore, cannot have extension nor, consequently, be in local motion—even though, as we shall see, certain "extrinsic changes" may legitimately be predicated of Him.

God can undergo no real change at all.   No true change at all is possible, whether accidental or substantial, without a passive, potential principle of change. Where there is substantial change, there must be a "prime matter" underlying the change of substance. Where there is accidental change (even an instantaneous one, such as the acquisition by a spiritual being of a new thought or a new volition), there is composition of substance and accident; the substance is the potential factor, the subject of actuations in accidental changes.

Where, then, a being is utterly simple, where a being is purely act, where a being is absolutely perfect, where a being is necessarily the entirety of whatever it here and now is, there is no possibility of any real change at all, substantial or accidental, material or spiritual. A necessarily existing being, whatever it is, is necessarily what it is; it cannot, therefore, become other than what it is. Change always implies composition: the mutual dependence of the components of the changeable being and the dynamic dependence of the whole composite upon some outside agent to which the union of the parts is due. The self-explanatory, necessarily existent being is necessarily independent of all outside influence and so cannot be intrinsically composite. Hence, all *real* change, any change properly so-called, is impossible within God, and this prerogative is called His immutability. It is the divine transcendence over change.

III. EXTRINSIC CHANGE

Earlier we mentioned "changes not properly so-called." Creation and annihilation, for example, although very radical processes, making a tremendous difference for the being that is created or annihilated, are not strictly changes; they are not changes "properly so-called." Even so, they cannot, as is obvious, possibly happen to a necessarily existent being, a self-explanatory reality. If the divine being, because of its necessity and simplicity and infinite perfection, cannot even undergo a real change, then *a fortiori* it is impossible for it to be created or annihilated. The "changes" (improperly so-called) that are creation and annihilation are completely ruled out in the case of Him who is the ultimate explanation of all reality, not because they are changes improperly so-called (for even "extrinsic changes" which *are* predicable of God are still changes "improperly so-called"), but because of the radical imperfection in being which they imply in the beings of which they are predicable. But the same is not true of all changes not properly so-called.

Predications that seem to imply change in God. Despite the necessity and pure actuality of God's being, there is a whole series of predications commonly made about God which seem to imply that He goes from one state of being to another and therefore "changes." The world begins to exist; hence God, Who prior to the world's existence was only potentially a "Creator," is now actually a "Creator." Again, God, Who from all eternity knew what events at this time *would be* actual, now knows that they *are* actual. God loves the man who is living a good life, but He is subsequently repelled by that same man when that man is in the state of grave sin.

Even simple words like "Creator," "Conserver," "Cooperator," "Providence," "Ruler," "Lord," "Judge," "Reader of the hearts of man," "Hearkener to our prayers," and so forth, seem to indicate a change in God. God could be without these denominations, for the perfection that these terms imply depends not on His necessary nature but on a free decree of His infinitely free will. These denominations are said to apply to God "in time" and not "from eternity"; they are sometimes called God's "contingent attributes," for they are denominations that He could be lacking.

Of course, if all that is meant by these terms is that God *can* create, conserve, cooperate, and so forth, then they are not "contingent attributes" but "necessary" ones. Often we name a thing by reason of its power even when that power is not actually terminating in a present effect. Thus a "doctor" is a doctor even when he is not doctoring, a cook is a cook even when he is asleep, and a lawyer is a lawyer even if he has never handled a case.

But even though the predication of such terms of God is justified, this does not imply any real change in God. The changes involved are extrinsic to God; they are changes occurring to beings distinct from God; God Himself is not intrinsically modified by them. New denominations, however, are rightly predicated of Him by reason of the new relations that creatures come to have with respect to Him.

Extrinsic change in general. To divide changes into "intrinsic changes" and "extrinsic changes" is perhaps useful in the present chapter, but it could be misleading—somewhat as would be a classification of men into "living men" and "dead men." For "extrinsic change" is simply not real change of the thing of which nevertheless it is predicated. A thing that is "changed" extrinsically is only the logical and grammatical "subject" of the change, not the ontological subject.

Examples. We say that *the sun is hotter* at noon than at dawn. But the real change is in us, not in the sun. Again, when the fog lifts from a valley, the valley "becomes" visible. Previously, it was invisible, and so the valley changes from being "not visible" to being "visible." Actually, the only changes are in the evaporation of the fog and in the vision of the onlookers; there is no change in the valley itself. The valley is not really any more passive, nor any more active, when it is "visible" than when it is "not visible." Our real seeing of the valley involves a change in us, and this new change— real in us, and conditioned by the real evaporation of the fog—furnishes the foundation for a new predication with respect to the valley itself. The valley is now extrinsically denominated "seen" or "visible" because of the intrinsic new form that exists in us, because of our act of "seeing" the valley. The valley has "changed" with relation to us, but this change, though it occasions the attribution of a new predicate to the valley, is really extrinsic to the valley. The valley is "extrinsically changed" when it "becomes visible."

Application to God. All this may seem trivial enough to the student, but there are some important applications to be made of this doctrine, serving to clarify difficulties that arise concerning God's immutable nature. Since "extrinsic" changes are not real modifications of the "subject" of which they are predicated, we can still maintain God's immutability and yet describe Him with predicates indicating various "extrinsic changes." New things have come into existence in total dependence upon God, new relationships have arisen between various creatures and God, but no addition or subtraction has occurred in God's own intrinsic perfection. God is infinitely good in Himself; He is none the better for the existence of creatures, and none the worse for their non-existence. Their possibility and their actuality are totally dependent upon God's perfection. Unless God were exactly what He is, creatures would be neither possible nor actual. God's infinite perfection is presupposed for the possibility and the actuality of creatures. Their existence or their non-existence is ontologically subsequent to and dependent upon His perfection. Hence nothing that affects them can affect Him.

The existence and the non-existence of creatures are equally within God's complete dominion. If they exist, this is because God wills them to be; were they non-existent, this would be because God would have willed them not to be. God *wills* the existence and nature of all actual non-divine existents, but He is not *motivated* (i.e., *moved*) in creating them; there is no outside influence that could induce changes in God's knowledge or will or power. God would be no better nor worse for producing other beings, whose possibility and actuality are eminently contained in Him.

Relations of creatures to the immutable God. Creatures are entirely dependent upon God, and He is entirely independent of them. God is absolute being and absolute perfection; but a transcendental relation of dependence upon God constitutes the very being of creatures. Contingent beings are not beings plus contingency; their very being is their contingency; their being is their dependence; their very "to be" is "to be from God"; for them, "to be changeable" is "to have had their changeability eternally willed by God." God loves His creatures, possible and actual, with an everlasting love, the possibles necessarily (as His essence is of its very nature imitable, furnishing the ground for the "possibles"), and the actuals freely (for the actuality of non-divine beings is contingent upon God's free will). He loves all creatures in perfect proportion to their lovableness. But their lovableness is totally dependent, totally participated. Since it is God's own nature that creatures participate in, and since they exist and are lovable only to the extent that they derive from God's infinitely lovable nature, God is not altered by their coming into existence, by their "transference" from the status of possibles to the status of actuals, nor by the vicissitudes that happen to them during their actual existence.

God's love and hatred.   For a man to become a sinner means that he becomes related to God as an object of God's displeasure; if he repents, he becomes related to God as an object of God's merciful forgiveness and love. By sinning, a man moves from the sphere of objects of God's love into the sphere of objects of God's hatred. The man changes, but the divine act itself is unchanged. Love of the lovable, hatred of the hateful—God's unique, infinitely perfect act is simultaneously both. But with every change in a creature's relation to God a foundation is given for a new predication about God. God knows Paul's virtuous living; God knows Paul's sins. God loves Paul, and then, God hates Paul. The succession and plurality of acts are not God's: they are Paul's.

Succession and plurality are in God virtually and eminently but not formally: God's unique perfection and actuality is the eminent equivalent of all kinds and all shades of individual successive acts, but formally there is only one, eternal, fully perfect act in God, and this is never intrinsically altered, even though we constantly give it new "extrinsic denominations." As St. Augustine says: "When God is said to be angry with men who are wicked and pleased with them when they are good, it is not God who changes, but the men; just as a light is painful to weak eyes but soothing when the eyes are strong, not because of any change in the light but because of change in the condition of the eyes." [1]

[1] St. Augustine, *De Trinitate*, Book V, Ch. 16, n. 17.

Justified ways of speaking. New denominations that are predicated of God, but based on changes in things extrinsic to God, are justifiable ways of speaking; but they do not mean—and it would be erroneous and anthropomorphic on our part to take them as meaning—that God Himself is really changed. If we say that at the first historical moment of the existence of non-divine beings, God changed from the status of *potential* Creator to the status of *actual* Creator, the "change" is purely extrinsic to Him. The newness of something extrinsic to God, but totally dependent upon Him, gives the foundation for the new predication.

Since that which, for an extrinsic reason, is denominated a change is not a change properly so-called, a predicate which explicitly or implicitly signifies such a change does not necessarily imply that the subject of which it is predicated is in any way imperfect, composite, finite, perfectible, contingent, or mutable. Neither does such a predicate deny that the subject in question is mutable. There is no *a priori* objection that can be raised, therefore, against applying to God words expressive of extrinsic change.

IV. MISCONCEPTIONS ABOUT DIVINE IMMUTABILITY

A. Mutability and Perfectibility.

We are so accustomed to change, and we are so used to seeing the finite data of experience become more perfect as a result of new acquisitions, that we tend to conclude that if something is immutable, it is extremely imperfect, and that its immutability, since it precludes perfectibility, is necessarily an imperfection. But even this statement needs qualification, for "we are always impressed by the sight of stability, firmness, permanence of strength and fitness, whether we see them in a grand building, in a political constitution, in a landscape, or in the character of a noble man. All this exists in a supreme degree in God." [2]

Of course, if a thing is finite, it will always be, at least in the

---

[2] James Bellord, *Meditations on Christian Dogma*, Westminster, Md., Newman Press, 1948, Vol. I, p. 16.

abstract, capable of further perfection, and since no increase in a thing's actual perfection is possible without change, it is true that, for finite things, to be "immutable" would be a serious imperfection. Recall our allusion to "Unwashable Jones" in *Chapter 2*. But where "immutability" is the result of infinite richness and of plenitude of actuality, where a being cannot acquire any perfection because He already possesses all possible perfection, then to call such a being "immutable" is not at all to use a derogatory term; it is rather a formal denial of the imperfection involved in all composition and passive potentiality.

God's eminence renders mutability impossible. God's being transcends all need to undergo change in order to be perfect. God is immutable, not through defect, but, if we may so describe His eminent mode of being, through excess of actuality or perfection. God is the complete source of all non-divine reality; all non-divine reality is eminently contained in God, both as regards possibility (since God's infinite essence is the exemplary cause of all creatures) and as regards actual existence (since God's omnipotence is the efficient cause of all creatures). Creatures are real to the extent that they mirror God's perfection. This perfection is not intrinsically modified by being reflected. God has the fact of the actual existence of creatures and the "fact" of their non-emergence into actual existence completely under His dominion. He is the Lord, the supreme master of all being. His own perfection is neither increased nor decreased when He creates. There is all the difference in the world, to the world, between God-creating and God-not-creating; but the difference is entirely in the world. God's dominion, God's freedom, and God's intrinsic perfection remain the same in all situations.

God, immutable in mind and will. Again, we tend to think of a person as stern and unattractive if he is immutable. When a person is unwilling to change his mind, when he sticks to his decisions no matter what new facts are called to his attention or what new circumstances arise, we consider him as stubborn, proud, self-willed, in a word, as lacking real virtue; his "strong will" is "bad will." Obviously it would be ridiculous as well as impious to think of God's immutability after that fashion.

God does not change His mind, and He does not make new decisions—that is true—but not because of any moral defect, but because infinite wisdom guided Him in His eternal decrees. Since He is subsistent truth, the rock and ground of all truth and intelligibility, nothing can ever present itself to His attention as "new and previously unthought of," no bit of news can now become manifest that His infinite wisdom has not already apprehended and weighed from all eternity. Decisions eternally made in the light of infinite wisdom, justice, holiness, and love, and executed through infinite power cannot be changed because of any unforeseen condition arising; if they are changed, this can only be through whim or caprice, but to act out of whim or caprice is a sign of imperfection even in a human, and it would involve a contradiction in the case of infinite wisdom and holiness.

B. Immutability Not Irreconcilable with Divinely Decreed Succession.

God, certainly, has willed that there be changes in the universe; but He never changes His will with regard to the universe. Changes that occur in the universe are not manifestoes of changed policies or changed attitudes on the part of God. God sees that changes in the non-divine world are good, even necessary, in view of the particular natures He wants actualized and the ends that He wills to be accomplished. And so He wills that there be changes; but His willing of change does not involve Him Himself in change.

From all eternity God has willed, for example, that A be followed by B, that C be followed by D, that E cause F, etc.; God willed that A be first, that B be second, that C be third, and so forth; but He did not first will A and then will B and then will C. God willed that there be succession and interrelationships, but He did not successively will them. Rather, from all eternity He elicited His one supereminent will-act, whose result is all the gigantic complexity of all non-divine reality, stretched out through the eons of temporal duration and teeming with interrelated processes.

A remote analogy. Certainly it is hard for us to understand all this, for it is shrouded in the mystery of God's infinitely fecund perfection. Yet some remote analogy may make the matter less puzzling to us. When a person consults a physician about his health, the physician will often prescribe certain medicines and give certain detailed directions regarding the time and dosage in taking the medicine. He decrees a certain regime to be followed. He will, for example, say, "During the first week, take two of these pills after each meal and two extra ones just before retiring at night. Then, the following week, just take one pill after each meal and only one before retiring at night. And for the third week, reduce the dose simply to one pill a day, to be taken just before retiring." The conscientious patient, influenced by the doctor's orders, takes two pills after each meal and two before retiring at night, for the space of a week. The next week, he reduces the various doses to one pill each time; and finally, during the third week, he takes only one pill a day, just before retiring. The doctor gave only one original but complex order, and it was not given at the precise moment that its effects occurred; but this one will-decree of the doctor has effects that are stretched out in time and that have various relationships to one another. The prescription is followed out to the letter, the succession and variations going all according to plan.

So too, but in an inconceivably more perfect and efficient and effective manner, God has in His eternal transcendence willed the created universe: its existence, its constituents, its succession and interrelation of events. Everything unfolds in time, but the will of God does not change in the unfolding; rather, the immutable will of God causes the unfolding.

C. God's Immutability Does Not Render Prayers Inefficacious.

Difficulty. A final consideration for this chapter is a problem that almost spontaneously arises in the mind of a devout person who has been taught from childhood that he should pray to God for what he wants and needs, and who now for the first time, perhaps, has come to grips with the notion of God's will being eternal and immutable. If God is immutable, then why pray? If God never changes His decree as to what shall eventuate in the created universe, then what is the sense of petitioning Him for this or that grace, this or that benefit, whether for ourselves or for others? If we are going to get it, God has already, indeed eternally, willed that we should get it; if He has eternally willed that we should not get it, not all the prayers of the most fervent saint in our behalf will change His immutable decree. Once one concedes the divine immutability, it would seem that prayers of petition are futile and meaningless. The "God of philosophy" has ousted the "God of religion."

Answer: Providence. Such a position is extremely erroneous and rests on hidden anthropomorphisms. God has immutably, but not blindly, willed all the things that occur in the present economy of His Providence. His will-decree is truly a *providential* decree, a foreseeing decree. It has provided for prayers, and it has provided answers to prayers. God was guided by an infinitely luminous wisdom in making His eternal "fiat!" He did not speak the "fiat" to creation without thought of the subject of the word (as though He said, "Let 'it' be"—"it," an indeterminate, unspecified it!). All the various patterns of events, with all the possible relations of causes and effects, were eternally known to Him. Within each separate pattern, particular effects follow their particular causes. Physical dispositions are followed by physical effects; moral dispositions are followed by moral effects.

Praying for some particular good is an act that puts a man in the proper disposition for receiving certain graces or other benefits. We should pray for what is good for us, for the same reason that we should use our tongue and lips to speak and our muscles to move our arms and legs. Prayer puts us in the disposition to receive what God has *conditionally* destined for us, the *conditions* being that we properly dispose ourselves and that the benefit requested be really a good in the light of our final destiny.

God from all eternity has seen the fulfillment of the conditions, He has seen us freely disposing ourselves, He has seen our cooperating with grace, and He has from all eternity willed His response to our dispositions. God from all eternity saw all possible worlds and all possible conditions. He saw various possible physical laws working out throughout possible universes and the various possible harmonies of gravitational attraction between possible natural forces; He saw the tendencies latent in all possible germinal cells (whether plant or animal), and He knew under what conditions what cells would find fruition and what ones remain sterile. He saw possible men turning to Him in request; He saw others refusing to acknowledge their creaturehood. All these possibilities He saw from all eternity. In saying "Fiat!" to the present universe, our actual universe—

one out of countless other possible universes—He foresaw our prayers, and they were taken into consideration when He decreed our universe, when He decided that this particular pattern of possibilities, and not some other one, should be realized.

Divine immutability a solid foundation for religion. God's immutability is a most solid basis for personal religion and morality. God's Providence will never forget us, never ignore us, never desert us. God will never deceive us nor grow tired of us. No deeper foundation for faith and confidence can be had, then, than the divine immutability. This doctrine finds beautiful expression in the following paragraph from Father Garrigou-Lagrange, and with it we shall close this chapter:

Providence . . . has determined from all eternity that there shall be no harvest without the sowing of seed, no family life without certain virtues, no social life without authority and obedience, no redemption without a Redeemer, no salvation without the application of His merits and—in the adult—a sincere desire to obtain that salvation. In every order, from the lowest to the highest, God has had in view the production of certain effects and has prepared the necessary causes; with certain ends in view He has prepared the means adequate to attain them. For the material harvest, He has prepared a material seed, and for the spiritual harvest, a spiritual seed, among which must be included prayer. Prayer, in the spiritual order, is as much a cause destined from all eternity by Providence to produce a certain effect (the attainment of the gifts necessary for salvation), as heat and electricity in the physical order are causes that from all eternity are destined to produce the effects of our everyday experience. Hence, far from being opposed to the efficacy of prayer, the unchangeableness of God is the ultimate guaranty of that efficacy.[3]

LEADING IDEAS of Chapter 8

1. Precisely because the data of experience are mutable, we realize that they are not self-explanatory and that, therefore, their adequate cause must be immutable.

2. God wills the changes that occur in the universe, but He does not change His own will with regard to the universe; God wills succession, but He does not successively will.

[3] R. Garrigou-Lagrange, O.P., *Providence*, St. Louis, Herder, 1937, pp. 206 f.

3. Intrinsic changes are possible only in a composite being and are the effect of some outside causal influence; hence the absolutely simple and uncaused and infinitely perfect being cannot undergo intrinsic change, whether substantial or accidental.

4. "Extrinsic change" is not change properly so-called; it is rather a new denomination given to a thing because of a real change undergone by something distinct from it but related to it.

5. God's unique perfection is the eminent equivalent of all kinds of individual successive acts, but formally there is but one, eternal, fully perfect act in God, and this is never intrinsically altered, even though we constantly give it new extrinsic denominations.

6. Instead of being a reason for our not praying to God for anything, the divine immutability is rather the guaranty of the efficacy of our prayers; for God foresaw these prayers and took them into consideration when He providentially decreed the succession and relationships of our universe.

SUGGESTED READINGS for Chapter 8

For Scholastic Exposition:

St. Thomas. S.T. I.9 (*Basic Writings*, Vol. I, pp. 70–73).

Wm. Brosnan, S.J. *God Infinite and Reason*. New York: America Press, 1928, pp. 93–108.

W. Farrell, O.P. *A Companion to the Summa*. New York: Sheed and Ward, 1945, Vol. I, pp. 65–70.

R. Garrigou-Lagrange, O.P. *The One God*, translation by B. Rose, O.S.B. St. Louis: Herder, 1946, pp. 268–275.

A.L. Reys. "The One God," *The Teaching of the Catholic Church*, edited by G.D. Smith. New York: Macmillan, 1950, Vol. I, pp. 95–98.

On Change:

V.E. Smith. *The General Science of Nature*. Milwaukee: Bruce, 1958, Chapters 4 and 5.

On the Excellence of Divine Immutability:

St. Augustine. *The City of God*, Book 12, Chapter 17 (translation by Marcus Dodds in the Modern Library Edition. New York: Random House, 1950, p. 400).

On Immutability and Difficulties of God's Knowledge and Freedom: Brosnan. *op. cit.*, pp. 115–122.

On the Reconcilability of God's Impassibility and His Compassion:

E.L. Mascall. *Existence and Analogy*. New York: Longmans, Green and Co., 1949, pp. 134–143.

C.S. Lewis. *The Problem of Pain*. New York: Macmillan, 1944, pp. 36–42.

CHAPTER 9

OUTLINE

I. *Time, a Characteristic Only of Contingent Being*

II. *Formation of the Idea of Eternity, or Transcendent Duration*

III. *Contrast between Human Duration and Divine Duration*

IV. *Contrast between Angelic Duration and Divine Duration*

V. *Proof of God's Eternity*

VI. *Other Meanings of the Term "Eternity"*

VII. *Application to God of Expressions Implying Time*

VIII. *The "God of Religion" and Philosophy's "Eternal God"*

God's Transcendence over Time— the Divine Eternity

I. TIME, A CHARACTERISTIC ONLY OF CONTINGENT BEING

Closely allied to creaturely change is time, the measure of a material creature's duration; closely allied to the divine immutability is eternity, the duration of God. Let us turn, then, to a consideration of this fifth "negative" attribute of God, His transcendence over time.

The measuring of change. Because the things of our experience undergo various changes, the relative permanence of their reality (enabling us still to speak of various *they*'s and *it*'s) can be measured. A changing being does not of itself have the full actuality of which it is capable; it is in a process of becoming, of being more fully actualized. The various sectors or the various stages through which the thing passes in its progress towards its complete actuation can be compared and contrasted with one another with respect to remoteness from or proximity to the terminus of the actuating process. The measuring of change, that is, of this progressive actuation, is what constitutes time. Time is "the numerical reckoning of the succession involved in motion." [1]

Time not an independent entity. Despite what our imagination may suggest to us, time is not an independent entity, a sort of duration that has always existed and that will always exist, an uncreated, yet non-divine, universal and eternal receptacle in which are contained the temporary durations of the various data of experience. What is real about time, independently of our mind, is rather

[1] Aristotle, *Physics*, IV, xi.

the foundation of time, namely the reality and measurability of the motion or change which time is used to measure.

Time is an essential concomitant, therefore, but not the conditioner, of mutable beings. We say of a thing that changes that "it is subject to time"; we use old sayings such as "Time heals all wounds" and "Time will tell." But these are figurative ways of speaking. Time is not a cause; it is rather an effect. It does not produce change, nor condition the data of experience; rather, it is produced by change, in the sense that change is what furnishes whatever objective foundation there is for the concept, time.

The kind of being that is measurable by time.   If, then, a being is measurable in terms of time, this is because the being is changeable, capable of "gradual" actuations. In this context the word "gradual" does not have the connotation of "slow," but simply of "continuously progressive" without any interruption or actual stoppings until complete actuation is had. When water is being heated, or when it is being changed from the ice state to the steam state, the process may be accomplished in a leisurely fashion over a "slow" fire, or it may be done exceedingly swiftly by putting the ice directly on a red-hot stove. In both cases the boiling is a "gradual" process, a successive actuation that proceeds, without actual stoppings, through "grades," or degrees, from near zero to the boiling point. At any one of these indefinitely multitudinous degrees, or fractions thereof, the heating process could have been stopped, but at none of them did the process actually stop. Otherwise there would have been as many motions as there had been actual stoppages; there would not have been merely one continuous process of changing ice into steam. Were it not for the potential nature of these intermediary stopping places, time would have nothing to measure, since all actuation would occur instantaneously. Water would become steam without *going through* any degrees of heat.

Time measures "gradual" changes; but it is also used as the measure of the duration of the substances that underlie these processes, the substances that are the "subjects" of these gradual changes. We humans, for example, remain substantially the same—are without any substantial succession—so long as "we" are "we," that is, from the first moment we are human to the moment of our death. But our substance would cease to be, we would undergo a substantial change and no longer be "we" at all, were it not for the accidental changes (for instance, those involved in the assimilation of food, in breathing, and so forth) to which our substance is subjected. Stop the circulation of the blood, or stop the beating of the heart, and *we* stop; we quickly lose our essential being and become corpses and disembodied souls. Now, these accidental changes, to the extent that they involve quantified matter, are themselves subject to succession and to motion and so make us as a whole measurable by time.

Time is strictly or properly characteristic only of changeable, therefore only of produced, therefore only of non-divine, beings. The perfection whereby the divine nature excludes measurability in terms of time, the transcendence of the divine duration over temporal duration, is what constitutes God's eternity.

II. FORMATION OF THE IDEA OF ETERNITY, OR TRANSCENDENT DURATION

Analogical knowledge of God's duration. Our concept of God's eternity is, we may say, a proper concept (for it applies correctly, literally, and formally, not metaphorically, to God); indeed, it applies only to God and is therefore even a concept of a property of God. But it is also a very analogical concept. It is not derived directly from God Himself, nor is it formed merely by abstracting from the data of experience. Its formation is somewhat complex.

In the first stage, we attribute *duration* to God—making sure, however, that our concept of duration does not positively include what is strictly characteristic only of the kind of duration which is "time," a magnitude integrated of parts outside of parts. Then we go on to judge that God's duration not only does not include, but necessarily and positively excludes, the characteristic of temporal duration, namely, continuous change, succession in actuation, and lack of simultaneously integral actuality.

Like all "negative" attributes, eternity at least implies the positivity of "being" or "existence." Eternity, because it is conceived as a duration, even adds something positive to "being" or "existence"; it adds the notion of "persistence" or "permanence" to being.

Purifying our notion of duration. Perhaps our first impulse is to think of duration as something that flows along, as something stretched out in a sequence whose parts come, successively, into existence. But in that case, we are not thinking of duration; we are trying to imagine it. Or, rather, what we are thinking of in that case is *predicamental* duration, the imperfect duration characteristic of the material data of our experience. Under the influence of our imagination, we tend to take for granted, paradoxically, that, unless a being is being continuously modified, it has no duration or permanence. But strictly speaking, duration means permanence: permanent identity of being, persistence in existing.

Duration, therefore, does not necessarily imply any succession (even though the idea of duration or persistence would, perhaps, have never occurred to our human intellects unless we had had some experience of its contrast, succession). The positive perfection of a being's duration is really in inverse proportion to the succession undergone by that being. Time, however, necessarily implies succession and change and therefore a relative non-permanence. Hence time is a falling away from the pure perfection of duration. Time is predicamental and cannot be positively included in the formation of a concept of a transcendent perfection. What is temporal is not completely abiding, not integrally permanent.

Transcendent duration. The pure concept of duration, the concept of *transcendental* duration, the concept that furnishes what is positive in the formation of the transcendent notion, is not the concept of time, nor that of temporal duration, but rather the concept of the permanent existence that remains when we prescind from change or when we consider not any non-abiding, non-stable, accidental forms, but the persistence of the substance underlying change.

The notion of permanence is a pure (precisively pure) notion, but like any transcendental notion, it is verified in the real order either in a predicamental, hence imperfect and contingent, manner or else in a transcendent manner that objectively excludes imperfection and contingency. When we have come to know that some being must exist permanently and yet cannot exist with any intrinsic succession, we forthwith have our conception of *transcendent* duration, or eternity.

Essential difference between temporal and eternal duration. It would be false to picture time as a finite line, with a definite beginning and a definite end, and to picture eternity as a line parallel with the temporal line but without a beginning or an end, as though, if time were simply without beginning and end, it would be commensurable with divine eternity. We would, in imagining such to be the case, be very much in error, for we would be trying to describe eternity by multiplying an element that is its contradictory. Further, what makes temporal beings essentially imperfect as temporal is not the having a first moment and a last moment to their duration, but that they have their actuality in a succession and not all of it together.

A beginning and an end are accidental in temporal duration; what is not accidental but essential to it is the possibility of succession. And, philosophically, the world teems with the possibility of succession and of change. The world is necessarily temporal, measurable in terms of time. The nature of God, however, is a nature which exists of inner necessity; it is the uncaused, self-sufficient actuality, positively excluding not only a beginning and an end but also all succession. It endures, certainly, and it endures in the best possible manner; it is indeed the only reality that completely, integrally endures.

III. CONTRAST BETWEEN HUMAN DURATION AND DIVINE DURATION

Our actuality is cumulative. It is especially in contrasting the fluid duration of our human existence with the fullness and necessity of God's duration that we best appreciate the meaning of eternity. We begin our substantial existence as a human being when our spiritual soul is infused into the matter properly disposed to be a human body. We start out in life as a microscopic cell, grow first into an embryo and then into a foetus, and after nine months are born into the world. We pass quickly from babyhood to childhood, adolescence, young manhood, and manhood. We become adults; then we slow down, we become middle-aged, we grow senile, and we die. From the moment of conception to the moment of death, from our generation to our dissolution ("corruption"), we are "stretched out" in being; our reality is constantly added to, but we never have all of it at any one moment. Our actuality, our historical existence, is parcelled out to us; our total perfection in being is cumulative. Any one moment of our life has snowballed from the past and is pregnant with the future. We are never absolutely the same from one moment to the next.

We recognize our utterly fleeting nature when we advert to our memories of what has already lapsed and to our plans and presentiments of what is yet to be. For the very moment in which we advert to the past is a moment that immediately lapses into part of that past. Before the twinkling of the eye, the act of trying, here and now, to recall the past has itself joined the past. Before we have even finished reading this sentence, we have been modified. We are actual, yes, substantially actual; but the full *we*, the *we* of history, with all our operations and all our acquired perfections—*this we* never exists at any one moment; it is not simultaneously existent. Our whole being is never had simultaneously as a whole; we are drawn-out existents, spatial and temporal *continua*.

Change, necessary for human life. There is, indeed, a relatively permanent underlying *ego*; we maintain some identity from the cradle to the grave, else *we* would have no duration at all. There is one and the same "I" who is subject to all the manifold changes occurring in *my* biography, but the totality of my reality—*my* past, *my* present, and *my* future—is something that never exists as one simultaneous whole. We are a flux of being. We cannot be simultaneously an embryo and an adolescent; we cannot simultaneously enjoy the buoyancy of youth and the experienced prudence of old age. Our life is essentially a progression; we build up our being. We start out with manifold potentialities, quite remote from full actuality. We develop, we mature, we grow old. We are creatures of time; our beginning and our end are marked off by a definite, limited span of duration, and the whole interim, from beginning to end, is constituted by succession and change. For us, change is vital, essential; to stop changing is to stop living; it is to cease to be ourselves at all.

God is always fully actual. God, on the other hand, is not at all changeable. He cannot, therefore, be measurable by time. He undergoes no change. He always is all of His reality; He has His total actuality totally and always. He has it without beginning, without end, and, most importantly, without succession. Moreover, He has all this of absolute necessity. He exists of Himself, or He could not exist at all, for He cannot have been created. His very essence is to exist; He is uncaused in His being, totally independent of all other reality; and so no cause can effect His cessation from being, He cannot be annihilated, and He cannot cease to be. He is immutable and incapable of succession, and He has no parts streaming after other parts; He is purely act, with no plurality and no possibility of the least alteration in His infinite perfection and utter simplicity.

Cross-sections of temporal being and of eternal being. Our temporal duration is but a pale "mobile image of eternity." Our "present moment" is a tiny part of "us," and our total duration is integrated by the complete accumulation of our succeeding instants. God's "present moment" is abiding—not, like ours, fleeting; in His permanent "instant," all perfection whatsoever is concentrated. We are never all of our perfection, but God is always all of His perfection. Any two cross-sections of our historical existence will be somewhat different; with God, no cross-sections are possible.

A duration that is not a process. A being that undergoes no change does not "age." For the created universe, years and years, centuries and eons have gone by, but God is the "beauty ever ancient, ever new." [2] No comparison or contrast between different sectors or stages or moments of development can be made in His case; for these are excluded by His full actuality, which excludes even a plurality of simultaneously existent *parts*. God has duration—His actuality endures—but it is not prolonged, nor is it a process or a progression. God's duration is infinite duration, but the entirety of it is simultaneously existent; it is not had through succession.

No past, present, or future to eternity. God's actuality is not stretched out; it has no parts. God does not accumulate perfection while our years glide by. Equally synchronous with any given moment of our time, God is outside all time, for He is not stretched out along our duration. He is rather the center around which the circle of time is being drawn. God is utterly permanent; He does not progress, for He is in the state of supreme, infinite perfection.

[2] St. Augustine, *Confessions*, Book 10, Ch. 27.

It would be an illusion to picture God's eternity as though a part of His actuality existed centuries ago, another part of it exists now, and yet another part will exist in the future. God's past, present, and future are concurrent. Rather, God has no past (for what is past is no longer actual) and no future (for what is future is not yet actual), nor even any present in our sense of the term (for our present is a fluid moment trailing off from the past and fanning out into the future). There is no flux in the divine being; all of God is an undivided, indivisible whole, which He possesses simultaneously, completely, and immutably as an infinitely pure and dynamic actuality.

IV. CONTRAST BETWEEN ANGELIC DURATION AND DIVINE DURATION

Instantaneous changes in accidental spiritual perfection. A form of predicamental duration to which we can argue if we grant the possibility of purely spiritual beings that are finite and contingent (namely, the angels, whose existence is known through revelation), is "eviternity." This is a duration, not of a substance that admits gradual accidental actuation, but of a substance that admits only instantaneous accidental changes (instantaneous acquisitions of thoughts and volitions). Finite spirits—precisely as finite— will be capable of accidental accretions to their perfections. Such accretions in these spiritual beings will be instantaneous, for it is only quantified matter that stretches out actuation and—giving the process a "before" and an "after"—makes it "take time." No single accretion to an angel's accidental perfection will be a successive actuation (that is, motion in the strict sense of the term); but a succession, that is, a plurality not simultaneously possessed, of instantaneously acquired accretions is quite conceivable.

Angels not in time. The duration of such beings will not be measured in terms strictly of time, for time measures continuous motion, motion that involves succession within one and the same actuation, and these spirits, because of their immaterial nature, cannot have a single motion that would be successive. Still, we cannot rule out the possibility of a succession of instantaneous changes (thoughts, volitions).

Eviternity an imperfect duration. Angelic duration, or eviternity, therefore, recedes from the perfection of duration. Like temporal duration, eviternity admits changes. Its changes are instantaneous, but precisely because these instantaneous changes are still changes, they are indications of real imperfection in their subject; they are signs of finitude and marks of contingency, as much as are the gradual changes in the accidental perfection of material substances. God, of course, is incapable of even the slightest accidental accretion. His eternal duration transcends even the order of angelic eviternity.

	with gradually successive actuaations	TIME
DURATION	with succession of instantaneous actuations	EVITERNITY
	without possibility of succession, full and permanent actuality	ETERNITY

V. PROOF OF GOD'S ETERNITY

Eternity follows upon necessity and immutability. Time measures the duration or permanence of imperfectly permanent beings; it measures such beings as undergo continual change; it measures deviations from pure permanence. Change is necessary for the perfection of the data of experience; hence time is a necessary corollary of the existence of these data. But where a being is by its very nature all-perfect, where a being is pure actuality and positively excludes all potentiality, change is not only not necessary, it is impossible. Without change, no measurability of change; without measurability of change, no time. God is necessarily existent and necessarily immutable; this forces us to conclude that God is outside of time. This perfection of God, negatively described as His excluding measurability by time (and eviternity), we call His eternity.

Or again: God is utterly simple; therefore He is pure actuality, admitting no passive potentiality (for this would indicate relativity, a *de jure* dependence on some distinct actuator). Being pure actuality, God is utterly unchangeable; change is possible only where a being has some potentiality. Being absolutely unchangeable, yet necessarily existent, God is essentially eternal.

Need of something always existent. If ever there had been absolutely nothing in existence, then there would still be absolutely nothing in existence. That absolutely nothing at all should yield place to anything at all is an utterly incredible situation. Something would be explained by nothing. Our intellect is not satisfied with any explanation of the present universe that would say that every individual being has been originated and that no being has always existed.

But granting that there has always been being, is there any *one* being that has *always* been? Is it necessary that "always" qualify some one particular being or, perhaps, class of beings? Might not many non-divine things have always been in existence? Even so, that would be no obstacle to proving God's eternity. We would not, as philosophers, gainsay the proposition that many non-divine things might have been always existent. But true eternity is not an "amount" of duration, it is a "kind" (or quasi-species) of duration. The real problem of proving God's existence and His eternity is not that of showing that something has always existed, but rather of showing that not all existent reality can be caused.

Not only no being that has had a first moment, but no being that is in any way originated or dependent in its being can give an ultimate explanation of the universe. Contingent being requires necessary being, and necessary being cannot possibly have ever been non-existent. Hence, some one being—at least one—not only has always been in existence but has been so of inner necessity. No being of finite duration, no, not even an everlasting being, could exist unless there is in existence, always, some being who has an inner necessity of existing, one whose existence is not caused but is self-explanatory, some one individual who is pure actuality.

Contradiction in the materialists' doctrine. The materialists would claim that eternity and necessity are attributable to the ultimate matter out of whose potentialities chance and the ironclad laws of nature have fashioned the present universe. In so doing, the materialists are making a monstrosity out of matter. Despite its potentialities, the materialists attribute strictly divine perfection to matter. Matter, they argue (if they even raise the question of its ultimate explanation), is absolutely self-explanatory, absolutely necessary in existence, simply uncaused, and independent of anything non-material; yet it has extension, divisibility, motion, change, relativity, and dependence of parts upon other parts of matter. And as for the ironclad laws themselves that are used by the materialists' chance in fabricating the present scheme of things, we saw in our proof for God's existence from "finality" that however "necessary" they may be when considered physically, they appear quite arbitrary and therefore not ultimately adequate when looked at metaphysically. The question: "Why?" is not answered merely by describing "how."

VI. OTHER MEANINGS OF THE TERM "ETERNITY"

As in the case with practically every word used in speaking about God, the words "eternal" and "eternity" are also less properly used in reference to creatures, or at least in reference to certain types of creatures. The words in their strict, non-metaphorical sense apply only to God. Eternity is a strictly transcendent perfection, something that in its primary signification is exclusively divine.

"Not having a first moment." The word "eternity" and its adjective, "eternal," are sometimes applied to creatures. We have seen, for example, that the question is seriously discussed among philosophers: Could the universe be eternal? or, Is an eternal world possible? or, Can something have been created and yet be eternal?— meaning, could something produced have been always in existence and have had no first moment of time, despite its total dependence upon God? An "eternal" world would be an eternally dependent world, an eternally created world, and its "eternity" should not at all be confused with the divine eternity. This is not only a duration that had no first moment and that is not measured by a finite amount of time in the past; divine duration is a necessarily existent duration, a totally independent, self-existent duration, one that cannot possibly have had a first moment. All other durations, even when they are called "eternal" and "necessary," could have had a first moment and can have a last one, since they exist only so long as God freely wills their existence. All time is "borrowed time." God could have willed that all non-divine beings have a first moment and a last one. He can will, absolutely speaking, the annihilation of any and every creature whatsoever. Their permanence in existence is due to His free causal influence; it is never a totally self-explanatory permanence.

"Everlasting" and "immortal." Again, the sanctions appointed for man after death are called "eternal." Thus Hell-fire is "eternal," meaning that it will never end, that it is "everlasting." Likewise, the soul of man, since it is spiritual and, therefore, intrinsically incapable of corruption, is sometimes said to be "eternal," meaning that it is incorruptible and immortal. The future life of man, the life of the soul after death, is often called "eternity" by ascetical writers. Many of the contrasts made by writers between "time" and "eternity" are contrasts between human life on earth and human life in Heaven (or Hell). Such "eternity" is predicamental: it is a product; it even has a first moment. Furthermore, a succession of accidental changes, it would seem, cannot be ruled out in the case of such an "eternity."

"A long time." Again, "eternity" is rather loosely used to describe a finite period of time that for some reason or other is, or seems to be, unusually prolonged. Thus a student complains that it will take him "an eternity" to finish all his home-work; a patient in a hospital finds his sufferings lasting for "an eternity." Things that have lasted a relatively long time, or that have remained substantially the same or have retained some striking characteristics for a long period, are called "eternal." Thus we speak of the "eternal hills" and of the "eternal city."

"Eternal" truths. True propositions are sometimes said to have an "eternity," or to be "eternal truths." This is especially the case when the propositions are statements of necessary truths, based on the intrinsic nature of the subject and predicate and pointing out necessary relationships or properties. These statements are "essentialist" propositions and are true no matter whether there are any temporal things in existence or not and no matter at what moment they are thought of. Their truth is not tied in with a definite time or place. They are true yesterday, true today, and true tomorrow; they are outside the actually existent realm of time. Yet such an eternity is a negative thing. It is not an actual duration, but a product of the mind. Its ultimate basis is God's eternal essence, imitable by countless beings outside Him, and God's eternal mind, where these "eternal truths" are so many ideas eternally known by God.

But even contingent, existential propositions, once the existential fact they describe has actually occurred, acquire, by our "hindsight," an "eternal" truth. The necessity of "having happened"—a mere "consequent necessity," a necessity established as a result of what actually has happened, a necessity based on the Principle of Identity (A = A)—makes us sometimes speak in fatalistic accents: "It is eternally true that the Ides of March, 44 B.C., is the day of the assassination of Julius Caesar." Everything in the existential order thus becomes just a case of *"Que será, será"*!

VII. APPLICATION TO GOD OF EXPRESSIONS IMPLYING TIME

Examples. It is commonplace to hear or read propositions like the following: "God created the world hundreds of centuries ago," "God will reward us when we die," "God knew that this was going to happen but did nothing to prevent it," "God will bestow His grace on the man who repents," etc.

Their meaning. These propositions are not meant to imply that God's actuality has a temporal extension of which one part was realized, for example, centuries ago (when the world began to exist), and then lapsed into non-being—as if God "grew older"!—and that there is another part of God's actuality which is not yet existent but which will have come into being by the time we ourselves are faced with death and which will then be ready to receive us into Heaven. God and the universe do not go along *pari passu*, side by side; they do not exist alongside each other. God transcends the universe.

Like the propositions that attribute change to God, propositions that describe God in terms of time are not literally correct, but they are not always necessarily misleading. Commonly enough, the speaker and hearer realize that figurative expressions are being used, and that phrases expressing past, present, and future are applied to God, not because of any change attributable to Him, but because of changes and succession in the data of experience which have their being, their order, their nature, their dynamism, and their relationships through dependence upon Him and which unfold in time in accordance with the unique eternal "fiat" of God.

God is the virtual, eminent equivalent of all that creatures are and have. Temporal expressions used of God are simply trying to express that fact. God's eternal, unique, free act is the virtual, eminent equivalent of a plurality and succession of human free acts. God did not successively will; He eternally willed the succession. He willed from all eternity and with but one will-act, but He did not will that the effect be eternal; He eternally willed that it be manifold and stretched out in time. What God eternally and freely wills is precisely the world of time, with all its changes and successions and interrelations.

Changes in creatures' relationships with God. Changes in creatures put new relations between the universe and God, and thereby give a basis for us to apply new denominations to God. These denominations do not affirm a new intrinsic form, and therefore change, in God, but furnish the justification for different predications of God indicating that the things related to Him are subject to time. Creatures change in their relationships with God, but the change is in them, not in God. Real mutual relations exist only between beings of the same order, beings that are mutually dependent on each other in some real respect. There can be no real mutual relation between the transcendent and the contingent. God, certainly, really causes the world; He, certainly, really loves mankind; He really has Providential care over the universe; but He is not essentially dependent upon the universe for any of His perfect reality. He is ". . . an infinite being in whom is only one act of will, which is identified really with his absolutely simple nature, and which though unchanged and absolutely unchangeable in itself, nevertheless, because placed in the light of infinite knowledge, makes provision for all the changeable events of time, and thus gives ground for our speaking in terms denoting time of the timeless duration of that being." [3]

[3] Wm. Brosnan, S.J., *God Infinite and Reason*, New York, The America Press, 1928, p. 116. See also *Ibid.*, pp. 137–139.

VIII. THE "GOD OF RELIGION" AND PHILOSOPHY'S "ETERNAL GOD"

William James would consider the attribute "eternal" one of those "pedantic dictionary adjectives," used in the construction of a "metaphysical monster" and "from the point of view of practical religion . . . an absolutely worthless invention of the scholarly mind." [4] We believe, on the contrary, that the philosophical notion of the divine eternity cannot but be of tremendous aid in man's religious appreciation of God, that the truly religious man realizes this almost instinctively, and the slightest bit of sober reflection will convince him that God's transcendence over time makes Him much more intimately engaged in man's welfare than could possibly be the case were God merely an aging super-man. Our past, present, and future are all equally present to God's substance, power, and knowledge. All of God is active in us and for us, every moment of our lives.

An apostrophe to eternity. The devout theologian Leonard Lessius (died 1623) was so overwhelmed when speculating on God's eternity that he closed his treatment of the subject with a beautiful apostrophe which we here transcribe, believing that it will convince the appreciative reader that "eternity" is not altogether worthless for "practical religion":

O Eternity! Thou are the primordial and unending reunion of all that is good; the total, perfect and simultaneous possession of a life that can never grow old; the supereminently complete fruition without beginning and without end of all happiness. For Thee there is no past nor future; for Thee there is no possible augmentation nor decrease. From the altitude of Thy *Now*, that actual moment which embraces infinite time, Thou gatherest together all things at once. Thou holdest them all present in such wise that they cannot flow away to the past, nor arrive at any thing new in the future. Thou precedest and anticipatest all things, present, past and future, and they are already present to Thee before they can have aught of the future in their being. For although whatever was to be in the future was such from all eternity, nevertheless it would not have been so, hadst Thou not known it, and either wished or permitted it.

[4] Wm. James, *Varieties of Religious Experience*, Modern Library edition, New York, Random House, p. 437.

In Thy *Now* all things are once for all considered and decreed. In it all counsel about all things is held and concluded. No deliberation remains to be made; all have been thoroughly scrutinized and examined. What is ever to be or not to be has been defined and decided. In that *Now* we have been numbered and weighed, and all our works have been placed in the balance. . . .

O Eternity! Be Thou ever present to my mind. Inhere in my innermost sense; be the rule of all my actions and of all my life; make me think of Thee so as to despise and regard as evil all that passes, be it of weal or woe; be my solace in all suffering; my help in all temptations; my light and counsel in prosperity.

To Thee who art the beginning of all beginnings and more ancient than them all, who art the Father of the ages, the King of the centuries, the dispenser of all time, the basis of all that subsists and abides and who givest a blessed eternity at the last, be all honor and glory for ever and ever. Amen.[5]

LEADING IDEAS of Chapter 9

1. The measure of the duration of changeable corporeal beings is time; time is a concomitant or even simply an effect of change, not its cause.

2. The perfection whereby the divine nature excludes measurability in terms of time is what constitutes God's eternity.

3. Duration does not essentially imply succession, but rather permanence; it is compatible (as in the case of corporeal creatures) with a certain succession or relative non-permanence, but in the case of necessary and immutable Being, it positively excludes even the possibility of succession.

4. We creatures never are at any moment all of the actuality that constitutes our being from the cradle to the grave; God is always all of His actuality.

5. Created spiritual beings, although not measured by strict time, have a duration compatible with some succession (of instantaneous accidental modifications of mind and will) and hence are not eternal.

6. Whereas a metaphysician sees no contradiction in the materialists'

---

[5] L. Lessius, S.J., *De Perfectionibus Moribusque Divinis*, Book IV, Ch. 5. (English translation by T.J. Campbell, S.J., in *The Names Of God*, New York: The America Press, 1912, pp. 156–158.)

position that matter has always been in existence, he must flatly deny that matter can be absolutely necessary, independent, and uncaused.

7. The word "eternal" is used metaphorically to mean a great length of created time or a successive duration that had no first moment or that will have no last one; necessary propositions are said to have "eternal" truth.

8. God's transcendence over time makes Him much more intimately engaged in man's welfare than could possibly be the case were God merely an aging super-man.

SUGGESTED READINGS for Chapter 9

For Scholastic Exposition:

St. Thomas. S.T. I.10.1–5 (*Basic Writings*, Vol. I, pp. 74–82); C.G. I.15 and I.66 (*Truth of the Catholic Faith*, Vol. I, pp. 98–99 and 218–219).

Brother Benignus, F.S.C. *Nature, Knowledge and God*. Milwaukee: Bruce, 1947, pp. 521–522.

Wm. Brosnan, S.J. *God Infinite and Reason*. New York: America Press, 1928, pp. 116–118 and 131–140.

R. Garrigou-Lagrange, O.P. *The One God*. St. Louis: Herder, 1946, pp. 276–292.

R. Kane, S.J. *God or Chaos*. New York: P.J. Kenedy and Sons, 1912, pp. 200–204.

A.L. Reys. "The One God," *The Teaching of the Catholic Church*, edited by G.D. Smith. New York: Macmillan, 1950, Vol. I, pp. 98–101.

F. Van Steenberghen. *Ontology*, translated by M.J. Flynn. New York: Wagner, 1952, pp. 106, 176–178.

On Time:

V.E. Smith. *The General Science of Nature*. Milwaukee: Bruce, 1958, pp. 312–322.

Classic Descriptions of God's Eternal Life:

Aristotle. *Metaphysics*, Book 12 (Lambda), Chapter 7.
Boethius. *The Consolation of Philosophy*, V, Prose 6.

CHAPTER

10

OUTLINE

I. *Ambiguity of the Term "Immense"*

II. *Existence in Place*

III. *Existence in Space*

IV. *Exclusion from God of Spatial Measurability and of Confinement in Place*

- A. God Cannot Be "Circumscriptively" in Place
- B. God Cannot Be "Definitively" in Place

V. *Transition to the Divine Omnipresence*

VI. *Various Meanings of "Presence"*

VII. *The Question: Where Is God?*

VIII. *God Omnipresent through Power, Essence, and Knowledge*

IX. *The Omnipresent God and the "God of Religion"*

God's Transcendence over Place and Space— the Divine Immensity and Omnipresence

I. AMBIGUITY OF THE TERM "IMMENSE"

Introductory remark. We saw in the last chapter that God's mode of duration is unlike the mode of duration of creatures. God is simply and absolutely independent of time; He is not measurable in terms of time; He transcends all contingent duration. Similarly, He is simply and absolutely independent of place and space; He is not confinable in place nor measurable in terms of space, but transcends all localization and all quantitative measurement. This transcendence over place and space we call His *immensity*.

Popular meaning of "immense." God is immense. Surely this is, at first hearing, a strange phrase for philosophers to apply to God, and one that could be anthropomorphic, since it popularly implies size, and God, as purely spiritual reality, can have no size. We commonly call something immense if it is a material substance that has a huge magnitude, that takes up a "lot of space." What is immense is rooted in matter and therefore teems with potentiality; it must, then, be at the antipodes of pure actuality and necessary being. Therefore, "immense" is scarcely a term to be used in philosophical language about God!

Technical meaning of "immense." Certainly it would be very misleading to think of God's immensity as an infinitely diffused, infinitely prolonged extension in quantity. Immensity, as an attribute of God, has no positive reference to magnitude or size or extension; paradoxically, divine "immensity" implies the negation of extension. God is "immense" in the technical, or Latin, sense of the word (the Latin *immensus* means "unmeasured," "not capable of being measured"). God has no quantity and therefore cannot be

239

measured in terms of quantity. Moreover, though a spiritual being may be restricted to a definite place if this being is finite in its power to operate, in the case of God His infinite power precludes such a restriction. God is not confinable in any place, and He does not occupy any space—not because He is more huge than any place or available measure, but because He is positively immaterial, that is, spiritual, and because He is infinite in power; He is, therefore, simply not in the order of place and quantity at all. God's being cannot be localized or spatialized. This is why we call God immense.

II. EXISTENCE IN PLACE

Confinement in place. The data of experience are related to place; they are "located": they exist *here,* or they exist *there,* or they exist *elsewhere.* Each material substance is at each moment in (or at least is passing through) a certain place to the exclusion of being in (or passing through) other places.

A thing is "in a place," in the normal meaning of the phrase, if it is an extended reality with its parts in contact with the extended parts of some other material substance. Thus, one thing's extension (or part of its extension) is another thing's place—when the other thing's quantity is in contact with it. It is a thing's contact through its own quantity with the quantified surface of another thing that gives us the foundation for asserting that this other thing is the first thing's place, or for denominating the first thing as "existing in a place."

But God is not "located" anywhere. He is not confined, nor confinable, in any place; for, not having any quantity at all, the divine being certainly does not apply His quantity, part after part, to the various parts of any extended surface—a procedure, nevertheless, which would be required if the divine being were literally to be circumscribed by some place, that is, if it were to be strictly localized in its existence.

III. EXISTENCE IN SPACE

Extended beings occupy space. Closely allied to the notion of existing in place is the notion of existing in space. The data of experience (except the inner experience of thinking and willing) are characterized by quantity or extension. Just as they are stretched out in duration and "take time" in order to have their total existence or actuality, so they are stretched out quantitatively or in extension; they "take up space."

This latter expression, to be sure, is non-literal, as space (unlike place) is not in itself a reality at all but (like time) a product of the mind with a foundation in the external world. This real foundation for the concept "space" is the existence of extended (or quantified) bodily substances; without their actual existence there simply is no such thing as "space."

It is because a thing has quantity that it is said to occupy space, to have spatial dimensions, to fill up a certain amount of room, to be measurable in terms of space. The extension or quantity of the data of experience is actually their own real or inner space, and their real extension is the exact measurement of their space; they occupy exactly such and such an amount of space because they themselves have precisely such and such dimensions.

Unextended beings and space.   In the case of a thing that is not extended, it would be meaningless to speak of it as occupying space or as being measurable in terms of space. At any rate, any meaning we might attach to these phrases, if used of unextended realities, would be quite different from their primary and literal meaning. It would be even less meaningful, for instance, than saying that a certain color tastes purple. The quantified and the unquantified simply cannot be compared according to quantity. God's being is not spatializable.

IV. EXCLUSION FROM GOD OF SPATIAL MEASURABILITY AND OF CONFINEMENT IN PLACE

Relations to place and space presuppose extension.   It should be obvious by now that attributing local and spatial denominations to an object can be done literally, non-metaphorically, and formally only if that object is endowed with extension, hence only if the object has the imperfection of being partly constituted by matter. Other conditions besides being material may also be needed (for example, contact with another's extension is a requisite for the predication "existing in a place"), but at least extension is an absolute precondition for relations of place and space in the ordinary meanings of these words. If a being has no extension, it is meaningless to say that it occupies place or that it is in space.

God is pure actuality and therefore has no potentiality, has no matter, and can have no extension. Without extension no measurement in terms of space, no spatialized existence, is possible; without contact through quantity with another body's quantity, there can be no existence in a place, no localized existence. God's positive perfection, the pureness of His actuality, excludes all quantitative extension, and therefore God is not localizable nor spatializable.

Differing interpretations of divine "immensity." At this point we must concede that among philosophers (and theologians) there is, in this rather abstruse matter, a certain amount of variety in describing what is meant by God's immensity. Some writers seem to speak of it as though it were a "possible" extension, a potency for limitless expansion, or an aptitude for being actually diffused if and when space exists or at least if and when other beings, especially bodily ones, exist.

This way of speaking may find its justification from an author's context and his own definitions and explanations, but unless it is carefully explained, it might well lead to the same kind of misrepresentation that is involved when one thinks of the divine eternity simply as a kind of time, though a time without beginning and end. God's immensity is not an infinite extension or diffusion, not even in potency. Just as God simply has no succession, so He simply has no extension, actual or potential. God's immensity, as we are defending it here, is fundamentally His spirituality—it is grounded in the negative attribute of the exclusion of matter—plus the non-finiteness of the divine power.

We may grant that writers have ample justification, in God's operation and knowledge and love, of speaking *metaphorically* of God as *diffused* everywhere, as *extending* infinitely in all directions. But these considerations pertain rather to the positive (strictly: negativo-positive) perfection, omnipresence, than to the negative attribute, immensity.

Points of agreement. No real theist, however differently he may prefer to describe God's immensity, will deny that God is spiritual or that He has infinite power; so none will deny that God has what we ourselves here designate as God's immensity. On the other hand, we ourselves do not deny what others concede when they describe God's immensity as the exigency of God's being in all things if, when, and where they should exist. This exigency seems to be a consequence of the unicity and the infinity of uncreated being, for these two qualities are responsible for the fact that it would be impossible for any non-divine being to exist independently of God.

Basis of disagreement.   In the final analysis, disagreement centers around whether there can be given any justifiable meaning to the notion, "absolute presence" (a real presence, possessed, supposedly, by a being even if it is the only being in existence), and, also, whether or not the formal reason why a spirit is "related to a place" is that his operation is affecting a definite quantified being. The answer a person gives to these questions determines whether he should consider immensity a negative attribute or a positive one.

Immensity a negative attribute.   We ourselves prefer to consider the divine immensity as a negative attribute and not as a positive one (remembering, of course, that no meaningful attribute can be entirely negative, just as no merely positively conceived one can be exclusively divine). Also, we regard immensity as an absolute attribute and not as a relative one. That is, it is something held by God independently of the existence of other things. Thus, in our description, immensity is not an "exigitive presence" (that is, the exigency or necessity of being present to other things if and when and where they are, even if their existence were not—per absurdum—the result of God's creative power). For immensity is not a presence at all—unless one wishes to say that God's creative omnipotence is a "virtual presence everywhere," and that God's infinite power which, as will be seen, we introduce as an element of God's immensity, is precisely creative omnipotence.

In this latter case our description of immensity would not be so different, after all, from that of other writers. The element making for a real difference of opinion is the admission or the negation of any meaning to "absolute presence" (had, according to its defenders, even when there is only one reality in existence), and the admission or negation that the "presence" of a spiritual reality to some place is possible in formal independence of operation, so that "to be present" for a spirit would mean something more than merely "to exist" and something less than "to be operating an effect in some subject."

We do not consider immensity as a positive attribute (such as an "exigency for being present everywhere" would be), for we are trying, in this part of our book, to find out the various aspects that make for the divine transcendence, and we believe that this is best done by developing a doctrine of negative attributes, in which, upon investigating the data of experience, we reason to what, in these data, cannot have a formal exemplar in the supreme being or first cause. The "immensity" of God is an aspect of His *transcendence*; "omnipresence" is His *immanence*.

Whatever is to be said later on about God's relation to place (His "immanence," His "presence" in all things), a meaning sufficient to constitute a separate attribute, immensity, is achieved by the necessary exclusion from God's being of confinability in terms of place or measurability in terms of space.

Immensity constituted by spirituality and infinite power. Of this negative notion, immensity, the primary constituent is spirituality, that is, positive (not merely precisive) immateriality. In itself, of course, *spirituality* is a most positive perfection. But we can form of it only a negative notion, through denial of materiality to a substance. The infinity of God's power must also be brought into the notion in order to maintain, with respect to place and space, God's transcendence even over other spiritual substances. For should other spiritual substances exist—and they do (angels, for example, and human souls)—still these will not be immense; they will not be measurable in terms of space, but they can at least be confined to place (because, in the view of those who hold for an "absolute presence," their *entity* is finite; according to our own contention, because their *power* is finite, and, since they can be in a place only through their power, therefore they can be confined or localized in terms of place).

In technical language, God is immense because He is purely spiritual (therefore not measurable in terms of dimensive quantity) and because He is not confined to place, actual or possible, since there cannot be what is called *circumscriptive* location in the case of a being who has no quantity to juxtapose to another's quantity and, more generally, since there cannot even be any kind of so-called *definitive* location in the case of a being whose power is not finite.

A. God Cannot Be "Circumscriptively" in Place.

Contact through quantity. A thing is said to be in a place circumscriptively if it is there by reason of its quantitative contact. Part of a material body is in contact with part of another material body, and the other parts of the first material body are in contact with the other parts of the second. There is part-for-part juxtaposition and contiguity in such occupation of place. Of course, the whole material body (or bodies) which is contacted by the located body may be larger than this latter, in which case it will have parts that are not in contact with the located body. It is only the amount of extension corresponding to the quantitative contact of the located body that constitutes the "place."

Now, in the case of God, this quantitative contact is essentially and entirely missing. God is positively immaterial, a spiritual being; hence He does not "occupy space" at all and cannot be circumscriptively in place, even in the hypothesis that other, and material, realities are co-existent with God. God is not quantified; there are no divine "parts" to be juxtaposed to parts of any material reality. There can be no contact through quantity where one of the beings in question does not and cannot have any quantity at all. Quantity is necessarily an imperfection; it makes a being divisible, capable of being divided and of ceasing to be itself; it puts a being at the mercy of many external forces; it is simply incompatible with pure actuality or necessarily existent, absolutely immutable being. It is impossible, therefore, for God to be circumscribed by any place, even after creation when place is available for any and every material reality.

Immensity is not merely spirituality. The spirituality of the divine being, plus the consequent impossibility of *circumscriptive* location, would be all that is needed to justify us in calling God "immense" and to say that He transcends place and space, were it not for the fact that there are other spiritual, but created, realities. The question naturally arises: Are these other spiritual realities "immense"? If they are, then immensity is not an exclusively divine attribute; it is a transcendental perfection but not a strictly transcendent one, since it is common to God and to some of His creatures. Hence, further investigation is called for.

B. God Cannot Be "Definitively" in Place.

Contact through operation. Finite spiritual substances have no quantitative dimensions. Still, they can be said to be in certain places and not in others, or they can be said to be "confinable in a definite place," because their power of operating is limited. If they are said to be in some place, it will be by reason of the operation of their power, for example, the human soul informing the human body or an angelic spirit effecting some change in a corporeal being. Confinement or definability in a place because of the finite operative power of the being which is said to be in the place is called "definitive location."

Difference between circumscriptive location and definitive location. To be in one place without the possibility of simultaneously being in another place is to be "confined" in place; it is to be *definitively* in that place. We believe that "confinedly" would be the better word here, but "definitively" (also "definitely") is traditional, despite the fact that in other contexts modern English usage gives the term "definitively" quite a different meaning. A thing may be confined in a place "through its contact of power," that is, because its operation therein proceeds from finite power. That is the only way a spiritual substance can be "confined in a place." A thing may, furthermore—and *a fortiori*—be confined in a place because it is quantified and has its own quantity unfolded alongside the quantity of the place. It is thus confined in a place "through contact of quantity." Induction seems to argue that "contact through quantity" is prerequisite for a corporeal substance's "contact through power." Where contact through quantity is made, the quantified being is in place not only "definitively" but also "circumscriptively."

In other words, "circumscriptive location" and "definitive location" should not be opposed as two contrary species, but as a species is opposed to a genus. Whatever is in place "circumscriptively" is also in place "definitively," though the inverse is not true. However, there is no specific traditional term to describe the location of finite spirits in a place; there is only the generic term "definitive." Common usage among Scholastic philosophers has so telescoped ideas about location that "definitive location" has come simply to mean confinement of a spiritual substance in a place, while "circumscriptive location" is the confinement of a corporeal substance in a place.

A comparison may be made with the term "angel"; this term serves not only as a quasi-generic term for purely spiritual (but finite) substances, but also as a quasi-specific term for the ninth and lowest of the choirs of "angels." Again, "animal" is often used as though it specifically denied rationality, whereas it is a generic term, with man (or rational animal) and brute (or irrational animal) as its species.

Spiritual substances and existence in place. Spiritual realities are not in place through any contact of quantity with another's quantity; being spiritual, they have no quantity. They have no parts to juxtapose to the parts of a place. They are wholly and entirely wherever they are, and they are wherever they are operating, wherever the effects that are due to them are being effected. "To be somewhere," for a spiritual substance, can scarcely have any meaning other than that of the relationship of causing an effect in some corporeal substance; the phrase is not inapt if the spiritual cause is acting independently of any medium or instrument.

Man's soul confined in place. All of my soul is in all the parts of my living body. My soul (*"anima"*) is solely, but wholly, where it is animating; that means that it is whole and entire in whatever part of me is really me, is really my living substance. My body is stretched out in space and occupies a definite place; parts of it are juxtaposed to parts of the floor, and other parts are juxtaposed to various parts of the atmosphere. But my soul is not stretched out. All of my soul is in my hand, all of it is in my head, all of it is in my little toe. But none of my soul is outside me; it is where it is operating, and it is presently operating only in my body. My soul, until death, stays within its proper "confines," namely, my body.

Angels confinable in place. If we consider the existence of pure angelic spirits (and philosophy cannot show their impossibility), then whatever else might be said about them, they will have to be created beings and, therefore, finite in their power. And if we go ahead and predicate of them the quality of "being in some place," the only intelligible meaning—it seems to us—that this phrase can have is that the angels are effecting a change in some definite corporeal substance. Alone to themselves, they are "nowhere." Since the effect of their immediate causality on a body is occurring in that body, the angel is said to be "in" that body, to be "located" there. At any rate, an angel's being and power are finite, and whatever meaning we choose to give to the notion of an angel being *in* a place, it would seem that God could make ever vaster places or bodies, so vast, indeed, that the angel's being would not be everywhere nor would the angel's power be capable any longer of dominating the place or producing an effect therein. Further, however broad and however deep the angelic power of operation is, it cannot immediately produce being as being; it is not creative power. In short, while an angel is not confinable in a place by reason of any quantitative contact, it is confinable at least because its powers of operating are limited.

Whatever meaning we give to the phrase, "to be somewhere," a spirit, if finite, cannot simply be everywhere. Whatever it is that constitutes a finite spirit as in a place will itself be finite, and therefore a finite spirit is essentially restricted to a finite place; it is not in all possible places. On the other hand, God's being and power are infinite; hence it is impossible for God to be "definitively" in place.

We can sum up all that we have been saying by the following schema:

GOD IS NOT	Measurable in terms of SPACE nor *Circumscriptively* in PLACE	Because He has NO QUANTITY
	nor *Definitively* in PLACE	Because His OPERATIVE POWER IS INFINITE

V. TRANSITION TO THE DIVINE OMNIPRESENCE

Reason for this discussion. Were the divisions and subdivisions of this textbook designed merely to furnish neatly isolated ideas arranged according to some primly geometric pattern, we should close this section on the negative attributes at the present point, after the above discussion of the divine immensity. A logical argument could be presented for relegating all discussion of God's actual presence in things to those parts of the book that deal with creation and conservation and knowledge. But ideas concerning the divine are so closely interrelated that, frequently, to discuss one aspect without pointing out a related one might give a distorted picture. And we believe that to treat of God's relation to place and space merely in the negative concepts included under the term, immensity, would not furnish us an adequate notion of the divine transcendence with respect to non-divine being.

Though not confined in place, God is present in things. God is not confinable in space and place—this is certainly true. But this does not cut off all relationship between non-divine beings and God. Although He is not in space, and although He is not in place, God is very much positively *present* to all places and all things, whenever and wherever they exist. To be *in space* would involve the imperfection of having quantity, and to be *in place* would involve the imperfection of having quantitative contact, or at least would presuppose a limited power of operating; but to be *present* (even, to be *present in* a place) does not necessarily involve either of these imperfections, nor indeed any imperfection at all. Presence is a transcendental perfection, hence not confined to creatures. To see how we pass from the transcendental notion of "presence" to the transcendent notion of "omnipresence" is now our aim.

VI. VARIOUS MEANINGS OF "PRESENCE"

Difference between being in a place and being present. The notion of "to be somewhere" or "to be in a place" primarily connotes the juxtaposition of one extended thing against another extended thing through contact of material part with material part. That is the sense we have been attributing to such phrases thus far, when we denied that God is "in place," "located," or "confined in place." On the other hand, the expression, "to be *present* at (or in) a place," may have quite different meanings—so different indeed that it no longer implies material contact, quantity, or finitude.

Sometimes, of course, "to be present in" means nothing more than "to be in" or "to exist in." We say very truly that "oxygen and nitrogen are present in the air" or "too many white corpuscles were present in his blood stream." But "presence" does not always demand the immediate physical contact of one material being with another material being. We also make such statements as: "Although he was miles away from us, we could still detect his presence; it was proclaimed by the orderly arrangement of the furnishings, by the choice of the designs, etc." Certain effects are due to certain persons; so those persons are said to be "present" when their effects occur. These persons are related to these places by reason of their power, their influence, their operation.

Presence through awareness.   Again, the notion of "being present" frequently has the overtones of "intellectually present," that is, of being endowed with consciousness and of being aware of what is going on, in short, alertness or knowledge. "Were you at the movie?" "Yes." "In other words, your nose was pressing up against the very screen?"—that would be a nonsensical deduction. That you were present at the movie is a true statement, even though you may have been in the middle row or the back row of the theatre. Immediate physical contact with the screen, however, would have kept you from seeing the movie at all and thus would have prevented you from being "present" for the showing.

Presence in a place, in the sense now under discussion, means a conscious awareness of what is going on; it does not demand that the one present be in immediate physical contact with the event. Presence can be of a cognoscitive nature and not merely of a physical nature. The hand of a corpse that has been near a fire may feel hot to you, but the corpse doesn't feel the heat. Pat and Mike have a conversation in the parlor. They are both present, each to the other. There may also be a pig in the parlor, but the pig is not present at the conversation, for it does not understand what is being said, nor does it know the conversants as such. It sees but does not witness; it hears the sounds but does not follow the sense.

Again, we speak of someone showing great presence of mind; we also speak, contrariwise, of absent-minded professors. So-and-so was there but was not really present! That is to say, he was physically within the place or its environs but was paying no attention to what was going on. "He was *there*, but he was *not present*; he is not able to testify." Knowledge (at least, intellectual knowledge) therefore is a factor giving additional possible meaning to the word "presence."

VII. THE QUESTION: WHERE IS GOD?

God present in several ways. When we ask whether God is present in the world, or simply whether He is present anywhere, the nuances we have been pointing out in the word "present" are of great importance. For, if "to be present" is taken as meaning to be stretched out quantitatively and to be juxtaposed, part to part, to some bodily substance, or even simply to be in one place—no matter how—but not anywhere else at the same moment, then we would have to say that God is nowhere; He is in no place at all. That is a consequence of His immensity. But truly God is everywhere; He is omnipresent, and that on several scores. He is present in all things by reason of the fact that it is His infinite power that, without any intermediary, gives existence to all existents. He is also present because He immediately knows all things: the past, the present, and the future. He knows them all as well as, indeed, infinitely more perfectly than, we ourselves know what is present before our very eyes. God being outside of time, His power and knowledge attain equally all things and all the relations among things. And since there is not even a conceptual distinction between God's essence (or substance) and God's power and knowledge, God is omnipresent by His very essence.

VIII. GOD OMNIPRESENT THROUGH POWER, ESSENCE, AND KNOWLEDGE

The three-fold division of the modes of God's presence mentioned in the above caption is traditional. It seems to be based on an ancient commentator's gloss on a remark of St. Gregory the Great (died 604 A.D.) and has received frequent and various interpretations. We shall give what is probably the most common one.

God's operative power giving being to all things. God is omnipresent, or present wherever there exists any other reality, for in the case of God, His operation is everywhere. If any non-divine being is in existence at all, that being is being made to exist, is being constantly actualized, by God's omnipotence. There is no real "where" (corporeal reality, serviceable as a locant for other corporeal realities) wherein God is not present by His operation. Hence, we say that God is everywhere. Yet, if our question were taken to mean, "What definite part of the actual universe—to the exclusion of the other parts of the universe—is God's habitat? Where is He exclusively located?" the answer is, "Nowhere!"

God is everywhere; and God is nowhere. Paradoxical—but not silly. God is "everywhere," that is to say, there is in existence no extended substance, nor indeed even any finite spiritual substance, to which God is not directly and immediately communicating being. God is "nowhere," that is to say, God is not confined to a part of the universe. He is not present in some one place to the exclusion of being simultaneously present in other places. Wherever there is reality, God is "present"—whether at the bottom of the ocean or on the tops of the mountains, whether in the nebulae billions of light years away from us or in the earth at our feet, whether in the heights of Heaven or in the very depths of Hell.

God, of course, is not contaminated by being in Hell. He is not in Hell by any consoling operation (indeed, separation from God is the pain of loss and is what constitutes the essential pain of Hell), but God is really there inasmuch as Hell is a reality, having real existence, that remains actual to the extent that God's power makes it exist.

God present by His essence. God is present in all these things primarily because of His operation. His operation is so important for creatures that without it they would not be existent at all. God is at the heart of every reality. And as God's omnipotence is identical with His very being, it follows that God Himself, not only His operation but also His essence, is intimately present to all things.

God is everywhere by what He does and what He is, by His power and by His essence or substance. He is not present through any "contact of quantity" but certainly through a "contact of power" (and, consequently, of His being). Without in any sense being confined in a place, He is at every instant making all existing non-divine things to be existent. He is the direct and immediate cause of their very being. He is conserving, or preserving, their existence. The moment He would cease to exercise His existentializing influence, at that moment all things would collapse into total nothingness. God is, therefore, most intimately present in all things. He is in them supporting their very being; He is more important for the existence of existing things than a soul is for the life of a living thing. He is, in the phrase of St. Augustine, "more profoundly present in me than that which is most my own (*interior intimo meo*)." [1] The bugler pauses for a moment to catch his breath, and at that moment the sound ceases to come from the bugle; the organist removes his finger from the keyboard, and the pipes give forth no further melody; God ceases to exercise His existentializing power, and the universe falls into nothingness. This fact of God's power, freely creating, conserving, and activating everything, justifies us in claiming that "God is everywhere."

Still, this does not mean that God is "stretched out"; His immensity excludes quantity. God is present as a spirit is present in a body (though, unlike other spirits, God is not "confined" but is simultaneously present everywhere); He is wholly and entirely in the whole body, wholly and entirely in each part of the body, not part juxtaposed to part and whole juxtaposed only to whole, but the whole wholly in each and every particular part and wholly in the whole. Such a presence, of course, is unimaginable; it has to be reasoned to.

---

[1] St. Augustine, *Confessions*, III.6 (11).

God present through His knowledge. Besides being present through operation (creation, conservation, cooperation) and essence, God is also present to all things by reason of His knowledge, His all-perfect, intuitive, eternal awareness of all things. As the Christian Scriptures put it: "All things are naked and open to His eyes." [2]

What exists contemporarily with us, and immediately in front of us, is "present" to us. We see it with a normally infallible eyesight. A teacher sees all his pupils simultaneously present before him. Some are in the back rows, others in the center rows, still others in the front rows. The teacher sees them all at once; practically speaking, all are equally present to his vision. So, too, in the case of God, all creatures, whether far away from other creatures or close to them, are seen by God with equal perfection, absolutely infallibly and utterly without any created intermediary. We saw earlier that knowledge, especially intellectual alertness and appreciation of things and persons, is a kind of "presence" to these things and persons. This being the case, we are justified in attributing to God a "presence" *par excellence* to all things; for his knowledge is utterly comprehensive of, yet not dependent upon nor subject to, the succession of time and the diffusion of space.

	through His POWER	immediately causing the being of all things
GOD IS EVERYWHERE	through His ESSENCE	since His power is His essence
	through His KNOWL-EDGE (or "presence")	immediately seeing all: past, present, future

Other modes of presence: supernatural and metaphorical. The thoughtful student will already have surmised that it would be very difficult to draw a line of demarcation between literal and metaphorical usages of the word "present." There can be no doubt that

[2] *Hebrews* 4:13.

the relation between all things and God's power, and also the relation between all things and God's knowledge, is so direct, immediate, and fundamental that if "presence" can justifiably be applied to conditions not involving, or not based on, quantitative considerations, then certainly immediate operation on, and intuitive knowledge of, all non-divine reality justifies us in saying that God has omnipresence as well as perfect spirituality and immensity.

Granted the existence of the supernatural order, other types of divine presence, likewise most real and proper, are possible. There is the Real Presence of Christ, God and man, in the Eucharist, effected by Transubstantiation. There is the presence of the Trinity in the souls of the just; there is the presence of the Holy Spirit in the infallible *magisterium* of the Church.

If to these one should add strictly metaphorical usages, the ways of describing God's presence become limitless. Witness the following excerpt from (pseudo-) Bonaventure:

God is in the soul of the faithful as a bridegroom in the bridal chamber, as the king in his kingdom, as a fortress in a camp; again, as a teacher in a class, as a fountain in a garden, as light in shadows; again, as a treasure in a field, as wine in a cellar, as a garnet in a golden setting; again, as the manna in the ark of the covenant, as a seal on a document, as medicine in a vial; also, as a harpist at a banquet, as a reflection in a mirror, as honey in a honey-comb; again, as fruit on a tree, as oil in a lamp, as a lily in the valley.[3]

IX. THE OMNIPRESENT GOD AND THE "GOD OF RELIGION"

As a conclusion of this chapter, we think it would be fitting to point out the complete compatibility between the "omnipresent God" of philosophy and the "personal God" of religion. We think this is done very well in the following excerpt from Father Walter Farrell, O.P.:

The ubiquity of God, in common with all the divine perfections, is not a cold, abstract thing meaningless to men. Its significance for human

[3] Translated from *Compendium Theologicae Veritatis*, I.17; *Opera Omnia Sancti Bonaventurae*, Paris, Vivès, 1866, tome 8, p. 74.

living is inexhaustible. In the concrete, it means, for instance, that God is in the surge of the sea, the quiet peace of hills and valleys, the cool refreshment of rain, the hard drive of wind-driven snow. In the cities He is in the bustling of crowds, the roar of traffic, the struggle for pleasure, for life, for happiness, in the majesty of towering buildings. In homes He is not to be excluded from the tired, drowsy hours of night, the hurried activity of morning, from the love and quarrels, the secret worries and unquestioning devotion, the sacrifice and peace that saturate a home. In every individual one of us God is more intimately present than we are to ourselves. Every existing thing within us demands not only the existence of God but also His constant presence, from every rush of blood from our hearts to every wish, every thought, every act. In other words, everything that is real must have God there as the explanation, the foundation, the cause of every moment of its reality. . . .

There is in this conception a majesty that transforms the earth. The mistaken exaggerations of Eastern philosophy made men walk carefully lest, treading on a living thing, they tread on the soul of a man. We have no fear of treading on the soul of man nor on God; but we do live in a world vibrant with divinity. We can give a real reverence to every being because within it, supporting its very existence, is the living God Himself. There is terror in this conception, the terror of moving in an atmosphere pervaded with divinity, of being ourselves wrapped about with divinity, penetrated with the infinite. But there is also courage and comfort here to be had from no other source. We bar the world in general from everything but the surface of our lives; friends are allowed to enter a few rooms of our palace; love throws open the gates as far as it is given us to open them—as wide as physical signs or clumsy, stumbling, inadequate words can open our souls, as wide as sacrifice and devotion can keep those gates open. Only God can walk freely about the innermost corridors of our being. And He does. Unless He be there, we could not be.[4]

LEADING IDEAS of Chapter 10

1. God's immensity or transcendence over place and space consists in this, that God is not confinable in place nor measurable in spatial terms.

[4] From *A Companion to the Summa*, Volume I, Copyright 1941, Sheed and Ward, Inc., New York, pp. 64–65. Reprinted by permission of Sheed and Ward, Inc., and Sheed and Ward, Ltd.

2. Without contact through quantity with another thing's quantity, there can be, strictly speaking, no location, no "existing in a place."

3. Space is not real apart from the actual extension of material bodies; God, being spiritual, is not measurable in terms of space.

4. The "contact through operation" that spiritual realities have with respect to corporeal realities gives a broader meaning to "being in place" and enables us to discuss whether spiritual substances can be confined in place; if this power of operating is finite, the answer is yes.

5. Since "to be in space" involves the imperfection of having quantity, and "to be in place" involves the imperfection of having contact through quantity, or at least presupposes a limited power of operating, God's existence is neither spatializable nor localizable; hence God is immense.

6. Though God is "nowhere" if being somewhere means confinement in a finite part of the universe, God is "everywhere" in the sense that He is omnipresent; He is *present to* all things by His operations, by His creative power that gives things their very being, and by His knowledge that eternally, comprehensively, and perfectly intuits all actuality: the past, the present, and the future.

7. God's omnipresence, that is, His *immanence* in all beings, is an attribute impressive especially when we are trying to see the identity between "the God of philosophy" and "the God of religion."

SUGGESTED READINGS for Chapter 10

On God's Presence—Scholastic Teaching:

St. Thomas. S.T. I.8 (*Basic Writings*, Vol. I, pp. 63–69).

J.F. Anderson. *The Cause of Being.* St. Louis: Herder, 1952, pp. 113–148.

R. Garrigou-Lagrange, O.P. *The One God.* St. Louis: Herder, 1946, pp. 253–267.

G.H. Joyce, S.J. *Principles of Natural Theology.* London: Longmans, Green and Co., 1934, pp. 327–332.

F.J. Sheen. "The Immanence of God," *God, Papers Read at the Summer School of Catholic Studies Held at Cambridge . . . 1930,* edited by C. Lattey, S.J. St. Louis: Herder, pp. 91–116.

On God's Presence through Knowledge:

L. DeRaeymaeker. *The Philosophy of Being.* St. Louis: Herder, 1954, pp. 316–319.

On God's Presence—according to St. Augustine:

St. Augustine. *Letter to Dardanus, Prefect of Gaul,* especially cc. 11–14. (A translation of these pages may be found in Sr. Wilfred Parsons' translation in *The Fathers of the Church,* Vol. 30, that is, *Writings of St. Augustine,* Vol. 12; Letters, Vol. IV, letter n. 187, pp. 229–231).

For Spiritual Inspiration:

Joshua Sylvester (1563–1618). *The Father.* This poem may be found in Nicholson and Lee, *The Oxford Book of English Mystical Verse,* Oxford: The Clarendon Press, 1932, p. 13.

CHAPTER

11

OUTLINE

God's Transcendent Life—
the Divine Knowing and Willing

I. INTRODUCTION: TRANSITION FROM THE NEGATIVE TO THE NEGATIVO-POSITIVE ATTRIBUTES

In the last five chapters we have been describing God's transcendence, investigating the various ways or modes in which God is necessarily unlike the data of experience. These discussions have yielded us the "negative attributes," so called not because they are not something positive in God Himself, but because we humans do not know these positive perfections except through negations of the strictly creaturely modes of being. We thus arrived at the "negative attributes" of God's infinity, simplicity, unicity, immutability, eternity, and immensity.

But besides our knowledge of these negative modes of God's perfection, we also know, in a positive fashion, certain positive notes that must be predicable literally of God. We know that God has existence, or being, and such transcendental perfections as are properties of being as being. We also know that God has power, that is, that He is active or is an efficient cause. But is there anything else that we can say about Him in a positive manner?

In *Chapter 3*, in the proof for the existence of God from finality, we saw that there must exist a being, distinct from the universe, with an intellect and will who has planned the order of the universe and has chosen and specified the nature and number of the beings that constitute the universe. Since we have some positive conceptions of what intellect and will are, and since these must be literally predicable of the ultimate cause of our universe, then we can say that not all of our knowledge about God is "negative," nor is our "positive" knowledge limited to the assertion that God *exists* and is the *cause* of the universe.

Still, we also saw, in *Chapter 5*—on how we come to know something about the nature of God—that even the positive concepts that are literally applicable to God must be qualified by the negative attributes if they are to describe God in the best way available to us or in a way rendering them predicable *exclusively* of God. In the present chapter, we want to investigate the negativo-positive concepts that we have of divine knowledge and divine willing.

II. PURIFICATION OF OUR CONCEPTS OF KNOWLEDGE AND WILLING

Imperfect kinds of knowing and willing. In us finite, composite beings, knowing and willing come to exist through a process of change (learning, deliberating), but the perfect act, the actual knowledge or the actual volition, is not itself a process. And if we had the perfect act without the process (if, for example, we were born with innate ideas), we should be no whit the less perfect. "To perfect" ourselves by learning and deliberating is to undergo change *prior* to having the perfections. The change is undergone with a view to the (relatively) stable possession of the perfect acts, the pure operations.

Learning and deliberating involve vital operations, but they also involve some passive reception; this indicates an imperfect subject of knowing and willing. Learning is a sort of perfection, but it is a "mixed" or "predicamental" one; its perfection is derived from the end to which it is ordered, namely, the actual knowing, the possessed knowledge. Knowledge is a perfect good; learning is an imperfect one. The vital operation *par excellence*, the perfect act in this order, is not the *process of learning* but the *act of knowing*; it is not absolutely essential, simply from the nature of the act of knowing, that it be a product, something acquired, or the conclusion of a process. Without some unoriginated knowing, the data of experience would not have their intelligibility and could not be known. Their being or perfection, and therefore their truth or intelligibility, presuppose as their ultimate origin self-existent being, infinitely perfect truth, and subsistent and creative knowledge.

Not necessary that knowing and willing be imperfect. "*To become* a knower" and "*to become* a willer" imply, of themselves, some imperfection, some radical contingency in being, for wherever there is any true "becoming," a subject is being reduced from a state of potentiality into actuality. A being that is subject to *becoming* wise or to *becoming* willing is a mutable and imperfect subject; he is not utterly simple, and he is certainly not all-perfect act. He is not self-sufficient in his knowledge and volition; he needs determination, specification, and motive coming from outside sources. However, "*to become* a knower" is not simply the same thing as "*to be* a knower" or "*to know*." "To be a knower" demands that the subject in question be conscious of an object's perfections; it does not necessarily demand that this awareness be derived from the things that are known. Indeed, like the case of "being," not all "knowing" can be *derived*. There must be some unoriginated, originative knowledge, some uncaused but creative (exemplary) knowledge, or there is no derived being, no order, and no intelligibly structured products. That which gives realities their being gives them their intelligibility.

Hence, although the "coming-to-be-wise" or the "coming-to-be-willing" is not a pure or transcendental perfection, the same cannot be said of the *state* of *being wise*, and of the *state* of *being a willer in act*. These, rather, are perfect states. In a word, "knowing" and "willing" do not of themselves imply imperfection.

Willing and knowing do not necessarily involve change. Since "knowing" is a pure perfection, a good in itself, the "coming-to-have-knowledge" is also good, but it is a good only inasmuch as it leads to a pure good. It participates in some degree in the perfection of the act in which it terminates. It is a good means to a good end, but it is good only as a means; it is not, in itself, an unqualified good nor a perfect act. Once we are constituted as knowing or as actually willing, we do not—at least, not necessarily—change. Actual knowledge and actual volition do not render their subjects continually changing nor continually changeable. Indeed, one cannot learn what he actually knows. While we are learning, we are in a process, an imperfect "state," a mobile condition; even when we are actually knowing, we are still a compound of our substance and its operations, and we quickly lapse from being actual knowers to being merely virtual knowers; we quickly lose consciousness of the actual knowledge of the moment. However, we do not, precisely as actual knowers and willers, undergo change.

Knowledge an intense form of life. However, just because we do not, as knowers and willers, undergo change, this does not mean that under this aspect we cease to be alive! Far from it! When we have finished our studying, when we have learned our lessons, we are, under this aspect, perfect; we are no longer being perfected; we actually know; and, as actual knowers, we certainly are not *eo ipso* inert or stagnant. Rather, he who knows is better off, is more perfect, and is living more intensely than he who is merely learning, that is, than he who is in the process of coming to the perfection of knowing. We are not intellectually dead just because we know our lessons and are no longer learning them. On the contrary—we are more alive. The masters, all other things being equal, are more perfect and more intellectually alive than the disciples. The former no longer acquire their knowledge; they already have it. Theirs is the happy life; to the pupils belong the pain and the toil, the imperfect mode of knowing, which is the coming-to-be-wise.

There is, then, no *a priori* reason for rejecting the possibility that God, though infinitely perfect, eternal, and immutable, has life, that is, the higher forms of life: intellectual life (knowledge) and volitional life (willing and freedom). Indeed, we saw in *Chapter* 3 that a being endowed with intellect and freedom is required as the source of our universe. As the uncaused, fully self-sufficient being, creator of the universe, He is the prime analog of being, truth, and goodness; from Him all other existents have their being, truth (intelligibility), and goodness. He knows them and loves them—not as having come to know and love, but as the infinitely perfect, intensely living, creative Artist from Whom they derive their truth and goodness. Let us turn, then, to a more detailed discussion, first of the perfection of the divine knowledge, and then of the perfection of the divine willing.

III. THE PERFECTION OF DIVINE
KNOWLEDGE

Mysteriousness of all knowledge. Knowledge is a transcendental perfection, human knowledge is predicamental, and divine knowledge is transcendent. *All* knowledge is puzzling! *All* knowledge is mysterious! Knowledge is said to be an "intentional union" between knower and thing known; it is a "living the perfection of other things"; it is a "conscious representation of other things." How frequently we are forced to shroud our descriptions of knowledge in figurative language, sometimes even in misleading language, or at least in language no clearer than the "knowledge" which we are trying to define or describe or explain! We find ourselves using terms (e.g., "intention," "representation") that presuppose our audience is already conscious of what knowledge is. This is quite understandable; something as fundamental and primitive as knowledge can be experienced by the least intelligent man but is scarcely describable by the most intelligent. We remain ourselves and yet, while remaining ourselves with our own subjective perfection, we endow ourselves with the perfection of other things, leaving, however, these other things themselves unchanged. It is indeed all very puzzling. And if human knowledge, so immediately present in our daily experience, is indescribable, what shall we say of the transcendent knowledge of God?

Complexity of human knowledge. Human knowledge, especially on the intellectual level, is a very complex process. Such knowledge presupposes all kinds of composition in man: that of matter and form, that of substance and faculties, that of faculties and operations. Man does not actually know intellectually without first undergoing a whole series of transformations: reception of sensible "species," unification of disparate species, formation of phantasms, abstraction of the intelligible species from the phantasms (with the complication of "agent intellect" illuminating and de-materializing the phantasms), impression of the intelligible species upon the "possible intellect," the expressing of the intelligible species. Now, all these transformations, described in Scholastic treatises of rational psychology, almost invariably give the impression of complexity. And we should not overlook the tremendous plurality of acts (simple apprehensions, judgments, and discursive reasonings) involved in human knowing. Even so, most of our human knowledge is habitual rather than actual.

Human knowledge is complicated, and it is also, as we have said, puzzling. It is not surprising, then, that the divine knowledge (although entirely without complication in itself, being utterly simple) is also puzzling. The problem is not so much whether God has knowledge (it would be preposterous that He should not have it!), as how He can know.

Qualities of divine knowledge. God, the origin of all other beings, the artist who has produced the structures of all non-divine being, has a knowledge that infinitely transcends in content and in mode the knowledge that is human knowledge. God's knowledge is unacquired: it is not physically caused by the objects in which it terminates; it is an eternal and immutable knowledge of what to us is past, present, and future. It extends even to what is merely possible and to what would be existent under other conditions. It is knowledge of things and of persons, it is knowledge of necessary events and of free acts, and it is knowledge of external appearances and of inmost responsibility and imputability. God knows all things, persons, and events, according to all their causes, circumstances, relationships, and modalities. God's knowledge is independent of time; it terminates in our future even while it is terminating in our past and present. God is a-temporal; His total being embraces, always, all durations of time; He is totally co-extensive with all actuality and every part of all actuality. He is conscious of all things possible, of all things actual, and of all their relations, dependence, succession, and subordination. Yet such consciousness does not imply any change in God but is an eternal, transcendent exemplifying, of all that ever is actual or possible.

The self-existent being, God, is absolutely adequate by His very nature for the operations of knowing (and willing). In Him there is no distinction between substance (nature) and faculty and between faculty and actual operation. God is subsistent intellection, always perfectly knowing all the knowable.

IV. GOD'S KNOWLEDGE OF CREATURES
NOT EFFECTED BY CREATURES

Creatures' operations are dependent, God's independent. The substances of dependent beings, creatures, are not identically their operations; at times creatures are acting, at other times they are quiescent and only in potency to acting. They are more perfect when they are operating (actually knowing and willing) than when they are inactive (with their faculties more or less remote from actual knowing and willing). Before living creatures become the principle of their actual operations, they require the reception of something outside themselves to specify their acts of knowing and willing, to determine their here-and-now act of knowing, and to motivate their act of willing. These creatures receive the specification of their operations from the terms with reference to which they are operating. They are not originative of what they know and love; rather are they dependent on these objects.

The situation is the other way round in God. God's knowledge is not derivative; it is originative. God does not learn from existent creatures the fact of their existence nor what perfections these creatures have; His knowledge is one of the very determinants—the exemplary cause—of their reality. His knowledge is not caused by them; it causes them—as the supreme exemplar, or prototype, of which creatures in their essential and accidental specifications are imitations. Things are true or intelligible to the extent that they have being or reality or perfection. This reality creatures have derived from God through participation in God's essence.

God, the exemplary cause. God is the creative source of all non-divine beings; He is the exemplary cause and the final goal of all non-divine reality. Reality, or being, and truth, or intelligibility, are correlative and coextensive; every being is true or intelligible, everything true or intelligibile is being. God is the source of being; hence He is the source of intelligibility. Conscious of Himself as the fountainhead of intelligibility and the omnipotent cause of all being, God is aware of all that is intelligible, to the degree that it is real or has perfection, that is, to the degree that it participates in, or mirrors forth, His own infinitely intelligible being. God's essence contains the patterns that things imitate when they exist. Things are real to the extent that their intelligible forms—their ideas— which are in God, have been realized as creatures. God's perfection is reflected in everything to the precise extent that the thing depends upon God; but every creature depends upon God for the fact that it exists and for the fact that it is what it is: for its being, its goodness, its truth, its beauty, its power, and its operations. These exist —they are real, they are what they are—to the extent that they participate in God through their dependence upon Him as their efficient, exemplary, final cause.

The divine "Fiat!" is not blind.   God is the absolutely first cause of all things; He made their inmost ingredients. It is His planning that gives them their order, the laws of their evolution and development. When He gives His "Fiat!" to creation, this verb is not an impersonal one; it has a subject, a definite subject chosen by God's providential decision from among the countless possible terms of His imitability. God does not have to wait and see what will eventuate from His "Fiat!"; He does not "learn" after saying "Fiat!" what the creatures are that result. Whatever added perfection one would imagine to accrue to God through a knowledge derived from the terms of His actual creation, is already had by Him in His eminent knowledge of Himself as the root of all that is possible and as the author of the primal distinction between what remains merely possible and what becomes at some time actual. An artist does not learn from his picture what he has painted; he is the "creator" of that painting.

V. GOD'S KNOWLEDGE OF THE FREE FUTURE ACTS OF MEN

Freedom, rather than futurity, the mysterious element.   When described in the rather general, perhaps vague, way that we have described them in the above paragraphs, the problems concerning divine knowledge may not seem so great; they are but a corollary of the problems of the infinity and immutability of God's perfections. But the mystery becomes particularly acute when we attribute to God an infallible knowledge of man's future free acts. It is certainly mysterious to us how God can know the *free future* acts of a man. Perhaps we should be satisfied in an undergraduate text such as this simply to make the unexceptional statement, "God's knowledge is infinitely perfect," and let the matter rest. At any rate, in what follows we most assuredly do not mean to be "dogmatic," nor do we claim to be settling age-old debates.

God's eternity and foreknowledge. God is eternal; He is not stretched out in time; He is equally present to every moment of our time. Past, present, future—God's eternity embraces all. For Him all events are present. God does not become present to them when they happen; God always is present to, totally contemporary with, all events. Now, this "eternal presence" of God to all things and events would be a ready explanation of how God knows the future—*except* that God's knowledge is not determined by these things, that is to say, it is not physically caused by them. God is not "enabled" by their presence to "learn" what they are. His knowledge terminates in them always and from all eternity, but He is not passively affected by them. Where events are not free, or to the extent that they do not involve any freedom other than God's very own, there is no particular difficulty about God's knowing them from all eternity; He knows them, however, not only as they are in their determined causes, but also as they are in themselves. This He knows by His consciousness of His own essence and omnipotent will. But once we introduce the idea of human freedom, the mystery arises, not precisely of how to reconcile that freedom with the "foreknowledge" that we attribute to God, but, rather, of how it is possible for God to know the freedom of these acts and to know the events that are modifiable through these human free acts.

It is difficult enough at times even for ourselves to estimate the freedom, the responsibility, with which we perform an act. Yet our instincts, our traditions, and our philosophizing on the infinite perfection of our Creator make us say that God is infinitely more *conscious* of our freedom and of what we freely do than we ourselves, who are *self-conscious* of it, are.

The Creator of free will must be able to know its free acts. God made us, and He made us *persons.* He gave us our spiritual soul, its intellect, and its freedom. Our liberty, therefore, is a produced liberty, not something uncreated; it is a loan, not an absolute and self-explanatory reality; at every moment of its reality, it is being made real by God. It is a genuine liberty, however, genuine enough to make the true responsibility, the true imputability, for our actions (virtuous or sinful) remain ours. God has, in His omnipotence, all that was needed to make finite persons endowed with intellect, free will, self-consciousness, and responsibility. Surely, then, His infinite perfection must have in itself all that is needed in order for Him from all eternity to know what these free wills are doing, whenever and wherever they are acting. Created freedom, freedom that would lapse into nothingness were it not for the creative and conserving omnipotent will of God, cannot elude the mind of God. God is conscious of all the possibles, even of those subordinate to our free will. God is also conscious of all actuals, including those which we ourselves freely produce. God knows them in the releasing of the energy—both His (eternal) energy and our own (temporal)— which actualizes the possibility of the free decisions of which we are the morally responsible determiners.

An analogy from Scripture. In the Christian Gospels,[1] we are told that on a certain journey of Jesus, a woman who had suffered for a long time from a pathological issue of blood made her way through the crowds surrounding Jesus and touched the hem of His garment, saying to herself that if she would but touch the hem of His garment she would be cured. Jesus halted the march and asked: "Who is it that touched me . . . ? Somebody hath touched me; for I know that virtue is gone out from me." Jesus was not referring merely to the physical contact of the woman who had touched the hem of His garment, for dozens of the people milling about Him had touched Him; rather, Jesus was particularly conscious of the surreptitious touch of this woman of faith, this individual who had deliberately touched Him in confident hope of a miraculous cure. "Who is it that touched me . . . ? . . . for . . . virtue is gone out from me," said Jesus.

Perhaps we may look upon this historial incident in the life of Jesus as a hint, or as a symbol, of the mysterious way in which God knows our human deliberate choices, a way differing from that

---

[1] *St. Luke* 8:43–48, and parallel *loci*.

whereby He knows necessitated events. When we exercise freedom, we are touching the hem of God's omnipotence; we are participating, in a most special way, in God's creative nature. Our free choices are what is most actual in us; hence, paradoxical as it may be, it is these free acts that are "most intelligible" to God, that is, they are what best imitate and participate in Him. Our free-will actions are not determined independently of the actual exercise by us of our freedom; hence they are still imputable to us as responsible persons. Yet neither are they independent of God's exercise of causality, and so neither are they independent of His knowledge. When we freely do something, God, too, is conscious of the exercise of His and of our causality; He "feels" power ("virtue") going out from Him; His concurrence with a creature's free-will actions is "felt" by Him as concretized, as taking on this or that dynamic form according as this or that is the creature's free choice.

Admittedly we are in a maze of mysteries here!

An argument from common consent. "To admit the existence of God," says St. Augustine, "while denying that God is aware of the future, is plain madness." [2] And humanity has from time immemorial attributed "foreknowledge" of all things to God. It has, of course, insisted that such knowledge is a property of divinity, is exclusive to divinity. The very word "divination" is testimony to the belief of mankind that God, and only God (and those to whom He has made special revelation), knows the future.

The fact that mankind has always prayed to God in the form of petitions bears witness to the universal belief that God knows the future. Men pray to God not merely that He ward off from them the physical evils that He sees impending, but also that He forestall them from doing foolish things—that He not allow them to be led into temptation.

Reconciliation of human freedom and divine foreknowledge. As for the reconciliation of human freedom with God's "foreknowledge," we should recall that God is outside of time. Where we say "God's *fore*knowledge," this is a condescension to anthropomorphism. All times, and all events and their sequences in time, are equally present to God; every event is a "contemporary" event for

---

[2] St. Augustine, *The City of God*, 5.9.2.

God. He is present to everything, including all the qualities, modalities, successions, and all the other relations affecting all things. Now, knowledge of what is occurring before one's very eyes is not a factor necessitating the occurrence. A scientist sees an eclipse occurring; his vision does not necessitate the eclipse. The scientist may even "foreknow" an eclipse; he may know that an eclipse will inevitably occur tomorrow at ten-forty, but the scientist's knowledge does not induce the inevitability.

Infallible foreknowledge and "consequent necessity." Pupils who are freely present in the classroom are seen by the teacher. He sees their relative positions: those who are in the front rows, those in the middle rows, those in the back rows; those who are on the right side, those on the left side, those in the center. He sees, simultaneously, those who are close by and those who are further away; he sees, simultaneously, the spatial succession and other relationships (we can here ignore the infinitesimal difference between the time required for light to come from the back rows and that required for it to come from the front ones; the human eye, even that of an experienced teacher, does not detect that difference!). The pupils, however, are freely present (despite the moral pressure that might have borne down on some of them not to absent themselves from further lectures). The teacher knows that they are present, and he knows their various relations of position; but this knowledge, infallibly certain as is such visual knowledge of the present, does not make the pupils lose their freedom. One may even very well argue: If the teacher knows they are present, then *necessarily* (for the teacher has good eyes and is not a victim of illusion) they are present. But such a "necessity" as this is not a physical necessity but only a logical necessity (forcing us, if we are to be logical, to draw the conclusion that pupils are present if they are seen to be present by the teacher); but it certainly does not keep freedom from being exercised by the present pupils. That they are present is a result of their exercise of free choice. The necessity of their being present if and when they are present may also be described as a "consequent" necessity, such as is had in the statements: "If it rained yesterday, it rained yesterday," "If it is going to rain, it is going to rain," "If I am going to have my dinner, I am going to have my dinner," "If I'm going to be damned, I'm going to be damned"—a necessity based on the banal truth, "What is, is," a necessity that does not determine events, but one that is determined by events.

Or again, just as my memory of what I freely did yesterday does not make what I did yesterday be something that was not freely done, so too God's knowledge (or anyone else's certain knowledge) of what will be freely done tomorrow does not destroy the freedom of tomorrow's actions. Things are not fated to occur simply because God has infallible knowledge of their occurrence; they are not inevitable simply because when they exist they are determinate. Certainly there is something mysterious about human freedom; most certainly there is something mysterious about God's eternal presence to all that ever is; but the deeper mystery yet remains: *How can* God know the *free* acts of other persons?

HUMAN KNOWLEDGE	DIVINE KNOWLEDGE
distinct from man's substance and intellect	identical with God's substance and intellect
the term of a process of learning	not acquired at all
derivative: receives the specification of its content from the objects known	originative: is not determined by the objects known but is their exemplary cause
fragmentary and fallible	total, comprehensive, and infallible
a plurality of acts and habits	no plurality: utter simplicity and unicity

VI. THE PERFECTION OF THE DIVINE WILL

Will, a pure or transcendental perfection. Will and, consequently, freedom are perfections that do not necessarily imply imperfection. They are "transcendentals." Furthermore, as has been shown in *Chapter 3*, the universe around us cannot be adequately explained except by the admission that it has been made and given its specifications by a being endowed with intellect and will (including freedom or power of choice). We attribute intellect and will, therefore, to God, the ultimate cause of the universe. We know that God has intellect and will in an infinitely more perfect manner than we humans do, but knowing this does not nullify the positive content contained in intellect and will as such. Of course, before attributing such a transcendent, negativo-positive perfection as "infinitely perfect will" to God, we should be careful to make sure that we are not merely unreflectingly deifying the predicamental notion "*human* will." "Will" and "freedom" as found in human beings do have deficiencies and imperfections; these are not, however, essential to the formal nature of will, which, therefore, can be a "transcendental" and which, when qualified by the negative attributes "eternal," "immutable," "utterly simple," "infinitely perfect," and so forth, is our description of the will which is divine will.

Desire and complacency.   The basic relation that a will has towards the good (therefore, towards being) is love. In human and imperfect wills, this love has a twofold aspect: it is a tendency towards such known good as is not yet possessed (a tendency that we call *desire*), and it is a *complacency* or a *rejoicing* in such good as is actually possessed. We should not insist on the necessity of *possession* if there is to be *complacency* of the will. The two aspects of love that we have just mentioned, and which conform to a fairly traditional mode of dividing volitions or acts of the will, seem practically to by-pass the possibility of a disinterested or altruistic love. There is still room, we believe, in Scholastic philosophy for further development of the doctrine of the love of benevolence.

At any rate, it is certainly not the element of *desire* that is essential to a will-act, no more than *learning* is the essential note of all knowledge. A young man loves the woman he is courting; he desires her as his wife. She has not yet consented to be his wife, but he does truly love her. Once married to her, he still truly loves her. Love does not necessarily vanish merely because desire has been transformed into possession. Complacency, then, is the perfect act of love. Desire is only relatively good; it is an essentially mixed good and can be had only in imperfect wills. God loves, but He does not desire.

Of these two aspects, desire and complacency, the first is due not to love as such nor to the nature of will as such, but to the finite and imperfect nature of the *human* will. The second aspect, complacency or joy, does not necessarily involve imperfection nor finitude; neither does it necessarily presuppose the first aspect—not, that is, in Him Who is the originator of being and Who is Subsistent Goodness. God is infinitely perfect and therefore cannot have any desires; but He can and does have complacency, and He rejoices in what is good. He can and does love whatever is lovable, to the extent to which it is lovable. For that reason He loves the divine goodness with an infinite love—and in this consists His sanctity or holiness.

Divine holiness. We are given an excellent exposition of this point by Father Edward Leen:

. . . (God's Infinite Holiness) consists in His Infinite Charity, that is, in His Infinite love of Himself. This statement needs a little explanation and expansion, for, as it stands, it might appear to the superficial to savor of an immense egoism. God is holy, not for the reason that He loves Himself but because That which He does love with an infinite intensity is what merits to be infinitely loved and chosen for its lovableness. God Himself embraces in Himself all that verifies the notion of Good. He loves that Infinite Good infinitely and in that lies His Infinite Holiness. He loves proportionately every created participation of that all-complete Good. He loves these created reflections of the Infinite Good, not for themselves, but as being ectypes of that which is the object of His Infinite complacency. In that lies His Holiness, and He loves Himself in these things. For men and angels also, sanctity lies in the love of that which is worthy of the most supreme love. It is synonymous with the love of God, and is measured by that love.[3]

God, therefore, has love, not as a desire for a good not yet possessed—for He possesses all good by His nature and omnipotence —but as a complacency and joy in good possessed. And He loves it for what it is, not precisely because it is His own possession. He loves it, indeed, with an absolute unselfishness, and it gives Him great joy to see this goodness communicated. Hence He freely wills to spread it abroad, to diffuse this goodness, by making created par-

[3] E. Leen, C.S. Sp., *Progress through Mental Prayer*, London, Sheed and Ward, 1935, p. 5f.

ticipants of it. God acquires nothing by creating; creatures, however, gain everything that they are. Hence the ancients say that "God alone is generous."

VII. DIVINE VOLITION NOT CAUSED BY CREATURES

We saw in the earlier sections of this chapter that God's knowledge transcends human knowledge, not only because God knows more than humans do, but because the very relations between knower and things known are, in the case of the creative intellect of God, in inverse order to what they are in the case of created intellects and the things they know. Things are ontologically intelligible because they have proceeded from God, in whose essence they have their exemplar, known as such by the divine intellect. Similarly, things are good because God has willed to communicate His perfection; He has freely decreed the existence of participated beings. Thus the relation between God's will and the good is, as with His intellect, in inverse order to that of finite wills and their goods. In the case of finite wills, lovable objects exist prior to the willing; they call forth an affective response of the finite will; they do not proceed effectively from these wills. But in God it is His will, both affectively and effectively, that calls forth things, thereby making them exist and be actually lovable. They are good because God wills them.

God, of course, loves all things to the extent that they are lovable, but only the divine essence, infinite and subsistent goodness, is lovable *absolutely*, for its own sake; all else is lovable only through its imitation of this goodness, and actual imitations presuppose the exercise of God's will. These actual imitations, that is, creatures, imitate the divine goodness and are therefore themselves relatively and secondarily good by the very fact that God has willed their existence; they thus derive their actual goodness from God's will, just as the possibility of their goodness is grounded in the perfection of God's subsistent goodness.

VIII. DIVINE FREEDOM

Aspects of freedom as such. Human liberty or freedom is our greatest natural gift. It makes us, in the natural order, most like to God.[4] It makes us to be moral beings, responsible agents, beings with dominion over our acts, beings with rights and duties. Freedom, however, is a quite mysterious thing, even in us. We should not be surprised to find some mysteries in divine freedom.

When we think of freedom in general, there are a number of aspects that present themselves to us; we think of active indifference, of self-determination, of deliberation, of choice, of a power to tend to whatsoever term suits its possessor's good pleasure.

Freedom cannot be exercised unless the agent has active indifference with respect to acting. That is, a free being has dominion over the terms that owe their existence to his choice. He is not determined by his intrinsic nature to will *this* particular term rather than *that* particular term; he can even will not to do anything at all; he can freely suspend his choice between alternatives. Liberty as such involves this active indifference, this dominion, this power of determining oneself, this power of choosing according to one's own good pleasure.

Imperfection in human self-determination. In the case of human liberty, however, the exercise of self-determination, the actual choosing, is never elicited in the light of infinite wisdom; it presupposes a certain suspension of the will prior to the choice, some hesitation or deliberation, some reasoning about the matter before one makes his choice, a weighing of the pro's and con's of an action. These are defects, however, of imperfect free agents; they characterize human liberty because it is human and not because it is liberty; they do not proceed from the nature of a free being as such, nor from active indifference as such. They proceed from the imperfect beings that we humans are, beings who have only finite, non-comprehensive knowledge, beings who not only "intend" things

---

[4] Divine Revelation tells us of a gift transcending anything in the natural order: "sanctifying grace," a quality which makes us supernaturally most like to God.

(tend towards things with our will-acts) but who are also "motivated" in our tendings, however freely we choose the motive to which we submit.

But self-determination as such does not demand "deliberation" in the sense we have just given to the word, that is, of hesitating and comparing the relative merits of various possibilities with a view to learning what is here and now the apparent best. We can, however, most correctly affirm that God does things "deliberately," if by this we simply mean that He does them with pure freedom, if by "deliberation" we simply mean intelligent choice or acting in accordance with an intellectually preconceived design.

Human freedom primarily regards internal acts. Liberty is a power: the power to choose. But in our own case this power is that of a faculty really distinct from the inner acts—the choices—to which it is related and which it elicits. Indeed, it is with reference primarily to these *inner acts* that we are said to be free, and only secondarily and derivatively with reference to our *external actions* and *external productions*. We say, for example, that we freely moved a desk, or that we freely built a house. But actually what we freely did was to choose to move the desk, or to choose to build the house; what we freely did was to elicit certain interior acts which, with the cooperation of certain physical causes (the material objects themselves with their physical laws, as well as various bodily forces), accounted for the external production. Indeed, what was strictly free about the "free moving of the desk" and the "free building of the house" was simply our internal act of choosing to move or to build. In other words, human liberty or freedom resides in a power to elicit internal acts rather than in a power to produce external effects.

Our own human free-will acts, our volitions, are contingent beings: they are entitatively (i.e., as realities) unnecessary, they are freely elicited by us, they are received in us, and we are internally changed by them. These internal acts of choosing are not permanent, nor are we always eliciting them. They come into being; they cease to be; when they come, they are, each of them, a newness which modifies us. Thus, when we exercise our freedom, when we actually choose, we ourselves undergo a change.

Divine freedom regards external objects. But suppose that freedom, the power of choosing, is not exclusively the power of eliciting internal acts; suppose that the power of choosing is the power simply of terminating or of not terminating one's dynamism in an external object, of terminating it in *this* external object or in *that* one, in accordance simply with one's own pleasure. In such a case, the free agent would not himself undergo change. He would receive nothing; he would only give. Whatever newness there is would be external to him.

Now, such is the case with God. Because of God's simplicity and His infinite actuality, there is no distinction among God's nature, God's faculty or power of choosing, and God's will-act or actual volition. God, as free agent, is a principle of external facts, or products, not of interior acts. Indeed, whatever is identical with divine substance is substantively necessary, and God's volition, as an interior act, is identical with the divine substance. It is, therefore, *entitatively* necessary. God is a free agent, not because He is the principle of His internal acts—there is but one internal act or volition in God, and it is identical with His necessary substance—but because He is the principle (and indeed, the *adequate* principle) of external productions or products, namely, creatures. These products exist only because God's will-act, though necessary as an entity, terminates in them freely and could equally well have not terminated in them; it could have terminated in some other created universe, or simply in no universe at all, had this been God's pleasure. And all because of the eminent perfection of the single divine act. This act is identical with the divine nature; it is not something elicited and received in the divine nature when God wills an external object. And so God undergoes no change, whenever the world begins and whatever the structure of the world is at any moment. God would have always been just what He now is, even if this world had never existed, even if some other world than ours had been created.

Plurality of human will-acts, oneness of divine will-act. Our human will-act or volition is not infinitely perfect. We cannot, through one and the same will-act, be both tending to this object and not tending to it. Also, we need a separate act for each tending. But with God, His power is identical with its operation, and that operation is so infinitely perfect that though it is but one eternal, immutable, simple operation, it accounts for the existence of all the things in the created universe as well as for the non-existence of the rest that are merely possible. It accounts for the fact that the particular things which exist are specified as they are, even though it could be accounting for other equally possible, but differently specified things. God's will includes in a simple unique act, identical with His very substance, all—and infinitely more than all—the perfection that we have in our one free faculty plus its immense plurality and succession of distinct individual acts.

Parallelism between human faculty and divine act. Even in us, however, it is good to point out that the *faculty* whereby we elicit this or that internal act, the faculty whereby we decide to do this or not to do anything at all, to do this rather than that, is *one and the same* faculty or power. That is, we do not have a separate faculty for each of our volitions nor for each of the terms of our volitions. Our one will is the same faculty which chooses *to do* this or which chooses *not to do* this and which chooses to do *this* or which chooses to do *that*. The faculty itself does not vary simply because of the differences in its acts and in their terms. So that if these acts were rather facts produced outside us, even we would not change when exercising our faculty of choice.

Our faculty, tending by *this* internal act towards *this* object, is still the same faculty that tends by *that other* act towards *that other* object. The faculty is the same; it is in itself, as such, unchanged by the plurality and variety of its acts. What further plurality there is in our being when we exercise our will, what change there is in us as total supposits, is due to the fact that our acts are not identical with our power and that this power or faculty is a principle not of external facts but of internal acts.

But in God there is only one will-act. This act is of such transcendent power that without any change it tends towards a plurality of different objects and could be tending to no objects at all (other than the Divine Essence, which is its primary and necessitating object), just as we, through one and the same faculty, elicit different acts and consequently tend towards different objects. With one and the same infinite act, one and the same entitatively necessary divine volition, God necessarily "intends" the Divine Goodness affectively and freely "intends" the participated goodness which is creatures, both affectively and effectively.

To sum up this section: no created universe is necessary for the divine Goodness; God does not necessarily will secondary goods, derivative goods, but only Subsistent Goodness, the Divine Essence itself. Hence the existence of creatures is contingent. One and the same divine will-act, therefore, is such that whereas it bears upon the Divine Goodness necessarily, it bears upon finite goods or creatures freely. It does terminate, secondarily, in these creatures, but it would be what it is even if it did not so terminate. It so terminates in the existence of this universe of ours that it could be not terminating in it (and thus our universe would be non-existent); it so terminates in this universe of ours that it could have been from all eternity, and without any change, terminating in some other and quite different universe. Such, then, is the perfection, the transcendence, of God's free volition.

HUMAN FREE VOLITION	DIVINE FREE VOLITION
distinct from man's substance and will	identical with God's substance and will
desires, as well as complacency	no desires, only complacency
motivated by its terms	intends its terms, but not motivated
self-determination after suspense and deliberative process	eternal self-determination in light of infinitely perfect knowledge
an exercise with regard to internal acts	a perfect actuality that regards external objects
plural	unique

LEADING IDEAS of Chapter 11

1. Besides the negative attributes of God, we also know a few attributes that are positive, e.g., intellect and will.

2. We learned from *Chapter 3* that our ordered universe needs an Uncaused Cause Who operates through intellect and free will.

3. Knowing and willing, unlike learning and deliberating, do not imply change but are indeed vital actions, the most perfect and the most intense forms of life.

4. God's knowledge is necessarily free of the composition characterizing human knowledge; it is eternal, omniscient, and immutable.

5. God knows creatures as does an artist who creates, not as an observer who learns.

6. How God knows the free-will acts of man is mysterious, but there is no *extra* mystery in man's being free "despite" God's foreknowledge.

7. God's infallible foreknowledge of man's actions does not make those actions inevitable.

8. Creatures can be good because Divine Goodness is imitable; creatures are good because God wills their being.

9. God's will has no desires, only complacency and joy in the known good.

10. Lovable objects exist prior to human willing, but subsequent to divine willing; human love is affective, divine love is both affective and effective.

11. Choosing, self-determination, in the case of finite persons presupposes hesitation, reasoning, evaluating, and the possibility of retracting; not so in the case of God.

12. Human will power is free in eliciting internal acts; divine will power is free in producing external facts.

13. One and the same infinite act of God, one and the same entitatively necessary volition, bears upon the Divine Goodness necessarily and terminates in the existence and specification of creatures freely.

SUGGESTED READINGS for Chapter 11

On God's Life:

St. Thomas. S.T. I.18.1–4 (*Basic Writings*, Vol. I, pp. 187–194).

On God's Knowledge:

St. Thomas. S.T. I.14 and 15 (*Basic Writings*, Vol. I, pp. 135–167).

C. Bittle, O.F.M. Cap. *God and His Creatures, Theodicy*. Milwaukee: Bruce, 1953, pp. 266–279.

G.H. Joyce, S.J. *Principles of Natural Theology*. London: Longmans, Green and Co., 1934, pp. 333–371.

R. Knox. *In Soft Garments.* New York: Sheed and Ward, 1942, pp. 9–18.

On God's Will:

St. Thomas. S.T. I.19 (*Basic Writings*, Vol. I, pp. 195–214).
B. Boedder, S.J. *Natural Theology.* London: Longmans, Green and Co., 1910, pp. 290–304.

On the Nature of Love:

D. von Hildebrand. *Christian Ethics.* New York: David McKay, 1953, pp. 34–63.
F.E. Crowe, S.J. "Complacency and Concern in the Thought of St. Thomas," *Theological Studies*, Vol. 20, 1959, pp. 1–39, 198–230, 343–395.

For Spiritual Inspiration:

Allan Wolter, O.F.M. *Life in God's Love.* Chicago: Franciscan Herald Press, 1958, pp. 11–21.

CHAPTER 12

OUTLINE

I. *Introduction: An Age-Old Problem*

II. *Need of Having a Hierarchy of Values*

III. *Need of Distinguishing Various Kinds of Evils*

IV. *Divisions of Evil*

- A. Moral Evil and Physical Evil
- B. Divisions of Physical Evil
- C. "Metaphysical" Evil

V. *Misguided Optimism and the Question of Choosing the Better World*

VI. *God's Willing of Physical Evil*

- A. Evil in the Sub-human World
- B. Animal Pain
- C. Physical Evil in the Realm of Man
  - 1. Moral values in physical evil
  - 2. Penal evil

VII. *God's Permission of Moral Evil*

VIII. *Post-Script: Hints from the Supernatural Order*

The Problem of Evil

I. INTRODUCTION: AN AGE-OLD PROBLEM

The problem not solely philosophical. At the beginning of her poignant essay, "Eviction," Dorothy Day writes: "It's all very well to talk about suffering, to write glowingly about suffering as one of the spiritual weapons we need today to alleviate the sufferings of the world. But if you get to the point when you can write about suffering, analyzing and explaining it to others—then it is no longer suffering. It has already been alleviated. Putting it down on paper has externalized it somehow, put it away from one's self."[1]

Still, philosophers, like fools, rush in (or at least saunter in) where angels fear to tread. People *will* talk about the problem of evil (even when pain or suffering is the only evil they are thinking of); they *do* ask the philosopher what he has to say on the subject. Anyone who wants to give a proper perspective to his treatment of theism must be willing to discuss, in however abbreviated, condensed, or sketchy a form, the problem that occasioned the writing, by Leibniz, of the first modern "Theodicy," the problem namely of showing that the evil manifest in creation is not in contradiction with the infinite perfection of the Creator.

Evil is a problem, however, that makes its impression on the whole man, particularly on the emotional man, on the sensitive man, and on the supernaturally minded man. And so the mere philosopher will never have the complete answer to the problem, or if you prefer, the mystery, of evil. Philosophy gives only certain rational elements of a solution. When people are suffering, however, they are usually not looking for "rational elements"; they want surcease.

And yet most people would consider it complimentary to John if it is said of him, "John has taken his loss quite philosophically,"

[1] Dorothy Day, "Eviction," *Jubilee*, Vol. 6, n.7, November, 1958, p. 29.

285

or "John is rather philosophical about his cancer." The implications are that, despite his tragedy, John has kept his human dignity, he has not let his imagination and his emotions overpower his higher faculties, and he has viewed, and is viewing, his loss or his affliction with a perspective that sees order and purpose, or at least opportunity, in all things and events.

Universality of the problem. At any rate the problem of evil is an ancient one. Indeed, philosophers from time immemorial have been expected to comment on it. And it is often some philosopher's formulation that words the problem of evil in its most acute and telling manner. For example, the sceptic David Hume (died 1776) states in a famous work: "Epicurus' old questions are yet unanswered. Is he [God] willing to prevent evil, but not able? Then he is impotent. Is he able, but not willing? Then is he malevolent. Is he both able and willing? Whence then is evil?" [2]

Hume refers us to Epicurus (died 270 B.C.) for this formulation of the problem, a formulation that seemingly puts the theist in a dilemma, or a trilemma, or even a tetralemma. Lactantius (died ca. 320 A.D.) also refers to "Epicurus" for this formulation.[3] We suspect that this is a copyist's mistake for "Empiricus"; for the idea attributed by Lactantius and Hume to "Epicurus" is extremely like that of Sextus Empiricus (died early 3rd century, A.D.).[4] Writers even more ancient wrestled with the problem. It is vividly presented in the book of *Job*. St. Augustine, a Manichaean before his conversion, always retained his interest in the problem.[5]

When St. Thomas Aquinas, early in his *Summa Theologica*, raises the question of whether God exists, he starts out by stating two objections, the first of which is precisely related to the problem

---

[2] David Hume, *Dialogues concerning Natural Religion*, Part X, p. 177 (of *Essays and Treatises on Several Subjects*, by David Hume, Esq., a new edition, Basil, printed and sold by J.J. Tourneisen, 1793).

[3] Lactantius, "De Ira Dei ad Donatum, Liber Unus," in *Opera Omnia*, Societas Ripontina, 1786, Vol. II, p. 197.

[4] Sextus Empiricus, *Outlines of Pyrrhonism*, Bk. 3, C. 2, nos. 9–12 (translation by the Rev. R.G. Bury in the Loeb Classical Library edition of Empiricus, Cambridge, Mass., Harvard University Press, 1955, Vol. I, pp. 331–332).

[5] St. Augustine, *Confessions*, Book 7, c. 5 (translation by Frank Sheed, New York, Sheed and Ward, 1943, pp. 136–137).

of evil: "It seems that God does not exist; because if one of two contraries be infinite, the other would be altogether destroyed. But the name God means that He is infinite goodness. If, therefore, God existed, there would be no evil discoverable; but there is evil in the world. Therefore God does not exist." [6]

The problem, then, as all should admit, is not a peculiarly modern one. It does seem, however, to be one to which modern man is increasingly sensitive, so much so that certain philosophers are concluding that the infinitely good God whom they acknowledge is nevertheless a God who cannot be infinitely powerful.

II. NEED OF HAVING A HIERARCHY OF VALUES

Good and evil must be distinguished. Good and evil would be meaningless terms, and there would be no problems concerning them, if one did not make at least some elementary distinctions, if, as far as he was concerned, all things, all persons, all places, all circumstances, and all events were simply discrete and independent isolates, "a-tomic" absolutes existing in and for their private individual selves, or simply juxtaposed as disparate, unordered, and equally unimportant phenomena that exist *for* nothing whatsoever.

Grades of value. Not only does a solution to the problem of evil demand that we at least admit some distinction between good and evil, it also demands that we further have such a hierarchy of values that—in general—we consider living things to be higher values, greater goods, and more important than non-living things. We must look upon plants and animals and men as more valuable —in themselves—than oxygen and hydrogen and carbon dioxide and uranium. Among living things, however, those that have knowledge are superior to those that have not; so that plants (including in this term everything that is of the vegetable kingdom) are to be evaluated

---

[6] St. Thomas, *Summa Theologica*, I.2.3, obj. 1 (translation by Anton Pegis, *Basic Writings of St. Thomas Aquinas*, New York, Random House, 1945, Vol. I, p. 21).

as inferior to brutes and men. And of the cognoscitive beings, those that are rationally cognoscitive and free—human beings—are very much more important and valuable than the non-rational, merely sensitive beings.

Indeed, the difference in value among all the beings lower than man is relatively insignificant in comparison with the enormous gap between the value of man and the values of all that is sub-human. For, as we are taught in Scholastic psychology, man, alone of visible creation, has a spiritual component; he is not a mere "vestige" of God, but a veritable "image and likeness" of God. Man, alone of visible creation, has intellect and free will and an immortal soul. He alone has rights, personal dignity, dominion, and responsibility; he alone has a destiny in eternity and not merely an end in time.

Man alone of the visible world has rights. Man is lord of the visible universe; other creatures are his instruments; they are intended for his necessities, his utility, and his rightly-ordered pleasures. They are all meant to help him perfect himself and achieve his destiny. With all their specific and individual characteristics, they still have a generic indeterminacy about them that enables man, through his intellect and bodily powers, to re-direct them, to compound or disintegrate them, to alter them, and to change their velocity and momentum so that myriad accidental and substantial changes result therefrom to the progress and perfection of man.

In the sub-human world, therefore, the individual as such is not very important. No mere *thing* is an end in itself; no being less noble than a *person* has any rights, responsibilities, or privileges. Sub-human individuals are subordinated to their species, and both the species and the individuals are subservient to the universe as a whole, and particularly to the visible lord of the universe, man. It should not prove to be so great a scandal, therefore, that many of the sub-human beings are "destroyed," "wasted," "sacrificed," and have "evil" inflicted on them—if thereby the necessities, utility, and legitimate pleasures of man are being fittingly served. Their incorporation into the world of man is not their degradation but their elevation, sublimation, and sacramentalization.

Creation ultimately theocentric. Without this humanist and anthropocentric view of the visible universe, we could not possibly say anything intelligent about many of the aspects of the problem of evil. Still, anthropocentric as the visible universe is, the finality of the whole universality of reality, visible and invisible, transcends even the order of human values; it is centered on the divine; creation is theocentric. All things proceed from God; they must in some way go back to Him, be directed to Him, and have their end in Him. He who is Alpha is also Omega.

While appreciating the fact, therefore, that man is the crowning glory of the visible universe and the lord of all he surveys, we must still realize that man is not destined merely for this world of which he is the master but for a higher realm wherein he shares in some way in the divine happiness. Even from the point of view of natural reason, unenlightened by revealed doctrine concerning the supernatural destiny of man, we know that some beatitude that is not finite and not of this world is the only reasonable destiny for the man who has successfully passed his probation on this earth. Man's soul is spiritual; hence it is immortal. Man exists, therefore, not merely for this visible world, but for something higher. Man did not make this world, and he did not make himself; he cannot consider as his absolute end the being master of the world. Like his origin, his destiny must come to him from his Creator. Man cannot establish his own absolutely ultimate end any more than he can create himself.

Temporal life an opportunity. Lord of the visible world, man is not the lord of all things. Man has freedom, but it is a human freedom, a created freedom, a "given" freedom; man is not his own law-giver. His freedom entails responsibility to his Creator; it means that man's actions are imputable to him. He must render an account of his overlordship of the visible world. His finite span of life on earth is his time of probation, of testing. It is man's chance to perfect himself, to become more and more worthy of his human dignity, and to become more and more clearly the image and likeness of God by developing the potentialities of his higher faculties (intellect and will) and by acquiring and strengthening those spiritual virtues that make him more and more like his Father, God. Temporal life is, for man, a magnificent God-given opportunity.

III. NEED OF DISTINGUISHING VARIOUS KINDS OF EVILS

Hierarchy of evils. Just as there is a hierarchy of values, so there is a corresponding hierarchy of "disvalues" or a corresponding "order" of disorders. Not all evils are equally evil; not all disorders are equally disorderly. This will become readily apparent if one will but relax and, instead of soberly reasoning about the universe, simply let his imagination go into play, lining up and associating in random fashion the various things or events that might spontaneously present themselves to his imagination as "evils." Such a list could go on indefinitely.

An imaginative list of evils. One "thinks" thus of hydrogen bombs, wars, Dachau, death, mutilation, torn ligaments, sprained ankles, stubbing one's toes; one thinks of murder, kidnapping, the ravishing of virgins, arson, airplane accidents, forest fires, lightning, sunburn, prickly heat; one thinks of afflicted children, drunkard husbands, broken homes, nagging wives, dog and cat fights. There are hunger, famine, drought, starvation; there are the croup and the pip; there are earthquakes, tidal waves, swimmer's cramps; there are typhoons, cyclones, whirlpools, tornadoes, hailstones, blizzards, buzzards, snow, cold, heat; there are headaches, stomachaches, heartaches, taxes. People are blind from birth, people become blind in accidents; people get smallpox, chickenpox, measles, dandruff. There are penance-hall, examinations, homework; there are theses, term-papers; there are germs, bores, poor relations and in-laws, road-hogs, glaring headlights, ill-fitting clothes, last year's fashions, chilblains, reveille, athlete's foot. There are wailings of infants, teething, wet diapers. There are plagues, the Black Death, hypocrisy, racial bitterness, jails, jailbirds, jail breaks, jail riots. There are treasons, robberies, divorces, orphanhood, widowhood, spinsterhood; quicksand, stagnant pools, rotting vegetation, fetid odors, narcotics, imbecility. There are insanity, remorse, guilt complexes, hit-and-run drivers, traffic fines, sleeping sickness, cannibalism; there is tipping, tippling, cacophony; there are weeds, arsenic, lice, wildcats, plant blight, fading flowers, snakes, lamb-tearing wolves, baseball umpires, poisons, butchers; there are typographical errors, linotyping mistakes, publishers' rejection slips, bookworms, lies, flies, chipped chinaware, hell and damnation. On and on the game of listing "evils" can go.

Call for distinctions. Obviously, a number of distinctions would be called for before one should even think of trying to answer so far-reaching a challenge as: "Now, tell me why, in just one word, WHY does God allow all these evil things?" One will probably not satisfy such a challenger by stating the blunt metaphysical truth, "All things are good."

In the case of many of these things, if they are taken in isolation, outside of a hierarchy of values, independently of their relation to man and to the rest of the universe, it would even be meaningless to call them "evil" at all. How can one answer the question: "Is *heat* really evil, yes or no?" or "If heat is evil, is *cold* good, yes or no?" or "Is alcohol an evil?" One must make distinctions; one must drag in relationships and circumstances; one must philosophize.

Before taking up the necessary distinctions, we would like to give a quotation from C.S. Lewis concerning the evil of pain:

We must never make the problem of pain worse than it is by vague talk about the "unimaginable sum of human misery." Suppose that I have a toothache of intensity X; and suppose that you, who are seated beside me, also begin to have a toothache of intensity X. You may, if you choose, say that the total amount of pain in the room is now 2X. But you must remember that no one is suffering 2X; search all time and all space and you will not find that composite pain in anyone's consciousness. There is no such thing as a sum of suffering, for no one suffers it. When we have reached a maximum that a single person can suffer, we have, no doubt, reached something very horrible, but we have reached all the suffering there ever can be in the universe. The addition of a million fellow-sufferers adds no more pain.[7]

[7] C.S. Lewis, *The Problem of Pain*, New York, Macmillan, 1944, pp. 103–104.

IV. DIVISIONS OF EVIL

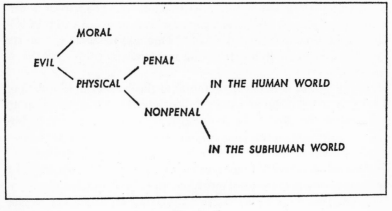

Figure 5.

A. Moral Evil and Physical Evil.

Their definitions. The first and most important division to make with respect to evil is the division into *moral* evil and *physical* evil. Moral evil is sin, that is, the deliberate violation of God's moral law. It is defined as the absence or lack of the agreement and conformity that should be present between human conduct and the rule or norm of what that conduct ought to be. Physical evil is a defect, or privation of a perfection, in a being, marring it in its natural integrity or in the exercise of its normal activities or in both. Physical evil thus consists in the destruction or impairing of material substances and in the pain (suffering), bodily or mental, of sensitive and intellectual substances.

Sin the only total evil. It is important to make this division. For sin, and not suffering, is the prime analog of evil. Indeed, sin or moral evil is the only real *total* evil in the universe. All other socalled evils can, under certain circumstances, be the positive object of a good will. But sin can never be willed positively, not even as a means to a good end. Moral evil cannot be rationalized into a system that would meet with God's unqualified approbation. It can exist if God permits it—that is, if He does not prevent its occurrence even though He has the power to do so and has certainly forbidden it— but it is caused only through the insolence of man defying God's prohibition. Physical evil, on the other hand, can be positively willed by God as a morally good, or at least as a morally indifferent, means to a (physically or morally) good end. Physical evil, therefore, unlike moral evil, is not an altogether unmitigated evil.

"Original sin" and personal sin. Moral evil, the transgression of the law of God, the deviation from the norm of morality, can be subdivided. Judaeo-Christian scriptures and tradition testify to an "original" sin on the part of the first parents of the human race, Adam and Eve, the consequences of which "original sin" were not, however, limited to Adam and Eve but had and are still having repercussions on the whole human race. These consequences are set forth in treatises of dogmatic theology. Many pious writers tend to ascribe most, if not all, the evils of the universe to the results of this "original sin." But that is a matter for dogmatic and ascetical theologians to discuss. When the philosopher refers to sin, he is referring to actual or personal sin, not to sin inherited from our first parents, but to sin that we ourselves personally commit. And these personal sins themselves, even apart from "original sin," go a long way to explain God's volition of many of the physical evils in our world, those namely which are either penalties for sin or concomitants of sin that, because of the solidarity of the human race, affect others besides the sinner himself.

Mortal and venial sin. Personal sins are divided into gravely serious (mortal) sin and venial sin. Mortal sin is a complete break from God; venial sin does not completely sever one's friendship with God. A person who commits mortal sin, so far as he himself is concerned, makes an absolute choice: instead of continued friendship with God, he chooses an apparent good which he cannot simultaneously have with the grace (friendship) of God. In making his choice of the merely apparent good, he rejects the infinite good, God. He puts himself in the ranks of the enemies of God. If such a sin is not repented, the sinner will not have, in his after-life, the beatitude that God had antecedently, but conditionally, willed him to have. His immortality will be that of an eternally displaced person, a lost soul, a being in Hell. So, unrepented mortal sin is the worst of all evils—not because of its dreadful eternal sanction, but because of its intrinsic malice, its consummate degradation of man, and its complete dissoluteness as a total final rejection of God.

B. Divisions of Physical Evil.

Non-penal evil. Physical evil, the definition of which we gave in the above section, can be subdivided into non-penal (or natural) evil and penal evil. Obviously, the problem concerning physical evil is not the same in the two cases. It should be easy enough to reconcile with God's infinite perfections His positive willing of physical evils as a punishment for the violations of His law. It is less immediately evident that God's positive willing of evils which are only "natural" (non-penal) is not in contradiction with one or other of His perfections.

These natural or non-penal physical evils can be subdivided into those that occur in the non-living world and those that occur in the living world, those that occur in the non-sensitive world and those that occur in the sensitive world, and, among the latter, those that occur in the sensitive world of the brutes and those that occur in the sense-life of human beings (whose sensitivity cannot be simply equated with that of brute animals).

Penal evil. Penal evil, that is, punishment inflicted or allowed because of sin or crime, can be corporeal (physical pain), and it can be mental (remorse). In either case it is positively willed by God, but only because the moral law has been violated by a creature's free defiance of God's antecedent will. The evil which is punishment, or penal evil, may be temporary, or it may be everlasting. The more dreadful, of course, is the latter; it is Hell.

God's will and the various evils. No moral evil can ever be willed positively by God; it can only be permitted. But all the physical evils that occur are, indeed, positively willed by God. However, none of these physical evils is willed for its own sake; it is willed only for the sake of a good; it is therefore willed only as a means and never as an end. And when the physical evil in question is a penal evil, it is a means for the vindication of right order and therefore is never willed by an antecedent will of God but only by a subsequent one, a "secondary" one, one that presupposes the occurrence of sin whose commission is never willed at all by God.

These various distinctions should be made if one is to carry on an intelligent discussion of the problem of evil and not merely indulge in outbursts of emotion and sentimentality. A perceptive soul can be brought to see that physical evils are willed because God loves the good and that moral evils are permitted because God respects human freedom.

C. "Metaphysical Evil."

Inaccuracy of the phrase. One other kind of evil may now be discussed, even though it is not properly an evil, as it does not really fit the definition. Especially since the time of Leibniz, certain authors speak of "metaphysical evil." By this so-called evil is meant simply the natural finitude or limitation of any creature. Any contingent thing, any non-divine being, will necessarily lack some absolutely possible perfection. No mere caused being, no creature, has all the perfection that is compatible with "being" as such or that is had by the Being Who is utterly subsistent in Himself and of Himself. This lack, this limitation, this "imperfection," is inherent in creatures. It is really synonymous with their creaturehood. To demand that God prevent such "evil" from entering into His creation is to ask for the elimination of creatures; it is to ask that God produce unproduced products.

Strictly speaking, however, no *being* is *evil*; rather, "every *being* is good." From the metaphysical point of view, evil is non-being, but it is not non-being in the sense of mere absence or limit or finitude, but in the sense of the negation, in a being, of something that this being, according to its nature, *should have*. Evil, properly considered, is a *privation* of good; it is the absence of some good or degree of being that *should be present*. Hence mere finitude, as such, in a creature is not strictly speaking an evil. It is not a privation for a creature, as such, to be finite; indeed, a creature cannot but be finite; finitude pertains to its metaphysical nature. If a creature does not have all the finite perfection that in the circumstances its nature calls for, then to that extent it is "evil," but merely to be finite is not to be evil. It is not an imperfection for a creature not to be God; it is not a limitation in God that He does not, and cannot, make an infinitely perfect creature, as this would be a contradiction in terms.

Reason for discussing "metaphysical evil."   It would scarcely be worthwhile even to mention the idea of "metaphysical evil," were it not for the fact that, as it seems, the difficulty some people have with evil in God's creatures is not really a problem of their "evil" but of their inevitable finitude. People ask: "Why didn't God make a *better* universe than ours?" Latent in this question, at least in the minds of many, is the justifiable belief that God, who freely creates, could have made a better universe than ours or could have made the substances of our universe accidentally better (ordered them better) than He absolutely willed to do so. But there is also latent an unjustifiable and unreasonable question, one perhaps not even vaguely formulated but nonetheless hovering in the background of their minds. They really want to ask: "Why didn't God create, instead of 'our world,' the *best possible* world?"

V. MISGUIDED OPTIMISM AND THE QUESTION OF CHOOSING THE BETTER WORLD

There is no special problem connected with "metaphysical evil." Creation is a problem, yes; the co-existence of the Infinite and the finite is a problem, yes; but neither of these problems is really the problem of evil. The problem of evil is meaningless if reduced to the question: "Why did not God make the best possible world?" If a person insists on calling finitude or limitation in being an evil—a "metaphysical" evil—then he should also admit that if it can be said at all that it is good for creatures even to be possible, or that it is not evil for God's essence to be imitable outside Him, then it should likewise be said that it does not contradict any perfection of God for Him to produce creatures and in this sense to will "metaphysical evil."

A "best possible" world not possible.   There is not, however, and there cannot be, an actual world which is the best possible world. Any world is a created being; created being is always finite; anything finite can be perfected. No finite thing, and therefore no creature, could be the best possible being. No actual world could be the best possible world. Suppose, then, God were to create a world better than ours, but still one that included our malcontent questioner as one of its inhabitants (if it makes sense to talk of someone from "*our* world" being an inhabitant of some "*other* world"); the mind of this person will still be disquieted, for his original question ("Why didn't God make a better world than this?") can be asked of any universe at all, since every possible and every actual universe is finite, is "metaphysically evil." Such a person would really be demanding that God make a universe better than which none is conceivable; thus he would not be asking for a possible universe at all; he would be demanding an impossible and absurd one (for we can always conceive a universe more perfect than any specified one)!

Rational, not "rationalistic." Scholastic philosophy, of course, seeks always to be rational, that is, reasonable, but it has no desire to be "rationalistic." A rationalistic philosophy demands that we be able to deduce, by strict logic, the consequence of *any antecedent*—even should that antecedent be an actively indifferent faculty, a self-determining free will, a power of making a deliberate choice. Rationalism "rationalizes" even God's freedom, so much so that God's "choice" of *our* universe is inevitable. That is to say, rationalism simply solves the problem of evil by doing away with God's freedom of choice. There is no problem of evil, it claims, since our world is the only possible world that, without contradicting His attributes, God can reasonably (that is, "rationalistically") create. According to the rationalists, God *must* "choose" the better thing, precisely because it is the better. Our universe, then, appearances to the contrary notwithstanding, must be the "best possible universe"—otherwise God would not have chosen it.

According to the Scholastic way of looking at things, however, it is impossible that God should be required by any of His divine attributes either to create at all or to *choose our* universe if and when He does will to create at all. No inevitable deductions can be made from an antecedently free will, not even when this is infinitely wise and infinitely good and infinitely powerful.

A banal truth. In one sense (reductively, a Pickwickian sense) it is perfectly true that *our* universe is "the best possible universe." It is the *best way*—indeed it is the *only possible way*—for a universe to be *our* universe. If it is *our* universe that God wants, then with this intention it is better that He create not some other universe but *this* *universe of ours*—otherwise, by creating, He would not have what He really intends. But none of God's attributes makes Him *intend our* universe *rather than some other* possible one.

"Sufficient reason" and "compelling reason." The rationalistic optimist really believes, and insists, that this world of ours is the best possible world. He thinks that it is philosophy's task to give not just a "sufficient reason" for God's choice of this world (e.g., "God chose this world because it is good to choose a world like ours that reflects so many of the divine perfections"); philosophy must further give a "compelling reason" why God chose this world *rather than* another, and this can only be because this world is the best possible ("God, being infinitely wise and infinitely good and infinitely powerful, could not have chosen this world if it were not the best possible; His own divine attributes absolutely prevented any other choice"). The rationalist, in eliminating the divine choice, really denies the divine freedom.

A less incautious but still speculative mind would say, with the Scholastics, that this world of ours is a very good world, though other and better worlds are nonetheless conceivable and creatable. Such a mind holds, reasonably, that if God chooses to communicate His goodness He can do so in myriads of ways and that He is utterly free to choose which way He shall communicate this goodness, i.e., He is free to choose how much of His imitable essence shall be imitated, how much communication or participation there shall be of its perfections. The reasonable view of free will, even of the free will of God, says that the "sufficient reason" for *a choice* is the same as the "sufficient reason" for *the simple willing* of an object, namely, its goodness, but that if there is a "compelling reason" why this object *rather than* another is chosen, this "choice" is not a true choice, and there really is no freedom. All choice (whether of this or that end— or of this or that indifferent means to an end) contains an element that cannot be "rationalized" if we are still to defend freedom of the will.

God wills to communicate His goodness. He can communicate it in degree A, and He can also communicate it in a higher degree, B, and so on. The only true answer that one can give to the question,

"Why did God will to create any world at all?" is to say, "To communicate His goodness." And the only sensible thing to say when asked the pseudo-question, "Why did God will to create world A rather than world B?" is likewise to say, "To communicate His goodness." The answer to the former and to the second, the psuedo-question, are completely the same. Justice, mercy, goodness—these virtues do not require that a rich man ask the beggar how much alms he would be most pleased to accept from his generous benefactor. Whatever it is that God gives, He gives out of sheer generosity and unselfish love.

VI. GOD'S WILLING OF PHYSICAL EVIL

Physical evils in the universe can be willed by God without any contradiction of His divine attributes. God wills such evils "accidentally" or "incidentally," that is, not for their own sake but for the sake of something else, something that is good in itself. God orders physical evils to the good of the visible universe as a whole and particularly to the good of man. Indeed, in many cases, if we prescind from the existence of man, it would be impossible to determine seriously whether we should call this or that thing, this or that event, good or evil. Is it, for example, good, or is it evil, that pigs eat acorns that would otherwise grow into sturdy oak trees?

A. Evil in the Sub-Human World.

Human life impossible without changes in the sub-human world. Without physical and chemical changes in the mineral world there would be no living beings. Plants require the breakdown of various minerals. But, in turn, without the destruction of plants, there would be no animals, no sentient life, and no men.[8] Without the possibility of changes in the mineral world, and without the possibility of the destruction of plants and animals, the universe would not have been adequately ordered as an abode for man.

[8] See Paul Siwek, S.J., *The Philosophy of Evil*, New York, Ronald Press, 1951, pp. 110–114.

Sometimes people talk about the problem of evil as though they would want each being, indeed each element, each molecule, and each atom in each being, to be willed and protected and cared for by God's providence for itself alone, exclusively, with no reference to other things in the universe, as though each thing must be cared for apart from and independently of all other things, indeed, with all other things subordinated to it. Certainly, one should admit that this would not be the only "intelligent" way to be busied about a universe. It would rather be an unintelligent, indeed, an impossible way; everything would be a universe in itself, yet everything would be for the sake of everything else while still being a complete end in itself.

God wills a system, not isolated goods. God does not will each and every creature absolutely, in total isolation from the rest of the universe, willing it no matter what means would be required for the triumph of that thing's isolated, individual good. God has, with respect to the terms of His creative activity, many intentions; He balances them off, restricting some by others, making a dynamic equilibrium in nature suitable for man. God certainly wills that the things that exist be capable of producing certain effects, even though He does not will that all these effects be produced.

God, for example, wants acorns to exist; and He wants some oak trees; but He never willed—and it could not be called wise for Him to have willed—to order all things in such a way that no acorns would ever come from oak trees except such acorns as would themselves in turn become oak trees producing other acorns. Acorns can become oak trees, and God wills that some of them actually do so. But He does not intend that man be crowded out of the world. He does not order woodmen to spare every tree. He has fashioned acorns in such a way that besides being potential oak trees, they can also furnish food for birds and animals, and their very decay, their death in sterility, helps in the formation of a fertile humus suitable for the growth of other kinds of living things.

A person may very intelligently and understandably want to learn both music and mathematics; he may decide to learn both. But evidently he cannot give full time to either without impeding the study of the other. He intends to learn mathematics—but only to the extent that it remains possible for him also to learn music, and not to such an extent that he will have no time or energy for the music. His volition to learn mathematics is a qualified volition, a conditioned volition. While all examples taken from created beings are inadequate when applied to the uncreated Creator, still we can speak of God's volitions as being in a sense conditioned or qualified. He does not will the various beings of the universe absolutely, but as components of a vast cosmos or system of mutually dependent beings, a hierarchized universe.

Had God willed all seeds to germinate, the world would have long ago become an uninhabitable forest. God never intended such a result. God intends primarily the order of the whole; He relates the various things of the universe to one another, coordinating them, subordinating them, and making a cosmos suitable for the propagation and development of the human race. There is nothing unintelligent in such a procedure, nothing incoherent, nothing that violates the integrity of any divine attribute.

With regard to certain evils that occur in the sub-human world, however, there are definitely some that create more of a problem than others. There is at least one which will probably never be adequately solved by philosophers. I am referring to the problem of animal pain.

B. Animal Pain.

Obscure area. Here, certainly, we humans can only grope our way about, for we are in a very obscure region. We must content ourselves with little more than clumsy guesswork. Constantly we are warned not to be anthropomorphic in our conception of God. But it would also be well that we be advised not to be anthropomorphic in our conception of animals.

It would be perfectly useless for *you* to try to imagine how *you* would feel if *you* were an animal. Humans have sensations, and brute animals have sensations; but humans do not have mere animal sensations and brute animals do not have human sensations. Animals manifest that they possess some form of sensations, that they hear sounds, see things, smell things, taste things, and feel things. But they do not have self-consciousness. Hence it is really impossible for them to sense like human beings, and it is impossible for us human beings to imagine how they are conscious of sensations—unless perhaps we should liken the "consciousness" of animals to that of a man who is thoroughly drunk.[9]

Sentimentalism. Much useless sentiment is expended by humans over animals in pain. Indeed, some humans seem really and truly to put greater value on animals—usually, certain pet animals—than they do on their fellow human beings. This, surely, is a perversion of the hierarchy of values. These people are insensitive to the suffering of their fellow man but resent deeply the pain they think unthinking animals suffer. But, truly, how are we to judge how much animals suffer? We do not commonly read of animals committing suicide! Presumably, they do not find their life unbearable. If we go only by external signs, we can be easily led astray; we can quickly be led to exaggerate animal pain. "In biology many of the so-called psychic experiences of animals have been shown by the experiments of Pavlov and others to be susceptible of a simpler explanation. . . . The simplest experiment with a dead frog, if seen by some sentimentalists, would make them write copious letters to the papers." [10]

Animal sensitivity and children's sensitivity. Sometimes when a very young child is in pain, it acts as if it were suffering the tortures of the damned; it screams, wails, and becomes hysterical with crying and howling. Then, when some adult, who can stand the noise no longer, gives the child a penny's worth of candy or a piece of bubble-gum, the wailing and howling immediately subside. From the pains of the damned to placid cherubic contentment—all in an instant! Surely the noisy child was not suffering as deeply as the wails would have seemed to indicate. In similar fashion, we might unthinkingly exaggerate the pain that animals are suffering when we hear them whimpering or moaning or howling. It is not unreasonable to liken their pains more to those of unthinking children than to those of reflecting adults. Let us not make bitter protests about Providence when we are not even sure that animals suffer bitterly. We really do not know what they suffer.

[9] Siwek, *op. cit.*, p. 125. See also *Ibid.*, pp. 99–100.
[10] M.C. D'Arcy, S.J., *The Pain of This World and the Providence of God*, London, Longmans, Green and Co., 1936, p. 61.

Balancing the accounts in the animal world. At any rate, the pains that animals undergo are of relatively short duration; the vast amount of their life is spent in perfect animal contentment. Their happy hours, their days of enjoyment, seem far to outweigh in quantity, intensity, and duration the pains that they suffer. Even their death is usually not a lingering thing, but rather something sudden. Nature is "red in tooth and claw," but gory as the deaths of many animals may be (wild animals, especially), there is no need to sentimentalize. Let us not judge the agony of animals from the aesthetic point of view. We simply do not know what it feels like to suffer and die as an animal.

To what extent is animal pain really an evil? Is it an evil that cannot fit reasonably into a providential order? Is not the possibility of painful sensations an entailment of the possibility of sensation at all? If an animal is to be able to feel comfortable, to be capable of pleasure, does not this demand that its constitution be such as to make it susceptible to pain as well, to feeling uncomfortable sense-experiences? The pleasures and satisfactions that animals have more than counterbalance their sicknesses and pains, but the former would be impossible without the kind of nature that makes the latter also possible. So, at any rate, it seems to the present writer. How could animals be sufficiently activated to flee dangers or to seek for food, if it were not possible for them to have any painful experiences? Even so, their pain is not to be likened to human pain, for animals do not have self-consciousness. Without self-consciousness, pain loses much of its intensity.

C. Physical Evil in the Realm of Man.

1. Moral values in physical evil.

Present life, a period of testing and developing. God has put us human beings on this earth for our probation, our time of testing and meriting. We should look upon physical evils in the realm of man as something willed by God *for the moral good of man*. They are the occasions for the exercise of the moral virtues and for the practice of those deeds that develop man as man, that bring out his heroic potentialities and actualize his latent greatness. If life on earth

is a time of probation, then opportunities must be furnished for acquiring, developing, testing, and strengthening man's virtue. Forti-
tude, courage, prudence, patience, unselfishness, family affection,
friendship, human solidarity, compassion, brotherly love, sympathy
—all these need to be practiced if man is to develop as man, if he is
to bring to the fore some of his most beautiful moral elements, and
if he is to make himself worthy of his eternal destiny. This idea
should not be too hard to grasp. It will, however, shed much light on
the problem of evil.

Opportunities—"trials" or "crosses," if you prefer—are needed to
make a man. Their very existence is a testimony to man's value. But
they may also break a man. In themselves, however, these trials are
something valuable, or at least something neutral, something useful
that, like a hatchet in the physical order, can be used or abused. At
any rate, they are necessary if man is to develop. Man is not subsistent holiness or substantial goodness, but he does have it in his
power to become holy and good. That power needs occasions in
which to be actuated.

A disease that lays a man low bodily can elevate him to sublime
heights spiritually. It may, on the other hand, be an occasion for
despair. An afflicted child may turn out to be a tremendous gift to
a family, binding the other members with a much closer bond of affection and mutual understanding than any luxury or comfort would
ever have done; it may unite the heart and soul of husband and wife
in ways past understanding. Yet it may, on the contrary, embitter
them. Always, always, there is question of *opportunity*. The spirit
of man, the freedom of the spirit of man, determines whether the
opportunity will redound to his *grandeur* or to his *misère*.

Our ignorance of God's vision.   One of the things that make
pain and sorrow, physical suffering and mental anguish, so difficult
for us humans to endure when they come our way, or even when we
see them happen to our fellow men, is our ignorance of just why a
supposedly all-good and all-powerful God allows them to happen.
But it is not unreasonable still to maintain that God, who certainly
sees things from a better perspective than we possibly can, is wisely
governing the universe even though this involves the willing of physical evils.

It is most unrealistic for a person to say, "If I were God, this is the way I would run the universe: I would not allow such and such things, etc., etc." The person who indulges in these anthropomorphic imaginings is usually sentimental; about the only useful thing to do for such a person is to instill in him the lessons of the book of *Job*.

If we could see the end God has in view in willing physical evils, we would not complain, for we would be seeing things from the divine viewpoint, which is infinitely wise and good. We ourselves put up more readily with evils when we see the advantages resulting from them, or when we see them as necessary means to, or correlates of, something that has a superior value for us. We have a better chance of seeing these advantages or necessities, and so are best prepared for facing these evils, if we have clear views and convictions about life's destiny. We too quickly forget that our span of life on earth is meant to be a period of training, a time of probation, and an opportunity for us to bring ourselves to the condition that makes us worthy of an eternal life of divine happiness with God, our Father. We quickly forget that, in God's plan of creating us, eternal beatitude is our goal. If we but remember the inheritance awaiting us as our final end, the physical evils that befall us *en route* will not immoderately perturb us.

2. *Penal Evils.*

Punishment not a disorder. Parents who truly love their children do not hesitate to chastise them if their proper training calls for this. God, who loves us more than any parent, will wisely chastise us. Indeed, much of the physical evil that befalls us has a moral purpose of a kind other than what we have been stressing above, for, besides being the occasion or stimulus of good moral action, physical evil in the realm of man can be reckoned as due punishment, sanction for the infractions of God's law.

As regards these physical evils that are of a penal nature, that is, that are punishment for violation of the moral law, certainly they do not constitute any disorder in the universe; there can be no recrimination against God's justice or His goodness or any of His perfections when He wills such so-called evils. Indeed, if the moral law were violated with impunity, then there really would be disorder in the universe.

God is not to be conceived after the fashion of a doting father who does not mind what his sons do so long as they have a good time. As Father D'Arcy says: "Such is the dignity of human nature that its freedom means business, a terrible business, and it is quite unworthy of man to suggest that this freedom is no more than a toy, that no matter what he decides to do with his life, God will soothe him as if he were an imbecile and clean up his mess." [11] God loves us as sons. True love of a true father for his son cannot tolerate moral disorder in the beloved son. Likewise, punishment motivated out of love and out of a desire for the repentance and conversion of the sinner is an effect of a perfect and benevolent Providence.

Punishment willed only "secondarily." God does not, of course, create a world with a view to punishment. He does create a world of free beings and gives them magnificent opportunities for making something worthwhile out of themselves. He foresees their coopera-tion and He foresees their perversity; He foresees, therefore, the need of proper sanctions. His volition of penal evil is, thus, "accidental," that is to say, it is not willed for its own sake, nor as something good in itself, but only as a good means for correcting the sinner and as a good means for vindicating right order, that is, for seeing that the exigencies of justice are met. We must add that God's volition of penal evil is only "secondary," that is, it presupposes that the sinner has freely, without any divine volition—and most especially without any divine approval, indeed, against the divine command—proceeded to sin. God never wills any sins at all; He merely permits them. But when He foresees sin, He wills that its sanction be applied. This willing of penal evil is something that proceeds out of God's love of righteousness, His love of goodness. Ordinarily it proceeds also out of His love of the sinner; but even when He foresees that the sinner is going to relapse, or is not even going to profit from the punishment, indeed is going to rebel against the punishment, God's justice still compels Him to inflict the punishment. Right order de-mands that He do so; it is fitting, it is called for, it is good—if the universe is to be rightly ordered.

In short, like all physical evils, penal evil is not under all aspects

[11] M.C. D'Arcy, S.J., *Death and Life*, New York, Longmans, 1942, p. 137. Compare C.S. Lewis, *The Problem of Pain*, New York, Macmillan, 1944, p. 28.

intrinsically evil; it is evil under one aspect, and it presupposes moral evil; but under other aspects it is good, and it is demanded by right order. It can, therefore, with no detriment to the divine perfections, be willed according to its goodness.

VII. GOD'S PERMISSION OF MORAL EVIL

The mystery. At the end of his magnificent essay on the goodness of God, C. S. Lewis has the following paragraph:

God is the only good of all creatures; and by necessity, each must find its good in that kind and degree of the fruition of God which is proper to its nature. The kind and degree of the fruition may vary with the creature's nature; but that there could ever be any other good, is an atheistic dream. . . . God gives what He has, not what He has not; He gives the happiness that there is, not the happiness that is not. To be God—to be like God and to share His goodness in creaturely response—to be miserable—these are the only three alternatives. If we will not learn to eat the only food that the universe grows—the only food that any possible universe ever can grow—then we must starve eternally.[12]

It is only the creatures that are endowed with intellect and free will that are capable of refusing to be like God and to share His goodness "in creaturely response." This refusal constitutes moral evil, or sin, and it involves Lewis's "to be miserable." Sin (and in this section we shall refer only to grave, or *mortal*, sin) is the consummate evil, the paradigm of all evil, the only complete disorder, the only *total* evil (since under no respect is sin a good). Sin is a choice of something forbidden by God as incompatible with the attainment of man's last end. It is the voluntary grasping after a good which, in the circumstances, is only a seeming good—"seeming," since nothing that is willed in conflict with right order can be a true good. Sin is thus the rejection of the supreme good; it is the alienation of a moral being from his intended destiny. God cannot positively will such an alienation; how sin can occur is the most mysterious and the most problematical element in the whole "problem of evil." How-

[12] C.S. Lewis, *op. cit.*, Chapter 3, pp. 41–42.

ever, almost inextricably interwoven with the mystery of sin is the problem of the eternal sanction against unrepented mortal sin, the sanction which is eternal loss, Hell, damnation.

God's esteem of human freedom. God permits moral evil, but He in no way wills it. He cannot will it, not even as a means to a good end. He does not will it under any aspect, He strongly forbids it, but He does not prevent it, even though there are some legitimate ways at His disposal (refusal to create at all, creation of other orders, placing men under different foreseen circumstances) whereby He could forestall the existence of moral evil.

Sin can occur because man has free will. God permits man to use his freedom as he wills, even to use it against right order. God does not constantly work miracles in the physical universe in order to prevent the physical ills that come from misapplying, or challenging, the physical laws of nature. In the moral order, He gives many aids, even many special interventions, but He does not eliminate freedom nor its consequences. God sees that it is good to create rational beings endowed with freedom; He foresees that abuse is possible; He forbids the abuse; He promulgates clearly the laws of right order; He warns of the punishments that are the sanctions for their violation—but nonetheless He so respects the privileged status and dignity of rational beings that not even when He foresees their deliberate abuse of freedom does He refuse to create them.

The risk involved in human freedom. Sin, we said, can occur because rational beings have free will. But this statement requires distinctions. *Human* free will is a wonderful perfection; still, it is not a "transcendental" one (as freedom, unqualified, would be). Rather, it is a "predicamental" or "mixed" perfection. For human free will includes the freedom to choose *between good and evil*, and not merely *to choose* between various goods. The freedom to choose between good and evil is not characteristic of freedom in the pure state and therefore is not absolutely necessary for all freedom, for freedom as such. It is found in *human* freedom, however, because such a "mixed" kind of freedom is what befits a being whose destiny is attainable only through probation.

Human freedom enables man to choose between various means that lead to his final end; it also enables him to choose a present, apparent good *instead of* a future, true good, a finite, immediate, and relative good *instead of,* and in opposition to, the Infinite, Ultimate, and Absolute Good. Sin, therefore, can occur not because man has *freedom* but because he has *human* freedom. As Father Phillips says:

Though it is true that freedom as such does not carry with it as a necessary consequence the capacity to sin, yet the freedom which would make man incapable of sinning is the fullness and perfection of freedom. Now it is not clear that it would not have been contradictory for God to have created a being which possessed such freedom as this of its nature, and of itself. For such an incapacity for sinning seems to come from a complete and perfect knowledge of the good, so that the bad loses all attractiveness. This, to be possessed by any being of its own nature, would demand in it infinity, so that it could not be a created or finite being. It would be a finite infinite, a contradiction, something to which God's omnipotence does not extend.[13]

And Father Joyce, in discussing this extremely obscure problem and while insisting that free will need not involve the power to choose wrong, goes on to say:

The existence of moral evil, however, becomes explicable, when it is admitted that man's life is a probation. . . . God, in other words, has created the present order such that man should have the glory of meriting his last end. We can see readily enough that in this He has conferred a great privilege upon us. To receive our final beatitude as the fruit of our labours, and as the recompense of a hard-won victory, is an incomparably higher destiny than to receive it without any effort on our part. And since God in His wisdom has seen fit to give us such a lot as this, it was inevitable that man should have the power to choose the wrong. We could not be called to merit the reward due to victory without being exposed to the possiblility of defeat.[14]

Perhaps it is not altogether unintelligible to say that a rational being cannot have a fully rational final happiness without some sense of meriting it, at least of having done something that enables him to be conscious that his beatitude is a reward for victory. But there is no victory without a struggle, without a risk.

[13] R.P. Phillips, *Modern Thomistic Philosophy,* Westminster, Md., Newman, 1948, Vol. II, p. 371.
[14] G.H. Joyce, S.J., *Principles of Natural Theology,* London, Longmans, Green and Co., 1934, pp. 600–601.

Sin does not triumph over God's will. To the objection that God could nonetheless have so disposed things that no one should be actually defeated, Fr. Joyce mentions, as a *possible* answer: "If all men eventually attained their last end and secured final beatitude, probation would have little meaning. The struggle would be but a mock struggle, if it were antecedently certain that, however a man might bear himself, God would bring it about that he should be saved from ultimate disaster." [15]

But Fr. Joyce himself goes on to invoke, as the sole reason that he considers fully conclusive, the idea that were God to abstain from giving existence to a soul because He foresaw that that soul would choose the path to evil, the perversity of the creature would have prevailed against the goodness of the Creator, and human wickedness have compelled God to modify His purposes. God, despite the infinite resources of His wisdom and power, would refuse to create because of foreseen evil—this would be like surrendering in advance to evil.

God could, indeed, prevent the occurrence of sin, but He does not—and none of His divine attributes requires that He do so. God prohibits sin, but He does not prevent it. He does, however, prevent the final triumph of sin; for unrepented mortal sin, by its eternal chastisement in Hell, is fitted into an orderly universe—not a universe that is a primary term of God's intention (for God does not antecedently will in its entirety any universe that contains sin), but one in which God's permissive will adapts the foreseen sin to a secondary providential order, one in which the foreseen and permitted sin is compensated for by adequate and inviolate sanctions.

Permission of sin not counter to divine attributes. The permission of moral evil—that is to say, the non-prevention of sin by Him who could refuse to create at all or who could create a different kind of universe forestalling all sin—does not go counter to any of the divine attributes. God has an excellent intention in creating: He wills to communicate the divine goodness at various levels; He wills that at the higher levels there exist beings with the supreme value of liberty, and, consequently, He wills that these beings have thereby the opportunity of winning unutterable eternal happiness. It is not against God's justice or wisdom or power or goodness or mercy to

[15] Joyce, *op. cit.*, pp. 601–602.

give a true probation, experiment, or test—most rightly called "opportunity"—to rational beings, even if He foresees that some will fail the test. This failure, it should be emphasized, is not a mere defect; rather, it is something freely and maliciously chosen by man. It is a creature's rebellion against his Creator; it is the deliberate refusal to accept one's finitude, one's creaturehood. It is foolhardiness, if you will, but it is deliberate malice shown against a most loving and generous Father. The stakes in the game of life are high—and the game is played "for keeps." But it is not a truly gambling game; everyone can be a winner, and victory is not determined by luck or chance, but by choice. No one loses by a mere mistake, a mere mischance; he loses only by his own free choice, his own malicious rebellion; God shares none of the responsibility.

God's wisdom. God's wisdom demands that He give a suitable, reasonable destiny to things. He has certainly done this in marvelously generous fashion, above all in the destiny He makes available for man. But does not such a possible destiny entail an alternate dreadful possibility? ". . . The deepest religious sense of mankind witnesses to the abiding consequences of free choice for the individual, and to the appalling possibility of eternal self-identification with evil as involved in the possibility of eternal self-identification with absolute Goodness." [16]

God's justice and holiness. God's justice demands that no man be tempted beyond that which he is able. Again, let us remark that sin is sin only if deliberately chosen, with a choice free of extrinsic and intrinsic necessitation. Justice demands that an arrangement of the universe—if it is to be providential—must contain sufficient means for the observance of the moral law. God's holiness, of course, demands that He promulgate His laws, that He establish due sanctions, that He clearly proclaim His prohibitions, and that He give to man suitable capacity for fulfilling the moral law.

God's goodness and mercy. Finally, God's goodness and mercy demand that the means, the aids He gives for observing the law, be sufficient and more than sufficient (but still compatible with the exercise of human freedom). God, surely, has been magnanimously generous in providing sufficient means. None of God's attributes are

[16] E.I. Watkin, "The Problem of Evil," an essay in *God and the Supernatural,* edited by Fr. Cuthbert, O.F.M. Cap., abridged edition, London, Sheed and Ward, 1954, p. 117 (or, p. 158 of the unabridged edition of 1920).

contradicted, therefore, by God's permission of sin in the universe. Sin exists only because man deliberately misuses a gift, excellent in itself and given him by God out of infinite love and esteem.

Hell. Infinite justice, however, demands that if the sinner die unrepentant, alienated from God, then his eternal life must be one fixed in bitterness of soul, alienation. The result of unrepented mortal sin is Hell, eternal damnation, the eternal loss of God Who is the only Good that can finally satisfy man. But the sinner cannot blame anyone but himself for his loss. No one can send another person to Hell; if the will were not free in the case of such and such an act, this act would not be sinful. Where there is truly sin, the sinner deliberately has chosen the sin despite the consequences. The consequences of unrepented sin are the inevitable reaction of what is good to what is evil. God cannot be the subsistent holiness and absolute goodness that He is, were He to be indifferent to mortal sin, or if He were to treat it in the same way as He treats good. Thus, in its own way, even Hell redounds to the honor of God.

It would be irrational for things to be otherwise. Suppose a man who knows that if he walks at a distance from, or even carefully along the edge of, a precipice, he will arrive safely at his destination, should complain that God has been cruel in making the physical laws of the universe, for, by taking a single step perpendicular to the path along the cliff's edge, he will topple over the cliff and dash to his death. Where is the proportion? A single step only, and then—death! But surely it would be completely stupid on his part to demand that God work a miracle should he, the wayfarer, decide to make the fatal step. If he perishes by deliberately making the foolish move, he has no one really to blame but himself. The laws of gravity and momentum are reasonably and wisely established for the orderly running of the universe. Similarly, the moral laws are reasonably and orderly established. Man knows these laws, and when he seriously violates them, this is like the action of the man who deliberately—against the known laws of nature—steps over the cliff. As far as the sinner is concerned, he severs his friendship with God irretrievably.

True, God has ways of enabling the man, if he sincerely repents, to regain the lost friendship, but it is unreasonable and unreal to demand that no time limits whatsoever be given in which the recovery is to be achieved. It is unreasonable also to demand that God should be more and more bound to give help, the more evil a man becomes

—as though the more malice a man shows, and the more insolent he becomes in his defiance of God, then the more obligation God is under of giving the man aid and securing his salvation. It has been well said: "Hell is the ultimate expression of the value of human liberty. To deny it is to say either that liberty is incapable of resisting . . . grace, or that sin is finally so absurd as not even to deserve punishment." [17]

To close this present section, on the mystery of iniquity, we would like to use another remarkable statement of C.S. Lewis: "In the long run the answer to all those who object to the doctrine of hell, is itself a question: 'What are you asking God to do?' To wipe out their past sins and, at all costs, to give them a fresh start, smoothing every difficulty and offering every miraculous help? But He has done so, on Calvary. To forgive them? They will not be forgiven. To leave them alone? Alas, I am afraid that is what He does." [18]

MORAL EVIL (SIN)	God does not will it, but merely permits it	OUT OF RESPECT FOR HUMAN FREEDOM
PENAL EVIL (PUNISH-MENT)	God wills it, incidentally and secondarily	FOR THE ORDERLY VINDICATION OF JUSTICE AND HOLINESS
PHYSICAL EVIL IN SUB-HUMAN WORLD	God wills it, incidentally,	FOR THE GOOD OF THE UNIVERSE AS A WHOLE, ESPECIALLY FOR THE GOOD OF MAN
PHYSICAL EVIL IN THE HUMAN WORLD	God wills it, incidentally,	FOR THE PHYSICAL, AND ESPECIALLY THE MORAL, DEVELOPMENT OF MAN

[17] M. Jouhandeau, quoted by Jean Danielou, S.J., in *God and the Ways of Knowing*, New York, Meridian Press, 1957, p. 88.
[18] C.S. Lewis, *op. cit.*, p. 116.

VIII. POST-SCRIPT: HINTS FROM THE SUPERNATURAL ORDER

No complete solution in this life. As we said at the beginning of this chapter, philosophy does not have the complete solution to the problem; it can at most furnish a few "rational elements" that make us distinguish various levels of evil, that more carefully explain for us just what is meant by "evil," and that establish enough facts concerning the divine nature that the sober-minded will conclude that there is no evident necessity of making the illation of the atheist: "If there is evil in the universe, then God, such as philosophy describes Him, cannot possibly exist."

But for a person who accepts the supernatural revelation given by Judaeo-Christian tradition and holy scriptures, the problem of evil receives much further light. Never, of course, in the present life will an absolutely ultimate solution of this problem be given, even by revelation. Still, much that is revealed is directed to the lessening of man's impatience with evil, to the calming of his emotions in face of trials, to preparing him for the purification that may be wrought by suffering, to the clarifying of his perspectives, to aiding him to appreciate the loving and orderly care of God, our Father, to encouraging him to bear his cross daily, and to the intensifying of his faith, hope, and trust in God. It will not be unfitting, as we come to the close of this book on the philosophy of God, to give two or three hints from supernatural sources. After all, a philosophy that claims it has said the last word on any subject, or that shuts the door to transcendent ways of communication between God and man, is not a true philosophy; it has an appreciation neither of the power of God nor of the dignity of man. Philosophy cannot prove the supernatural, but it must remain open-minded to all possibilities.

Helps from revelation. Now, from the supernatural viewpoint, furnished by faith in revelation, several additional elements can be brought forth to explain, and to render more tolerable, the existence of evils in the world. One who has the supernatural viewpoint will know that God has destined man not merely for perfect beatitude but for an ineffable sharing in the divine life itself. He will, therefore, realize much more deeply than the philosopher that the real evil in this world is sin, since sin alone can prevent a man's incorporation into the divine life. He will also appreciate, far more than the philosopher, the fact that "the sufferings of this life are not worthy to be compared with the glory to come." [19]

Reparation. From supernatural revelation man also learns how the bearing of suffering with patience and resignation atones for sin, and how it can be reparation not only for one's own sins but for those of others; one learns that he can assist the souls in Purgatory, and that he can win graces for his loved ones and even for his enemies by his own endurance of suffering and by the making of sacrifices. In a family that has a wayward son or daughter (a "black sheep"), the others will try to make reparation or amends for the wayward member; family solidarity makes the other children kinder, gentler, and more patient and attentive to the deeper feelings of their parents and of one another. This is a beautiful response, the only proper reaction, of children in the case of such family tragedies. The supernatural viewpoint can make us see, in analogous fashion, the beauty of the doctrine of reparation to the Sacred Heart of Jesus. The solidarity of the whole human race as at least potential members of the "Mystical Body of Christ" can motivate the supernaturally minded soul not merely to accept suffering, but to welcome it, out of a spirit of atonement or reparation.

Jesus Christ. Finally, and above all else, the example of Christ —of Christ scourged, mocked, crowned with thorns, spat upon, and dying on the cross—gives the lie forever to anyone who would dare to assert that God is indifferent to human suffering. The divine nature, it is true, cannot strictly suffer, but He Who is divine can also have a human nature; He can really and truly, literally, become *incarnate*, and in this human nature that He assumes, He can live and suffer and die as any man. And God did just that: He became a real man; He took a human nature, not a make-believe body and soul, but a real body and a real soul; He had real, physical flesh and blood; He had human nerves, human sensations, and a human heart. God became, in the God-man Jesus Christ, the human sufferer *par excellence*, the Man of Sorrows, the sublime prototype of suffering

[19] *Romans* 8:18.

humanity. Christ's death on the cross may not explain to our mere human intellects why God allows anyone to suffer, but it does speak to our inmost heart and soul, enabling our faith to triumph over our natural misgivings; it proves the extent of God's love, and it shows that He understands our sorrows and pains and has the most intimate compassion for them. We can endure much, very much indeed, when we know that Jesus Christ is enduring with us, in us, and for us.

The last word in the natural explanation of the problem of evil was simply: "God loved the world." In the supernatural explanation, the last word is, "God so loved the world that He gave His only-begotten Son." [20]

LEADING IDEAS of Chapter 12

1. Although evil presents a problem for the whole man, it is necessary that a theistic philosopher discuss it from the philosophical point of view, at least in order to show that there is no contradiction between the presence of evil in creation and the existence of an infinitely perfect Creator.

2. Although the problem is very much alive in modern times, it is an age-old problem; most people, however, seem to think merely of pain and not of sin when they think of the problem of evil.

3. To have a solution to the problem, we must have a hierarchy of values, realizing that the sub-human world exists for man and that man himself is destined for immortality, the present life being his proving-ground.

4. A rational discussion of the problem demands that we distinguish moral evil and physical evil, physical evils that are sanctions and those that are not, and physical evils in the kingdom of man and in the sub-human world.

5. If mere lack (and not strict privation) of possible perfection were metaphysically evil, all creatures would necessarily be evil.

6. Since any world is finite, an absolutely best world is not possible; a better world than any given one is always possible.

7. The rationalists' doctrine would destroy God's freedom by its insistence that God must choose the best possible world.

[20] St. John 3:16.

8. The reason for a free choice is the same as the reason for the simple willing of an object, namely, its goodness.

9. The same answer should be given to the question: "Why did God will our world?" and the question: "Why did God will *this* world *rather than some other one?*" the answer, namely, that He willed this world and could have willed some other one, He willed this world out of love and He could have willed some other world out of love.

10. God does not will the various individual beings of the universe absolutely, in isolation, but as components of a vast cosmos of mutually dependent beings, a hierarchized universe.

11. The pain of brute animals is quite mysterious, but it should not be exaggerated, nor should we become anthropomorphic in the matter.

12. The freedom of the spirit of man determines whether physical evils—trials, opportunities—will redound to his *grandeur* or to his *misère*.

13. God does not will moral evil at all, He permits it out of respect for human liberty, and He sanctions it with the penalties right order demands; God wills penal evils not for their own sake but for the orderly vindication of justice and holiness; God wills non-penal physical evils in the sub-human world not for their own sake but for the good of the universe as a whole and particularly for the good of man; God wills non-penal physical evils in the case of man not for their own sake but as probations, opportunities, for the physical and especially the moral good of man; in all of which there is nothing contradicting God's infinite power, justice, wisdom, goodness, or mercy.

14. The problem of evil receives much further light from the supernatural revelation given by Judaeo-Christian tradition and holy scriptures.

15. The last word in the natural explanation of the problem of evil is simply, "God loved the world"; in the supernatural explanation, the last word is, "God so loved the world that He gave His only-begotten Son."

SUGGESTED READINGS for Chapter 12

For Scholastic Exposition:

St. Thomas. S.T. I.22.2; I.48 and 49 (*Basic Writings*, Vol. I, pp. 231–234 and 464–479); C.G. III.71 (*Truth of the Catholic Faith*, Vol. III.1, pp. 237–242).

G.H. Joyce, S.J. *Principles of Natural Theology*. London: Longmans, Green and Co., 1934, Chapter 17.

R.P. Phillips. *Modern Thomistic Philosophy*. Westminster, Md.: Newman, 1948, Vol. II, pp. 364–375.

Paul Siwek, S.J. *The Philosophy of Evil*. New York: Ronald, 1951.

For Popular Exposition:

M.C. D'Arcy, S.J. *The Pain of This World and the Providence of God*. London: Longmans, Green and Co., new impression, 1936.

C.S. Lewis. *The Problem of Pain*. New York: Macmillan, 1944, especially Chapter 3.

J. Rickaby, S.J. *Studies on God and His Creatures*. London: Longmans, Green and Co., 1924, pp. 109–134.

For Discussions by Classic Writers:

F. Dostoyevsky. *The Brothers Karamazov*, Book 5, number 4, "Rebellion."

G.W. Leibniz. *Selections*, edited by P. Weiner. New York: Scribner's, 1951, pp. 509–522.

J.A. Mourant. *Readings in the Philosophy of Religion*. New York: Crowell, 1944, pp. 339–401.

L.A. Seneca. *On Providence* (in the Loeb Classical Library: *Seneca, Moral Essays*. Cambridge, Mass.: Harvard, 1958, Vol. I, pp. 3–47).

On Animal Pain:

Cecil Gray. "The Meaning of Pain, Consciousness and Death," *The Downside Review*, Vol. 79, 1961, pp. 189–193.

J.H. Cardinal Newman. *Discourses Addressed to Mixed Congregations*, sermon, "The Mental Sufferings of Our Lord," found in M.F. Egan, *Prose and Poetry of John Henry Newman*. New York: Houghton Mifflin Co., 1907, pp. 151–153.

On Hell as Penalty for Sin:

C.S. Lewis. *The Great Divorce*. New York: Macmillan, 1946, especially pp. 123–125.

Index

Numbers in boldface type refer, in the case of proper names, to direct quotations and, in other cases, to the more important definitions or descriptions.

319

324